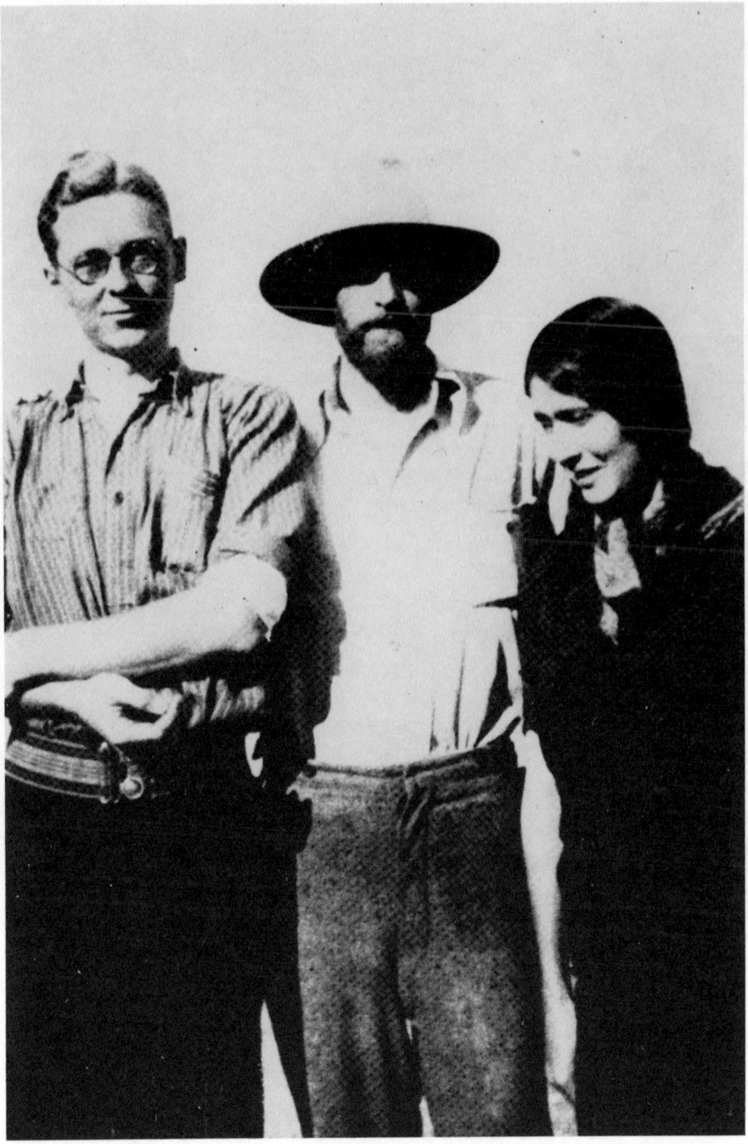

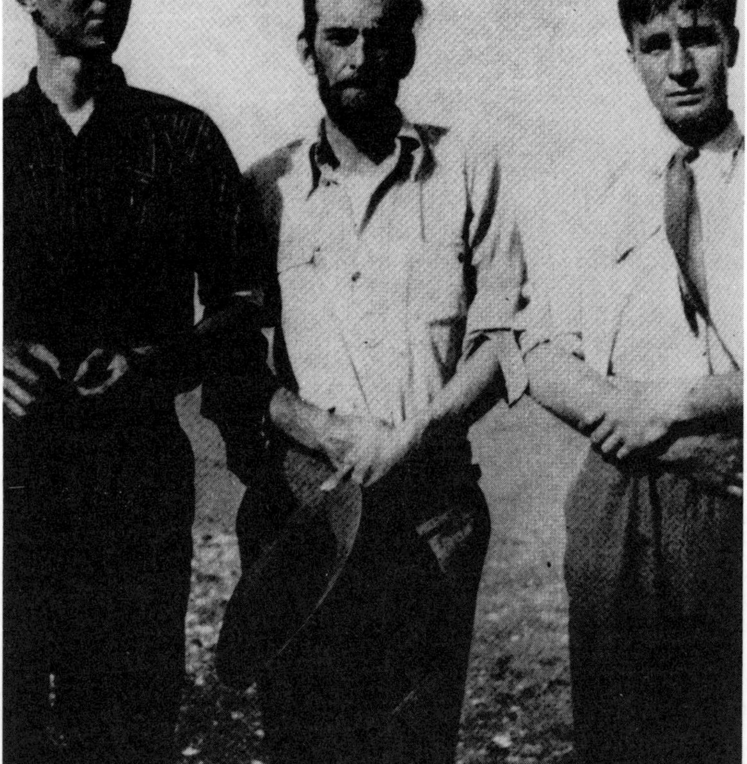

VOORSLAG

A MAGAZINE OF SOUTH AFRICAN LIFE AND ART

Facsimile Reprint of Numbers 1, 2 and 3 (1926)

Edited by

ROY CAMPBELL, WILLIAM PLOMER

and

LAURENS VAN DER POST

With an Introduction and Notes by

COLIN GARDNER and MICHAEL CHAPMAN

UNIVERSITY OF NATAL PRESS

PIETERMARITZBURG

and

KILLIE CAMPBELL AFRICANA LIBRARY

DURBAN

1985

Introduction, Notes and Index

Box 375, Pietermaritzburg, 3200
Natal, South Africa

ISBN 0 86980 423 5

Typeset in the University of Natal Press
Box 375, Pietermaritzburg, 3200
Printed by The Natal Witness (Pty) Ltd
Box 362, Pietermaritzburg, South Africa

CONTENTS

LIST OF APPENDICES

PREFACE

The Killie Campbell Africana Library Reprint Series sets out to make accessible important source materials which are now out of print.

The literary journal *Voorslag* was produced in mid-1926, near Durban, by the then youthful Roy Campbell, William Plomer and Laurens van der Post, all of whom were subsequently to establish themselves among South Africa's most prominent writers. Disagreements between Campbell and the sponsors of *Voorslag* soon led to the resignation of the young authors; but not before the first three issues, under their editorship, had provoked immediate controversy in artistic and journalistic circles.

The present volume makes available almost sixty years later, in facsimile and with editorial notes, numbers 1, 2 and 3 of *Voorslag*. An Introduction describes the founding of the journal and assesses its significance in the context of South African literature. In addition, appendices of press reviews and – published for the first time – letters by Campbell and others interested in the venture help to convey something of the atmosphere surrounding this out-spoken 'little magazine'.

In this facsimile reprint all the original typographical errors and unevennesses in type have been reproduced. Editorial material precedes and follows the reprint; pages have been numbered in one sequence with *Voorslag 1–3* falling between pages 26 and 27. Biographical information on the editors and certain other people has been placed in the index in order to avoid repetitive notes.

The publishers are indebted to Messrs A. C. Braby (Pty) Ltd, the original publishers of *Voorslag*, for permission to reprint the first three numbers of the journal. Acknowledgement for the use of letters by Roy Campbell is hereby made to Francisco Campbell Custódio, and to Mrs I. Keet for the use of letters by Edward Roworth. The originals of these letters are held by the Killie Campbell Africana Library, Durban, and the South African Library, Cape Town.

INTRODUCTION

I

Voorslag, the literary journal produced in 1926 by Roy Campbell, William Plomer and Laurens van der Post, has unusual significance both in itself and in the history of South African English literature. The present volume offers a facsimile reprint of Numbers 1, 2 and 3 (those under Campbell's editorship) together with Appendices of contemporaneous reactions in the press to the new journal, two letters by Edward Roworth, and – published here for the first time – a few of Campbell's letters pertinent to *Voorslag* and its attempt to provide a forum for literary and socio-political comment and debate. This edition is a response to the fact that *Voorslag*, although one of the most celebrated of South African literary journals in English (neither is it unknown in Britain and the United States), had a real temporal life of only two or, at the most, three months, and very few members of the present generation seem to have seen it. (Only a few complete sets of *Voorslag* are known to exist.) By attaching Appendices of press reviews and correspondence, we hope also to convey something of the emotional and intellectual atmosphere surrounding the appearance of the journal.

The interest in *Voorslag* resides of course most obviously in its initial editors and authors – Campbell, who was the presiding spirit, Plomer and, to a lesser extent, Van der Post. Number 1 appeared in June 1926 and was written largely by Campbell and Plomer. *Voorslag* Number 2 came out in July; again it was mainly the work of the two chief contributors, and there was also an article, in Afrikaans, by Van der Post. (*Voorslag*, incidentally, can claim to be one of the first attempts at a bilingual journal in South Africa, and Campbell had plans to introduce as well articles in Zulu.)[1] In the initial numbers

Campbell appears under his own name, but also as Mary Ann Hughes and as Lewis Marston, while Plomer features also as Pamela Willmore, almost an anagram of his name. On July 25 Campbell, speaking for his two colleagues as well as for himself, refused to accept the decision – taken apparently by Lewis Reynolds, the sponsor, and by Maurice Webb, whom Campbell and Plomer regarded as the business manager – to put Webb in charge of the journal (Webb had penned the introductory note to Number 1, 'Why *Voorslag*?', a piece described by Campbell as 'such an apologetic little preface').[2] *Voorslag* Number 3 duly appeared in August, but with the following curt statement on page 2: 'I have much pleasure in announcing my resignation from *Voorslag*. Roy Campbell.' The number contained contributions by Campbell, Plomer and Van der Post, but a new editorial control had begun to be exercised: the concluding section of Plomer's story 'Portraits in the Nude' had been tampered with,[3] while articles and creative pieces were included which, as various remarks and jibes tend to confirm, would not have met with the unqualified approval of the three young authors – for example, Sarah Gertrude Millin's short story 'Pumpkins',[4] Theodore Haarhoff's translations of Catullus,[5] and the verse of David Gamble.[6]

In contrast to Number 3, the first two numbers contained much that was daring, dashing, challenging, yet profound. *Voorslag* means 'whiplash', and the lash had sting and zing, its aim (to quote Plomer) 'to sting with satire the mental hindquarters, so to speak, of the bovine citizenry of the Union [of South Africa]'.[7] The contributions of Campbell and Plomer themselves set the tone of Numbers 1 and 2. Campbell, for example, displayed his percipience as a critic (an aspect of his literary capacity so far largely ignored), particularly in his reviews of Plomer's novel *Turbott Wolfe* (1925) and T. S. Eliot's then recently published poem 'The Waste Land'. In addition, Campbell's call for modern expression in literature informs his article '"Eunuch Arden" and "Kynoch Arden"', in which he deals with what he saw to be the demise of a challenging English poetry after the Romantics and the rise of a second-rate Georgianism, something at odds with the vital new tendencies of the French Symbolists. (All of these articles are important to a full understanding of Campbell's own practice as a poet.)

Similarly Plomer's contributions offer illuminating insights into his literary personality: his review-article on Dr Leys's book *Kenya* ('Dr Leys and the Colour Question') affords him the opportunity (which he had previously made use of in *Turbott Wolfe*) of severely indicting the Colour Bar, as it was called, while his serialized story 'Portraits in the Nude' is a satire on white bourgeois values in life and letters, with the 'portraits' introducing certain structural and thematic features present also in a 'tradition' of South African fiction, in Olive Schreiner's *The Story of an African Farm* ('Portraits' employs the motifs of isolation and the questing human spirit, both seriously and parodically), Pauline Smith's *The Beadle* (Takhaar literally strips himself naked at Nagmaal) and Sarah Gertrude Millin's *God's Stepchildren* (Plomer's tale concludes with a brutal presentation of desires and actions inspired by the idea of miscegenation).

Almost certainly the article in Number 1 by General J. C. Smuts ('Beauty in Nature') was included as something of a gesture. (Reynolds had been Smuts's secretary at the Versailles Conference in 1919, had political ambitions of his own, was on good terms with Prime Minister General J. B. M. Hertzog and Colonel F. H. P. Creswell, the leader of the South African Labour Party, and was conscious of the need for *Voorslag* to attract the favourable attention of men of influence, as indeed was Campbell in the initial stages of the venture.) Campbell was to attack Smuts's concept of Holism in some of the most amusing lines in *The Wayzgoose* (1928),[8] the satiric poem, written soon after Campbell's resignation as editor, in which he lampooned various figures who had annoyed him during the production of *Voorslag*. Another contributor to Numbers 1 and 2, Edward Roworth, the well-known South African painter and academic, was also to feature in Campbell's satire;[9] at the time of the first issue of the journal, however, the two men were given to lengthy and sympathetic exchanges on the subject of European art.[10] Roworth's articles on Cézanne and Gauguin were (as Campbell was aware) largely paraphrased from books by French art historians; nevertheless the emphasis given to the French modernist painters, as romantic figures devoted entirely to their art, is interesting in that it represents the underlying philosophy of *Voorslag* itself, in its attempts to confront what was seen to be a complacent 'grocer's mentality' with avant-garde ideas, usually emanating from Europe, on art and thought.

By Number 3 the strokes of the whiplash had grown not weaker but considerably fewer. In the remaining numbers of *Voorslag* – and the journal came to a halt only with Number 11, May–June 1927 – it is difficult to see the point of the title at all. (There are however several pieces of some interest in the later issues, including a letter by Campbell[11] and contributions by Mary Cowley Hewitt,[12] Pauline Smith, Ethelreda Lewis, Sarah Gertrude Millin, J. D. Rheinallt Jones, T. J. Haarhoff and Gandhi's friend C. F. Andrews: we have appended the contents pages of Numbers 4 to 11.)

The Campbell-Plomer phenomenon in South African literature is inextricably connected with *Voorslag*, even if some of the best work produced by the pair during the mid-1920s does not appear in the journal itself. (As far as poetry is concerned, Campbell contributed only 'The Albatross', 'To a Young Man with Pink Eyes' – apparently aimed satirically at Lewis Reynolds – and a few translations of Baudelaire and Rimbaud; Plomer offered one poem, 'The Strandloopers', which he was not to include in his *Collected Poems*.) Despite this, the brief glowing partnership of Campbell and Plomer – and of Van der Post, though he was at the time perhaps little more than an intelligently observant acolyte – is one of the striking events in South African literary history. For three bright winter months in 1926, at a small cottage in Umdoni Park near Sezela on the then fairly deserted coast about sixty kilometres south of Durban, the three of them generated a fine corporate imaginative energy.

The '*Voorslag* Days' have been chronicled (vividly if at times a little romantically) by Plomer, Van der Post and, most recently, by Campbell's biographer Peter Alexander, and the reader is referred to their articles, all of which are readily available.[13] Briefly, Campbell after an unsuccessful spell at Oxford had returned to Natal in June 1924, his long poem *The Flaming Terrapin* (1924) having attracted considerable attention in British literary circles where it was felt to possess the kind of vitality necessary to rescue English poetry from the gentility of Georgianism. Son of an influential family in Durban, Campbell had expected to be fêted on his return, and to some extent he was, his lecture to the town, 'Modern Poetry and Contemporary History',[14] receiving prominent coverage in the press despite the fact that many of his comments on 'modernity' in literature and life were rightly interpreted as a direct assault by enlightened youth upon the older generation of white, middle-class South African society (the youth-age issue was to dominate subsequent press reactions to *Voorslag*). In his public lecture and in several night classes he conducted at the technical college founded by his father, Dr Sam Campbell, he anticipated the approach *Voorslag* was to adopt towards the mediocrity of 'colonial culture' – an attitude that did not impress his frank, commonsensical father, who had little patience with his son's notions of artistic bohemianism. It was Sam Campbell's insistence that his son earn a living, possibly in journalism, that was to a degree responsible for Roy's begging Lewis Reynolds, the son of a local sugar-millionaire, for money to establish a literary journal. Reynolds, who had left Oxford shortly before Campbell arrived there, had been impressed by *The Flaming Terrapin*. Moved by the poet's plight he invited Campbell, together with his wife and baby daughter,[15] to occupy a seaside bungalow at Sezela on one of his father's estates, Umdoni Park. (Near the bungalow was a rondavel which had been occupied by Roworth, who was to become the art editor of *Voorslag*.)

In May 1925 the idea of a journal along the lines of *The Dial* and *The Adelphi* received Reynolds's support; Maurice Webb, a friend of the Campbell family and the producer of a commercial directory, was to be business manager and publisher. (*Voorslag* was printed by A. C. Braby of Durban, a firm renowned for its business directories.) Shortly afterwards Campbell met William Plomer, whose parents ran a trading-store in Zululand and who had recently completed *Turbott Wolfe*, a virulent attack on colour prejudice in contemporary South African society.[16] When he met Plomer Campbell had not yet read the novel, but he would include his seminal review 'The Significance of *Turbott Wolfe*' in the first number of *Voorslag*. Plomer, who shared Campbell's contempt for South African white middle-class values and his conviction that art was what really mattered, has in retrospect described his relationship at the time with Campbell:

> Propinquity had brought us together. It is unlikely that we should have been mutually attracted at Oxford or in London: the differences in our backgrounds, temperaments, outlooks, ambitions, and tastes were great. But in South Africa we were isolated, and isolation can be a social cement. We were of about the same age, and both high-spirited. Each was dedicated to the written word, to the recognition and perpetuation of the first-rate in literature, and to the art of creative writing. We liked the same sort of jokes, and agreed that the cultural pretensions of English-speaking South Africa at that time were mostly absurd. Campbell, instantly recognizable as a poet, began to widen and enrich my understanding of poetry. At the same time, an evident intensity in my feelings about racial conflicts in South Africa, and my open sympathy with Africans, was not without its effect, its temporary effect, upon him. This short period of our close association was in fact remarkably fruitful for both Campbell and myself. Every moment was fertile.[17]

Campbell prevailed on Plomer to move into the bungalow at Sezela as joint editor, and a period of intense literary activity began, the result of which fills the pages of the first issues of *Voorslag*. (The two also had plans to produce a series called *The Conquistadors*, satirizing the course of white settlement in southern Africa, but all that was to materialize from this project was Campbell's poem 'Solo and Chorus from "The Conquistador"', in his *Adamastor* volume, and Plomer's title poem 'Conquistadors'. Of more importance is the fact that Plomer, at this time, wrote his story, 'Ula Masondo', one of the more innovative treatments of the 'Jim comes to Jo'burg' theme.)[18] Plomer introduced Campbell to Laurens van der Post, who was working in Durban as a reporter on Henry Wodson's daily newspaper *The Natal Advertiser* (which has continued as *The Daily News*). Van der Post, who had written little, was immediately accepted by Campbell and Plomer as a kindred spirit and became Afrikaans editor, a gesture by the young authors, respectively, of *The Flaming Terrapin* and *Turbott Wolfe* that Van der Post was never to forget:

. . . I could not put *Turbott Wolfe* down until I had read it from cover to cover. This establishment of a difference between Wodson and me was never erased, though we remained friends until his death. Almost daily we quarrelled over the book and inevitably all sorts of other latent differences were drawn to the issue. I found it in a very real sense a book of revelation. Art, to me, is a magic mirror wherein suddenly are made visible aspects of reality hitherto invisible, and this *Turbott Wolfe* was for me and some of my generation in South Africa. For my editor and his contemporaries, no matter how we argued and pleaded, it remained a work of total darkness. They would not even give it the conditional admission to their understanding that Calvin gave the Book of Revelations, with the fearsome proviso that though divinely inspired it was also 'a dark and dangerously obscure book'. Within a few months our differences had grown so acute that I was writing letters under my own name disagreeing with Wodson and his literary critic in the columns of *The Natal Advertiser* and he was answering back in his leading articles! And both the fact that he allowed this and could take this particular issue so seriously seems to me today considerably to his credit. . . .

All this I think shows what sort of impact *Turbott Wolfe* had for me on all levels of life. For a start it brought me and Plomer together, and through Plomer I met Roy Campbell. For the first time in my life, instead of reading about literature in books, I was to be in intimate touch with it through the work of contemporaries – Plomer was three years older than I was; Campbell a year or two older than Plomer. However much one can learn from the old and the experienced, there is nothing comparable to the dynamics of learning from people of one's own time, themselves caught up and struggling in the baffling process of expressing immediate apprehensions of a common reality. I could hardly have done without the companionship of mind and interest which Plomer and Campbell gave me, nor their example of how to set about the difficult business of self-employment as a writer. Consequently my debt to the

> two of them is immense. The debt of South Africa was to be even greater.[19]

When the first number of *Voorslag* appeared, Campbell (Maurice Webb's directories in mind) spoke of 'a coffee-coloured [magazine] which would have disgraced a tradesman's catalogue'.[20] In fact the cover of each number was to depict an example of San rock-art copied by the South African painter Hendrik Pierneef (the San or 'Bushman' later provided Plomer with a metaphor to sum up the *Voorslag* movement: '. . . perhaps like twentieth-century Bushmen [we] had left a few vivid paintings on the walls of that dark cave, the mind of the white South African').[21] Certainly the journal achieved its purpose of stinging the 'bovine citizenry'. As the press reviews in the Appendices suggest, it attracted immediate and very often hostile comment in the pages of newspapers in Durban, Johannesburg and Cape Town, the strong reaction prompted by its outspoken criticism of the Colour Bar and by the fact that the young authors had branded their enemies as a philistine mob. If one of the functions of the little magazine is to stir up controversy, *Voorslag* had succeeded – as had its short-lived but illustrious predecessor of the 1820s, Pringle and Fairbairn's *South African Journal*, as would several literary journals to follow *Voorslag*, notably some whose titles were obviously inspired by the metaphor of the 'voorslag', for example Stephen Black's *The Sjambok* and Bosman and Blignaut's *The Touleier* (both of which appeared soon after Campbell and Plomer's journal, in the late twenties and early thirties).[22]

As attacks and counterattacks appeared in leader articles and among readers' letters in the press, Reynolds (who had invested £1 000 in *Voorslag*) became increasingly alarmed. Having plans to stand for parliament in his father's old seat, South Coast, and having secured the support of Smuts and Creswell, he saw the journal developing into a forum for the 'radical' views of Plomer and Campbell. Consequently, and evidently in the light of Campbell's threat to resign as editor,[23] Reynolds, together with Webb and Roworth, met on Sunday 25 July 1926 to tell Campbell that the sponsors wanted greater editorial control over the contents. (There had been disagreements over editorial interference, as Campbell's letter to Webb – Appendix D – indicates. Campbell, in his letter to Sibbett – Appendix F – also speaks of Roworth's having betrayed him by siding at the last moment with 'management'.) The meeting was interpreted by Campbell, who had been having organizational difficulties in the production of the journal, as the final attempt to make art the handmaiden of grubby commercial interests, and, though he had no prospects for the future, he quit the journal. With his family he was allowed to stay on at the bungalow for a month, until the end of August 1926, during which time (according to Plomer)[24] he wrote several of his most powerful and haunting poems, 'The Serf', 'The Zulu Girl', 'To a Pet Cobra', 'The Making of a Poet' and 'Tristan da Cunha', all treating the themes of lonely genius and exceptional energy, in a way the 'themes' of the *Voorslag* adventure itself.[25]

II

Campbell and Plomer were in some ways very similar, in other ways extremely different. Perhaps the conjunction of 'sameness with difference' is what accounts for the vitality but also – as it turned out – the brevity of their association. They were both very young: Campbell was twenty-four and Plomer twenty-two (Van der Post was only nineteen). They had both been born in South Africa, but had lived in Britain, Plomer for important periods of his childhood, Campbell for several years after he had left school. By mid-1926 they were both authors who had published in Britain and were widely admired there and in the United States. Yet they felt themselves to be South Africans and were intensely concerned about the cultural and political problems of the country – but at the same time, with a youthful mixture of perceptiveness and arrogance, they took some pleasure in adopting a larger view of local affairs and in deriding the earnest expounders of typically South African attitudes. (One of Campbell's letters to Sibbett – Appendix I – provides an interesting perspective on the author's concern also with South African, as opposed to European, literary tradition-making.) Both Campbell and Plomer had read and thought a good deal, and their imaginations were exploring a wide range of issues. They felt deeply, wrote eloquently and often wittily, and were not afraid to shock or to be aggressive. Above all they saw themselves – perhaps Campbell especially – as representatives of youth, individuality and creative intelligence in the fight against the somnolent values of middle-class conformity and prejudice. And, as one reads nearly sixty years later the poems, stories, articles and reviews that they wrote in those months, one can only conclude that they were in almost every respect quite right in their estimate of themselves and their role. Many of the things that they say are memorable and prophetic:

> The publication of the 'Waste Land' marks a new era in English Poetry. It is one of the most relentlessly honest works of the age. For in it the spirit of historical culture is made to recognise its futility: the soul of man shrinks horrified from the gulf to which it has been advancing so unconsciously with flags and banners for the last two hundred years. Mr Eliot's enormous erudition and imaginative power concentrate with a horrified and hypnotised glare on the naked spectre of the truth. One hears the crash of falling ruins, the querulous expostulation of the old ideals and idols against the powers of a new and inscrutable darkness. High over the sleepy self-satisfaction of middle-age one hears again and again the agonised searching question of youth now rising into a hoarse shout and then breaking off into an exasperated hyena-like chuckle – mocking, blasphemous, unanswerable.
>
> Mr Eliot has invented a new form in which he aptly captures the rhythms, the bewildering kaleidoscopic movement, of modern life.
>
> (Campbell, 'Marginalia', No. 1, p. 60.)

> How much longer is the colour of a man's skin to influence his rights as a man? It will not be enough to elevate the Cape Coloured people to an equal status with Europeans. It will be

> necessary to learn to recognise every man's human qualities as a contribution to the building up of an indestructible future, to judge every man by the colour of his soul and not by the colour of his skin. Otherwise the coloured races of the world will rise and take by force what is denied them now by a comparatively few muddle-headed money-grubbers.
>
> (Plomer, 'Dr Leys and the Colour Question', No. 1, p. 56.)

Some of the challenging statements in *Voorslag* would produce today, unfortunately, in many white South African readers almost the same angry and guilty explosion as they did when they were first written. It is good to be able to put the early *Voorslag* – the *real Voorslag* – back into circulation.

But the intense vitality which animated Campbell and Plomer – and Van der Post – grew to some extent from the sense, which seems to have been dimly present to them (especially to Plomer), that their paths, which coincided at that special moment, were in fact pointing in different directions. Campbell's imagination was powerful, romantic, at its best very sensitive, sometimes rather assertive, with a tendency towards either dramatic or comic hyperbole, whereas Plomer's spirit was more quietly penetrating – intelligent, fine yet sharp, essentially compassionate but moving often towards a fairly intellectual and detached kind of irony. The two Umdoni Park photographs, reproduced here – one showing Campbell and Plomer with Mary Campbell, the other showing them with Van der Post – tell one a great deal. Campbell stands in the centre, a strong, handsome, brooding figure, looking straight into the camera, with his slightly histrionic hat; Plomer, at his side, is relaxed, confident, nearly smiling but in a guarded way, unwilling to be caught up too fully in the mystique of photography. Mary and Van der Post are not so easy to describe: they both seem conscious of being in the presence of two strong personalities (though, interestingly enough, in the world of practical, day-to-day affairs it was Mary who usually took the initiative).

As the three magic months came to an end and Plomer and Van der Post left for Japan, and the Campbells after some months in Durban went back to England (Campbell's plans, mentioned in his letter to Sibbett – Appendix I – to start another journal called *Boomslang* having not materialized), and then as the twenties ended and the thirties began to pass, it became clear that the trajectories of Campbell and Plomer were getting further apart. Differences of personality and attitude were to lead to their eventual estrangement.[26] Campbell found Britain stifling: he disliked both what he felt to be its urbanized tameness and the cliquishness and the sexual ambiguity of its literary people (*The Georgiad*, published in 1933, turned out to be a fiercer satire than *The Wayzgoose*). He moved to the south of Europe, where he found and participated in what he felt to be a more equestrian and traditional civilization. Plomer, on the other hand, returned to Britain in 1929 and chose to live and write, fairly contentedly though by no means uncritically, in the very environment which Campbell had denounced.

The stories of the lives of Campbell and Plomer have been told elsewhere,[27] and it is not our intention to retell them here. It is perhaps worth noting however, since we are looking at them from a South African point of view, that the differences between the two men were shown up sharply on visits that they paid to South Africa in the mid-1950s. Campbell travelled from Portugal to Natal to receive an honorary doctorate from the University in 1954: he struck those who met and heard him as warm, expansive and yet jaded, and rather wild in some of his statements (particularly on political matters, where he expressed flamboyantly right-wing views which embarrassed his mainly liberal audiences).[28] Plomer visited South Africa in 1956, primarily in order to address a conference at the University of the Witwatersrand: he came across as observant, critical (his political views had not changed fundamentally) and interested in new South African writers, both black and white.[29] He later told John Betjeman that his hands were clenched the whole time he was in the country, because the atmosphere was so tense.[30] (Notwithstanding or perhaps because of this, the visit inspired two of his most impressive poems, 'Transvaal Morning' and 'The Wild Doves at Louis Trichardt', reminiscent in their evocations and their concern of his important 'African' poems written closer to the '*Voorslag* Days' in the 1920s. Plomer in fact continued to respond emotionally to the South African situation, and another great poem, 'The Taste of the Fruit', dealing with the deaths of two South African writers, Ingrid Jonker and Nat Nakasa, appeared in 1966.)[31]

Laurens van der Post – who is, incidentally, the only surviving member of the Umdoni Park threesome – also moved to Britain in the late 1920s. (Campbell was killed in a motor accident in 1957, Plomer died in 1973.) Though London has been Van der Post's main base, he has returned to South Africa on a number of occasions and has travelled widely. His first book, the novel *In a Province*, was published in 1934 and, following in the tradition of *Turbott Wolfe*, is a reflection of his commitment to the ideals of *Voorslag*. His subsequent writing, which consists largely of partly symbolic fiction and partly philosophical non-fiction, is very different from that of his two colleagues – yet a book such as *The Lost World of the Kalahari* (1958), in its tendency to mythologize and idealize aspects of indigenous southern African culture (especially those relating to the San or 'Bushmen'), does evoke a spirit of romance similar to that which, during the *Voorslag* period, produced poems from Campbell like 'The Serf' and 'The Zulu Girl'. In addition Van der Post has said that his piece on whaling in *Voorslag* Number 3, 'Nimrods van die See', was to form the basis of his book *The Hunter and the Whale* (1967).[32]

III

This Introduction has suggested that *Voorslag* is significant and therefore has been influential in South African literature in English, a view with which many writers and critics would concur (dissenting views have, however, also been expressed).[33] Yet, as the brief account given here of the life of the journal will have indicated, the influence of *Voorslag* is very difficult to delineate precisely, for two main reasons. First, *Voorslag* appears to have been for many people a legend rather than a concrete reality; it seems likely that the journal was not actually read or even seen by many of the writers who responded in a general way to its appeal and challenge. The second reason is related to the first and is more pertinent: it was impossible at the time, and is impossible now, to disentangle the influence of *Voorslag*, such as it was, from the considerable effect produced by the more readily available publications of Campbell and Plomer: Campbell's *The Flaming Terrapin* (1924), *The Wayzgoose* (1928) which owes so much of its material and inspiration to the *Voorslag* period, and *Adamastor* (1930) where are to be found the striking poems composed in the white heat of the poet's frustrations and disappointments at the demise of the journal; and Plomer's *Turbott Wolfe* (1925), *I Speak of Africa* (1927) and *Notes for Poems* (1927), all of which are informed by social and racial criticism such as had also characterized the author's contributions to *Voorslag*; there are also (as was mentioned above) some later works by Plomer and those of Van der Post.

It would hardly be appropriate, in these introductory pages, to attempt an assessment of the overall importance, and the impact in South Africa, of Campbell, Plomer and Van der Post. Instead we shall conclude by reiterating some of the ways in which *Voorslag* – whether as an actually experienced reality or as a semi-mythical event – has proved significant in certain areas of South African imaginative and intellectual life. The journal was brought into existence by two fine and thoroughly committed writers, and it set high standards: it was fresh, lively, alert and bold, its boldness shown partly by its willingness, indeed its eagerness, to see aesthetic, cultural, social and political questions as wholly interrelated. It is of course necessary to see the three young authors as circumscribed in various ways, by their upbringing, by their class and indeed by the very society which they disdained: we do not, for example, find in their writings the in-depth critiques of working-class formations such as had characterized several of the writings of their near-contemporaries Olive Schreiner, Douglas Blackburn and Sol. T. Plaatje;[34] nor do we find attempts to appropriate to 'literary' modes typically South African speech rhythms and forms of 'folk' culture such as one discerns, variously, in the works of Pauline Smith, Stephen Black and, shortly afterwards, Herman Charles Bosman.[35] Yet Campbell, Plomer and Van der Post must by any reckoning count as innovative and liberating figures. *Voorslag* has become a symbol of the creative artist's necessary independence – a symbol of importance in the development of writers and writing in a 'new' country. The three young authors expressed what they believed and, when their 'managers' tried to interfere, they resigned and walked out. (The shortness of the real life of *Voorslag* and the fact that its creators soon left the country are all important components of the story; exile, either voluntary or forced, is of course a common experience that must be taken account of in any understanding of South African writing.)

The variety of the contributions written by Campbell and Plomer (Van der Post's have their importance too) – poetry, fiction, social commentary, literary criticism – can be said to have re-animated, or in some cases even to have set in motion for the first time, various impulses in South African writing. Campbell's pieces can be seen on the whole as expressions and evocations of power – of awe, of passion, of scorn – while Plomer's work is above all acute – in insight, in probing analysis, in irony. It is these tendencies – power and acuteness – which represent two of the main thrusts in a good deal of South African literature of the last fifty years or so. To look more closely at the late twenties and the thirties, several critics have been inclined – notwithstanding the achievements of Olive Schreiner and Pauline Smith – to see Campbell and Plomer as the initiators of a sustained 'new wave' in South African English literature, and also as an important influence on Afrikaans literature (Campbell in particular offered a vivid example to the Dertiger poets, one of whom was N. P. van Wyk Louw).

Voorslag plunged vigorously into a discussion of South African literature and culture. Its attitude towards local culture – 'colonial culture' as it tended to call it – was very far from being protective or reverential. Understandably Campbell and Plomer viewed events largely from the perspective of whites. Yet were they right to insist so confidently on what they felt to be metropolitan standards? Were they insensitive to other aspects of South African life and literature? Certainly their contemporary Stephen Black had reservations about the direction and assumptions of journals such as *Voorslag*, when he remarked of the journal which he himself founded and edited:

> ... *The Sjambok* has not yet received the compliment of passable mimicry; but we hear that a positive small-pox of

> imitators now threatens to afflict the unfortunate public. Some of our imitators will be too high-brow (oblivious of the fate that befell Roy Campbell's eclectic venture in Durban); and some will be too low in every way, heedless of the fate that has befallen the various attempts to mix ink with mud instead of brains.'[36]

His lively, challenging and often libellous journal (even if its title makes some overture to *Voorslag*) deliberately adopted a 'non-élitist' line and, appearing as it did each week from 1929 to 1931, no doubt reached a numerically larger readership than did Campbell and Plomer's journal. Black's comments are a useful reminder of 'alternative' directions in South African literature and thought, some of which are only now in the process of being rediscovered and which involved writers who, from the start, were prepared to stay in South Africa and to see this country, not Europe, as the yardstick by which artistic value was to be measured.

To recognise this, however, is not to deny the crucial importance of *Voorslag*, but rather to appreciate something of the complex task of drawing a comprehensive map of South African literary influences and developments. (This task has been made even more complex and interesting by a greater general knowledge of the work in English produced, in the late twenties and the thirties, by black creative writers and journalists.) What is significant in the end is that Campbell, Plomer and Van der Post backed up their declarations about international standards and the integrity of the artist by the unusually high quality of their own performance, both in the creative and critical fields. *Voorslag* had the courage to enter the realms of serious and probing questioning on matters of art, human feeling, and society; it is the substance, temper and tone of its involvement which this facsimile edition seeks to convey and re-create for present-day readers and students of South African literature.

Colin Gardner
Michael Chapman
(University of Natal)

NOTES

To avoid repetitive notes, biographical information on people who are mentioned frequently in the text of *Voorslag*, or in the editorial material, has been given in the Index.

1 Laurens van der Post, Unpublished letter to the University of Natal Press (1979).

2 See Appendix D, Campbell's letter to Maurice Webb, June/July 1926. (Campbell Collection, Killie Campbell Library, Durban.) In an unpublished letter to Edward Roworth, 1925, Campbell wrote: '[Plomer] and I are writing a Manifesto for *Voorslag* which we both think is more concise and less rambling than Webb's. Unless you are perfectly satisfied with Webb's try to dissuade him from getting it printed until we can have a proper confabulation together.' (Campbell Collection, South African Library, Cape Town.)

3 The evidence we have of 'interference' and 'textual alterations' is contained in Campbell's letter to Maurice Webb (Appendix D) and in Plomer's Preface to *I Speak of Africa* (1927) – for details of alterations to Plomer's 'Portraits in the Nude' see the note to page 58 of *Voorslag*, Vol. 1, No. 3, as reprinted here. In a note to *The Wayzgoose* Campbell with characteristic hyperbole said: '*Voorslag* nevertheless retained some of our MSS. to which they claimed a legal right, and we allowed them to be published after exacting the *promise that they would not be tampered with*. After having both solicited and accepted our MSS., the founders, without asking our permission and before publication, read them aloud at their public literary debauches. Then, after that, they made considerable alterations to the proofs, spoiling everything we wrote either by their bungling "improvements" or by neglecting to correct the proofs' (*Collected Poems*, Vol. 1, 1949, pp. 293–294).

4 See Appendix D, Campbell's letter to Maurice Webb, in which are mentioned Sarah Gertrude Millin's possible contributions to *Voorslag*. Campbell's famous epigram 'On Some South African Novelists' (*Adamastor,* 1930) refers of course to Millin's 'restraint' as a novelist:

You praise the firm restraint with which they write –
I'm with you there, of course:
They use the snaffle and the curb all right,
But where's the bloody horse?

(Incidentally, one can perhaps see the genesis of this epigram towards the end of the first paragraph of Campbell's letter to C.J. Sibbett, Appendix K.)

5 Van der Post, in his unpublished letter to the University of Natal Press (1979), remarks that Campbell objected to Professor Haarhoff's translations of Catullus ('I am not going to have any "mossies", even Roman ones, twittering in the pages of *Voorslag*').

6 David Gamble worked, as Van der Post did, on *The Natal Advertiser.* Van der Post liked him and respected his poetry, but Campbell disliked both.

7 *Double Lives: An Autobiography* (1943), p. 43.
Robin Hallett makes a useful point: 'Campbell's friend, Wyndham Lewis, had already launched a number of tough satirical journals, the latest of which was provocatively entitled *Blast*. Wyndham Lewis's example must have been at the back of Campbell's mind when so aggressive a title as *Voorslag* . . . was chosen.' 'The Importance of *Voorslag*: Roy Campbell, William Plomer and the Development of South African Literature', *Theoria,* Pietermaritzburg, No. 50 (May 1978), p. 31.

8 Smuts published *Holism and Evolution* in 1926. In *The Wayzgoose* Campbell writes:

Statesman-philosopher! I shake thy hand –
All tailors envy thee throughout the land
Whose Button-Holism, without reverse,
Undoes the Trousers of the Universe!

9 Campbell scorned Roworth's over-coloured paintings and, in *The Wayzgoose*, satirized him as Pollio.

10 Campbell's unpublished letter to Edward Roworth, 1925. (Campbell Collection, South African Library, Cape Town.)

11 We reprint O. Bunn's letter (*Voorslag* Number 5) and Campbell's reply (Number 6):

A PLEA FOR THE HISTORICAL NOVEL
To the Editor of *Voorslag*,
Dear Sir, –

It seems to me a pity that, in the first number of *Voorslag*, the type of novel advocated as an example for the South African novelist should be that of *Turbott Wolfe.* This novel can only be read or understood by an esoteric coterie who can never represent a public in the best sense of the word. So-called realism is often merely obscenity, and is then decadent; and destructive criticism, such as that of Mr Campbell, is almost obstructive, and may defeat its purpose (if there is one?). The whole trend of philosophy and thought of the present day, in spite of the differences dividing such thinkers as Croce, Troeltsch and Whitehead, to name only three, is towards 'insistence on the union of time and space – and on the event as the unit of reality'. The type of novel, for which there is a marvellous wealth of material available in South Africa, is one which has scarcely been touched at all – I mean the historical novel. In England it is immensely popular. In Paris last autumn, the most discussed novel was the romance written round Mme Récamier and Mme de Stael by the Socialist Premier Edouard Herriot, and there has appeared a successful series of this type on the lives of the famous women of the XVI and XVII Centuries, one of which at least is a *tour de force*. In Germany Spengler's colossal historical work is widely read and discussed now.

Few people know much about South Africa's history – most know nothing, therefore much research and careful enquiry would be entailed. Our history holds a wealth of romance and adventure equal to that of any country in the world. The conflicting forces of race and religion, of which our problems today are the outcome, keep their secret well. Is it because the authorities in Cape Town and Pretoria are most unwilling to disclose any of their valuable sources of information?

As to the native point of view, which is so insistent in *Turbott Wolfe.* The native, in regarding this story, can be left with nothing but scorn and disgust for the degenerate white race, whereas, in spite of being infuriated – perhaps even more though differently – by the utterly brutal treatment of his ancestors, he cannot but admire the courage, enterprise and perseverance of the conquering race in olden times. Courage he has. Might this not help him to attain enterprise and perseverance – two qualities without which he cannot progress –

. . . Thou shalt die, but these almighty forces
That meet to form the two for evermore,
They hold the state in their eternal courses,
And shape the long sand grasses on the shore.
Be calmly glad thine own true kindred seeing,
In fire, in storm, in flowers with dew impearled,
Rejoice in thine imperishable being,
One with the essence of the boundless world.

Yours faithfully,
O. BUNN

Broadmoor,
Wartburg, Natal.
Sept. 14th, 1926.

Dear Sir, –

Your correspondence pages seem to have become the resort of all those who are anxious to commit *hari-kari* in public by means of their arguments. I have a life-long experience of South African art, literature and other forms of suicide: and as I seem to be the innocent cause of so much trouble, I hasten to offer my services as undertaker to those who are past hope, and to administer first aid to those who are not. The 'Vaalman',* it

* Campbell refers here to an item in the Correspondence pages of *Voorslag* Number 4.

DENOUEMENT

Some great man said: 'Whoever a portrait draws,
Unconsciously produces two because
He draws the sitter's and his own.' Did he perhaps allude
To William Plomer's 'Portraits in the Nude'?

VAALMAN

seems, has been waiting a long time for his coffin, but here it is. Let us bury him, as he perished, in rhyme and metre:

> Vaalman, though warned by Plomer's self-portrayal
> Hastens as rashly to his own betrayal:
> Four lines suffice his stature to declare
> And frame his person in a wooden square:
> I offer here six more to close him in:
> Proceed, and let the funeral begin.

Mr O. Bunn is altogether too good to be disposed of in this cursory manner. He is still within reach of first aid, or, at least, of taxidermy. Mr O. Bunn asserts that *Turbott Wolfe* can 'only be read or understood by an esoteric coterie,' and immediately proceeds to air his views on a book which he has, therefore, neither read nor understood. Were it not that this confession amply excuses the incoherence of his remarks, I should have left him at the mercy of his own arguments. The 'public' is volubly 'represented' by its journalists; and it cannot hope to be represented by first-rate artists while it clings to third-rate ideas. It has only itself to blame that clear-thinking and intelligence are confined to a 'coterie.' If there were anything creative in the attitude of the public to the native question – there would be no native question by now: *Turbott Wolfe* would never have been written, and the South African 'public' would be able to claim the honour of being 'represented' in English literature by Pringle, Olive Schreiner, Plomer and myself, who, though we represent English literature in Africa, cannot be said to represent white South Africa in English literature. Our work is opposed to public opinion not because we are 'obstructive' but because public opinion is. As long as public opinion is retrograde, so long will international literature be hostile to it. If Mr Bunn were as anxious to claim kinship with the native, as with 'fires,' 'storms,' and bits of 'long sandy grass on the shore,' he would make more impression than by trying to induce the native to read unwritten historical novels. Mr O. Bunn preaches about the 'union of time and space.' How can an artist be in 'union with time and space' by writing about the past? Does Mr O. Bunn live so far in the past that he finds it an effort to 'unite' with the present? If Mr Bunn is more in union with historical novels than actual ones, neither Plomer nor myself can make ourselves responsible for the precise epoch in which his development was arrested. Let us revise Mr O. Bunn's inspiring finale and bring it into closer union with time, space, the present occasion, and Mr Bunn himself.

O Bunn, live on: but those almighty forces,
Thine arguments, will clash for evermore,
And though they stun the planets from their courses
And scare the sacred muses from our shore,
Be calmly wise, thine own true kindred seeing
In fires and storms and accidents: O seer,
Rejoice in thine inexplicable being
And have a glass of beer.

ROY CAMPBELL

12 Interestingly, the sympathetic views of Mary Cowley Hewitt, in her contributions on Olive Schreiner ('The Soul of Olive Schreiner' in Number 4 and, in Number 6, where she appears as 'M.C.H.', a review 'Olive Schreiner's Posthumous Novel' – on *From Man to Man*), accord well with Campbell's own views at the time on Schreiner's writing (in his poem 'Buffel's Kop', printed in the *Adamastor* volume of 1930, he designated Schreiner's 'silver plume' an emblem of fearless honesty and truth). Furthermore, in both articles Mary Cowley Hewitt makes slightly derogatory references to Cronwright; similar remarks are made by Campbell in his letter to C. J. Sibbett, December 1926 (Appendix I).

Geoffrey Haresnape has suggested several ways in which Olive Schreiner inspired the *Voorslag* trio, in 'The *Voorslag* Movement and Olive Schreiner', Van Wyk Smith, Malvern and Don Maclennan (eds.), *Olive Schreiner and After: Essays on Southern African Literature in Honour of Guy Butler* (1983).

13 Plomer, '*Voorslag* Days', *London Magazine*, Vol. 6, No. 1 (July 1959). See also *The South African Autobiography* (1984), pp. 164–178.

Van der Post, Introduction, *Turbott Wolfe* (1965), reprinted in the most recent edition of *Turbott Wolfe*, edited by Stephen Gray

(1980). See also 'A Remarkable Team and a Remarkable Period', *Cape Times Centenary Supplement* (27 March 1976), pp. 16–22. Alexander, 'Campbell, Plomer, Van der Post and *Voorslag*', *English in Africa*, Grahamstown, Vol. 7, No. 2 (September 1980). See also *Roy Campbell: A Critical Biography* (1982), pp. 42–75.

14 *Natal Witness*, Pietermaritzburg (19 March, 26 March, 2 April, 16 April, 23 April, 1925).
Campbell's return to Durban was greeted with the headline 'A South African Poet: Author Visits his Home in Durban', *The Natal Advertiser*, Durban (14 June 1924).

15 Campbell had married Mary Garman in 1922.

16 In *Double Lives* (1943) and his *Autobiography* (1975 and, as abridged, 1984) Plomer gives fairly full accounts of the press reaction to *Turbott Wolfe*.

17 '*Voorslag* Days', p. 48.

18 'Ula Masondo' was printed in *I Speak of Africa* (1927).

19 Introduction, *Turbott Wolfe* (1965), pp. 19–22. *Turbott Wolfe* was greeted in Natal by Wodson in *The Natal Advertiser* (19 March 1926) under the headline 'A Nasty Book on a Nasty Subject'.

20 Campbell's unpublished memorandum to William Plomer, August 1926. (Durham University Library.)

21 *Double Lives*, p. 166, and *Autobiography*, p. 172.

22 In the Preface to *I Speak of Africa* (1927) Plomer says: 'In 1926 I began, together with my friend Mr Roy Campbell, the first literary movement in South Africa.' In his *Autobiography* (1975) he adds: 'Certainly nothing remotely like *Voorslag* had confronted its readers before, nothing so European, so cultivated, so forceful, ironical, and direct' (p. 172).

It is possible to concur with Plomer's views, especially that he and Campbell began the 'first literary movement in South Africa'; nevertheless his remarks, which are characteristically disdainful of his South African origins, might suggest that the *Voorslag* trio were unprepared, and probably insufficiently informed, to see their journal in a context of South African literary magazines, a point with which Stephen Gray for one has taken issue (see Note 33, below). In fact *Voorslag* had been preceded by several literary journals in South Africa, most notably by the *South African Journal*, which was suspended by the editors Pringle and Fairbairn after the second issue of March–April 1824 because they were not willing to submit to censorship. Other independent periodicals to appear prior to Campbell and Plomer's journal were Alexander Johnstone Jardine's *Cape of Good Hope Literary Gazette* (1830–1835), James L. Fitzpatrick's *Cape of Good Hope Literary Magazine* (1847–1848) and Roderick Noble's *Cape Monthly Magazine* (1857–1862; 1870–1875) which was taken over without a break in publication by Noble's brother John and finally ceased in 1881, to be replaced by the *Cape Quarterly Review*.

23 In a letter received by C.J. Sibbett in August 1926 Campbell writes: 'In fact I had sent in my resignation a week before and Ned [Roworth] had specially organized the meeting in order to try to persuade me to reconsider my resignation.' (Campbell Collection, South African Library, Cape Town.) See also Campbell's letter to Sibbett, received in July 1926 (Appendix F).

24 '*Voorslag* Days', pp. 49–50.

25 These poems appeared in the *Adamastor* volume of 1930.

26 In his *Autobiography* Plomer writes: 'In later life Campbell and I were estranged. I blame myself, and am ashamed to have been an unfaithful friend to one who had been generous to me, but there was too sharp a divergence in our opinions and in what might now be called our life-styles' (p. 176).
For details see Alexander, *Roy Campbell: A Critical Biography*, pp. 113–115. See also Geoffrey Haresnape's Introduction to *William Plomer: The South African Autobiography* (1984), pp. x–xiii.

27 See the respective autobiographies, Campbell's *Light on a Dark Horse* (1951), Plomer's *Autobiography* (1975) and Van der Post's *Yet Being Someone Other* (1982), as well as Alexander's *Roy Campbell: A Critical Biography* (1982) and H.D. Jennings's 'The Enigma of Roy Campbell', *Contrast*, Cape Town, No. 57 (July 1984), pp. 63–82.

28 'Poetry and Experience', *Theoria*, Pietermaritzburg, No. 6 (1954), pp. 37–44.

29 See Plomer's 'South African Writers and English Readers', *Proceedings of A Conference of Writers, Publishers, Editors and University Teachers of English* (1957), pp. 54–72.

30 'About William Plomer', *London Magazine*, Vol. 13, No. 5 (December 1973–January 1974), p. 14.

31 These poems all appear in the revised edition of Plomer's *Collected Poems* (1973).

32 Unpublished letter to the University of Natal Press (1979).

33 See for example J.M. Miller and Howard Sergeant's *A Critical Survey of South African Poetry in English* (1957), pp. 106–111, Robin Hallett's 'The Importance of *Voorslag*: Roy Campbell, William Plomer and the Development of South African Literature', *Theoria*, Pietermaritzburg, No. 50 (May 1978), pp. 29–38, Peter Alexander's 'Campbell, Plomer, Van der Post and *Voorslag*', *English in Africa*, Grahamstown, Vol. 7, No. 2 (September 1980), and Geoffrey Haresnape's doctoral thesis 'The Writings of Roy Campbell, William Plomer and Laurens van der Post with Special Reference to their Collaboration in *Voorslag* ('Whiplash') Magazine in 1926' (University of Sheffield, 1982).

A dissenting view is offered by Stephen Gray in his forthcoming article 'William Plomer's Stories: The South African Origins of New Literature Modes', *Journal of Commonwealth Literature*, Leeds, Vol. 21, No. 3 (1986) and in his *Southern African Literature: An Introduction* (1979): 'All three writers have subsequently much publicised *Voorslag* as a unique literary revolt against the stagnant conformism of the colonial backwaters of Southern Africa, despite the fact that Pringle and Fairbairn had enacted the same declarations of the artist's independence a century before, and the fact that, to the present day, with the exception of some conservative magazines, virtually all literary reviews in the history of English literature in Southern Africa have regularly collided with popular taste and the institutions of officialdom' (p. 193).

Our own response to Gray's strictures has been to allow the *South African Journal* and other literary magazines their due and to make no claim that *Voorslag* was the first or the only important journal in South African literary history (see Note 22, above). At the same time, we do point to what seems to us the unique distinction of the *Voorslag* phenomenon: that its authors backed up their declarations by the high and sustained quality of their own performance.

34 For example Schreiner's *Trooper Peter Halket of Mashonaland* (1896), Blackburn's *Burger Quixote* (1903) and Plaatje's *Native Life in South Africa* (1916).

35 For example Smith's *The Little Karoo* (1925), Black's many stage plays, the best of which are to be found in *Three Plays* (1984), and Bosman's *Mafeking Road* (1946), a volume comprising stories many of which had appeared in little magazines during the 1930s.

36 'An Epidemic of Imitators: *The Sjambok*'s Success and Why', *The Sjambok,* Johannesburg, Vol. 1, No. 8 (7 June 1929), p. 14. See also Sarah Gertrude Millin's concern about 'the extremely narrow appeal' of *Voorslag* (Appendix B) and Campbell's reply (Appendix C).

VOORSLAG

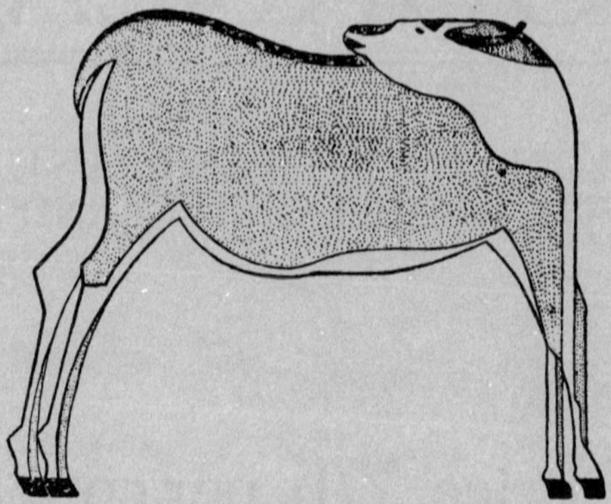

Vol. I JUNE 1926 No. 1

Two Shillings and Sixpence

VOORSLAG

Vol. 1 JUNE 1926 No. 1

Contents

VOORSLAG

A MAGAZINE OF SOUTH AFRICAN
LIFE AND ART.

Published by A. C. Braby, Durban.

MSS. and all communications should be addressed to Box 731, Durban.

Why Voorslag?

Voorslag has come into existence because it has been felt that there is need for it in South Africa. If that apparent need proves to be real it will continue. Voorslag will be devoted to the Life and Art of South Africa and the development of the South African people.

Voorslag will also attempt to keep in contact with contemporary thought in Europe and America, it will present articles on the most important European painters and review the most important European books.

Some little concern has been expressed at the choice of title. This must not be taken too literally. The name has the virtue of being short and being South African. It must not be taken to imply that Voorslag will be content to lash; Voorslag will, necessarily, be critical upon occasion; it hopes, however, to be genuinely constructive as well.

In its pages Voorslag hopes to present original work of South African writers, each in his or her own sphere, and readers are invited to submit MSS. for consideration.

In Politics Voorslag has no party. It offers an open platform for the consideration of social and political questions free from party or racial prejudice. Whatever concerns South Africa is the concern of Voorslag.

As with political parties, so with the two languages of the South African Union. Either language will be represented and contributions, accepted for publication, will appear in the language of the writer, be it English or Afrikaans.

Those to whom this new enterprise appeals are invited to make it known to others likely to be interested. This first issue is presented, with a full knowledge of its shortcomings, yet without apology.

M.W.

The Albatross.

Stretching white wings in strenuous repose,
Sleeving them in the silver frills of sleep,
As I was carried, far from other foes,
To shear the long horizons of the deep,

A swift ship struck me down: through gusty glooms
I spun from fierce collision with her spars:
Shrill through the sleety pallor of my plumes
Whistled the stinging buckshot of the stars.

Thrashing numbed wings my shattered wreck was strewn,
And conquered by the envious winds at last,
A rag upon the red horns of the moon,
Was tossed and gored and trampled by the blast.

Flapping the water like a sodden flag,
No more to rise, shot down by stormy guns,
How shamefully these great sprained sinews drag
That bracketed my purpose with the Sun's. . . .

To the dark ocean I had dealt my laws
And when the shores rolled by, their speed was mine:
The ranges moved like long two-handed saws
Notching the scarlet west with jagged line.

The minarets of Asia, as I passed,
Like toadstools rose, to shrivel in an hour:
Lopped by the steel horizon from their fast
Rock-rooted bases, toppled peak and tower.

Feathered with palm, and eyed with broad lagoons,
Fanned open to the dimly burning sky,
A peacock-train of fierce mesmeric moons,
The coast of Africa had rustled by.

The broad curve of the West with nightward tilt
Wheeled down, and nations stood upon their crowns;
Each spire a crutch, each chimney-stack a stilt,
Across the nether sky their fog-red towns

Went striding—while up far opposing seas
I by earth's sunward wheel was steeply borne
To see the green foam-heaved antipodes
Capsize their thousand islands on the morn.

Then through the gloom wherein, like tiny spiders,
Webbed in their flimsy rays, the systems spawn,
Up dim blue rocks of cloud with scarlet fibres
Crawled the gigantic lichens of the dawn.

Striped with the fiery colours of the sky,
Tigered with warpaint, ramping as they rolled,
The green waves charged the sunrise, letting fly
Their porpoises like boomerangs of gold.

The cliff-ringed islands where the penguins' nest,
Sheltered their drowsy legions from the foam
When evening brought the cormorants to rest,
Gondolas of the tempest, steering home.

To sleep or cackle grouped in homely rings
I left them, roosting warm in their own dung:
And while they fattened there—with homeless wings
The great harp of the hurricanes I strung;

Towering far up among the red star-sockets
  I saw deep down in vast flotillas shoaled
The phosphorescent whales like bursting rockets
  Bore through the gloom their long ravines of gold.

Far coral islands rose in faint relief
  Each with its fringe of palms and shut lagoon
Where with a running fuse of spray the reef
  Set off the golden crackers of the moon.

By nameless capes, where the slow thunder prowls,
  I dared the shapeless phantoms of the storm,
Relentless as the noon to dazzled owls,
  Inflicting beauty on their hate of form.

Squelching like sodden shoes, with stoven flanks
  Doomed vessels swung their tetering yards on high,
Sucked the grey surges through their rifted planks
  And thrashed their crippled turbines to the sky.

I read my doom in their gaunt stoven ribs
  Nor with vague fancies drugged my truth-of-sight—
I knew the stars for momentary squibs
  In the perpetual horror of the night.

I saw how vile a thing it is to die
  Save when careering on their sunward course,
The strong heart cracks, the shivered senses fly
  Stunned by their own expenditure of force.

Erect, unterrified, though robbed of breath,
  In those wild hours of triumph had I died,
The shades around as in a meteor's death
  Had seen annihilation glorified.

My stiff quills made the hurricane their lyre
Where pronged with azure fire, the black hail screams;
Huge brindled shadows barred with gloomy fire,
Prowling the red horizon of my dreams,

Thick storm-clouds threatened me with dense eclipse;
The wind made whirling rowels of the stars;
Over dark waves where sky-careering ships
Gibbet the moon upon their crazy spars,

A white velocity through roaring glooms
My breast was trolleyed on a rail of light;
I felt the laughing trades inflate my plumes
Rolling new leagues of azure into sight;

Through calms that seemed the swoon of all the gales
On airy frills that softest winds had spun
I floated like a seed with silken sails
Out of the sleepy thistle of the sun.

I had been dashed in the gold spray of dawns
And hit with silver by the stars' faint light;
The red moon charged at me with lowered horns
Buffalo-shouldered by the gloom of night.

Broidering earth's senseless matter with my sight,
Weaving my life around it like a robe
Onward I drew my silken clues of flight
Spooled by the wheeling glories of the globe

The world revolving like a vast cocoon,
Unwound its threaded leagues at my desire;
With burning stitches by the sun and moon
My life was woven like a shawl of fire.

Clashing the surf-gold fringe that round it runs,
Its giant mesh of fire-shot silk, unfurled
And braided with a chain of flashing suns,
Fleeces the craggy shoulders of the world.

How dimly now its threads are ravelled out,
Its gorgeous colours smoulder from my brain,
While my numbed memory the world about
Rays forth its thin meridians of pain.

My thoughts with wild funereal trophies blaze
Like dying torches—spoils of azure nights
And the slain suns my speed has shorn of rays
And dashed to bleed upon the western heights.

Night surges on the black reef of the world;
Shaking the sky in ponderous collapse,
I hear the long horizons, steeply hurled,
Rush cataracting down through starless gaps.

No more to rise, the last sun bombs the deep
And strews my shattered senses with its light;
My spirit knows the silence it must keep
And, with the ocean, hankers for the night.

ROY CAMPBELL.

Beauty in Nature.

Natural Beauty, in spite of its importance and pervasiveness in the universe, has so far received but scant notice from Science; and this unfavourable treatment stands in marked contrast to the very great attention which has been devoted to other aspects of Nature. Our knowledge of Nature has to do either with facts or with values and meanings. Now our knowledge of physical facts is almost uncanny in its fullness and completeness. But about the other aspect of Nature, which has to do with values and meanings, we know very little indeed. And yet this is a most important aspect. Of Beauty we know very little except insofar as it is practised in the Arts of sculpture, painting, music, poetry, etc. But when we go beyond our human art and beyond Beauty from our human point of view, we enter a world which is still largely unexplored by science. Beauty in Nature is and remains largely *terra incognita*. What is its nature and what are its sources? What purposes does it serve in the order of the universe? What is its *raison d'être?* Beauty in Nature clearly has not a mere human reference; things beautiful are not merely such to us humans. Beauty would be there even if we were not there to behold it. The beautiful colours and shapes and sounds of Nature were not meant for us, and were there long before we had appeared on the scene. The wonderful plumage of birds was not meant for our eye but for the eye of birds and other animals, just as their wonderful songs were meant primarily for themselves and not for us. The thrilling notes of the nightingale were meant to pierce and soften the heart of the coy beloved mate; and thousands, perhaps hundreds of thousands of years before they had stirred the sad heart of Ruth, they had exercised their irresistible spell in the quarter for which they were intended. In trying to find an explanation of organic Beauty we must abandon the human reference as entirely irrelevant; we must study Beauty in its native home in Nature and not in the human mind; both the source and the appeal of natural Beauty are in their essence extra-human, however much we may be affected thereby. This is true of organic Beauty, of the beauty of living things. It is just as true of Beauty in inorganic Nature. The colours of sunrise and sunset were not meant for our eye; the lines of sea and land. the changing lights on the mountains, the moonlight sleeping on the bank, the wind on the heath—are there in their own right in the order of Nature. What unearthly sunsets there must have been over the warm Silurian seas which covered much of the globe millions of years before the human advent! What indescribable lights must have played on the Algonkian mountains, of which only the stumps and roots remain to-day to remind us of their existence in the abyss of time! No, the human approach is the most useless and irrelevant of all to this great problem of Beauty in Nature. These things were not meant for us, however we may enjoy them, now that we too have arrived on the scene.

Having ruled out the naive human point of view, let us now ask what Science makes of the problem and how it approaches this subject of Beauty in Nature. Now Science sees no meanings or values in the Beauty of inorganic Nature. It sees no purpose which could be served by the lights and shadows on the mountains, or the colours of sunrise or sunset, or the beautiful contours of the mountains or the seas, of the hills and the valleys. These effects are to her the products of natural forces and situations; they are part of the mechanism of Nature and are not capable of further explanation. The iridescence of crystals, the wonderful colourings of minerals are due to their inner chemical and physical constitution and serve no external purpose. For Science they are facts and not values in the order of Nature; and we must accept them as facts, as what they are, without asking childish questions about their meaning or value.

When, however, Science comes to living things it sees more than mere brute facts, it admits and accepts the existence of values too, and it accepts the beautiful as one of the aspects of value in Nature. But here it puts a very limited sense on this aspect of value. It accepts the beautiful in a restricted limited sense which must come as a shock to all real lovers of Art. We know the catch phrases of Artists, "Art for Art's sake," "Beauty for Beauty's sake." For them ethical or utilitarian considerations have nothing to do with Beauty. The beautiful is such, apart from all considerations of whether it is good or useful. This is not the view of Science, at any rate as applied to organic Nature. Science is profoundly utilitarian; its philosophy is the philosophy of utility. For it none of the poetry and the mysticism so dear to the artistic soul. It is severely pragmatic and utilitarian in its outlook. It asks only what is useful for, what helps in, the organic struggle and advance. That is its test and standard of value.

Applying that test and standard, Science gives the following account of organic Beauty. Beauty has been evolved as a bye-product in the struggle of existence. In that struggle Beauty has proved a useful weapon; and this fact accounts for its rise and progressive elaboration in the course of organic evolution. Its usefulness in the grim game of life has been its title to existence and the cause of its continuous growing expression. But for this close and vital connection with the exigencies of life it would have seemed a mere freak, surplus cargo to be jettisoned at an early stage of the voyage. And in that case it would only have persisted, if at all, as a sort of vestigal survival instead of the powerful, wide-ranging, pervasive factor which it undoubtedly forms to-day in organic Nature.

Beauty is useful in the organic struggle in various ways. In the first place, some beautiful colouring and patterns have been evolved by insects and animals as a means of protection against their enemies. Through these colours and forms they imitate or harmonise with their beautiful natural surroundings and thus escape detection. In the second place, animals or insects evolve beautiful protective colourings for another reason; that is to say, they mimic the colourings of some other animal or insect which is nasty to the taste of their enemies, and through this imitation avoid their attentions. While the imitated species has evolved conspicious colours in order publicly to advertise its unsavoury and odious presence, the imitating species, which is savory or palateable, has put its enemies on a wrong scent by concealing or disguising its true nature.

Butterflies which are palateable often mimic in their colourings unpalateable butterflies, and thus afford most curious and interesting instances of this form of Beauty which is meant to deceive, though in a sense very different from that in which the expression is sometimes applied to human female beauty.

All these and similar cases fall within the principle of Natural Selection as ordinarily understood. That is to say, Beauty in these cases is directly useful as a means in the struggle for survival and helps its possessors in that struggle. But there are other far more numerous cases of organic Beauty which have no direct connection with Natural Selection, and they must therefore be useful in the game of life in some other way. In the grim struggle a weak or otherwise unfit and unsuitable organism will not, apart from the above cases, be saved by its looks. Mere Beauty will not help or save an organism out of harmony with its surroundings. Natural Selection is conceived as essentially blind and ruthless, and not all the Beauty in the world will move it one inch from its course.

The existence of Beauty is therefore one of the facts which have shown up the inadequacy of Natural Selection as the cause of organic progress. A still more dominant fact is sex, which in its powerful appeal seems to call for a factor of its own in the organic situation. Hence the theory of Sexual Selection to which, in spite of the opposition of Wallace and others, Darwin attributed ever more importance as his views matured. Sexual Selection means that females select the more powerful, beautiful, attractive males as their mates; these males therefore have a superior advantage in breeding and propagating their kind, and in that way their characters confer on them a superior survival value. Beauty is thus a powerful motive force in Sexual Selection and a primary cause of organic evolution. The forms, size, colours and song of males help to influence females in their choice of mates, and to excite them to sexual union. And this influence on and excitation of females thus accounts for all that wonderful outgrowth of beautiful forms and colours and songs which we see in organic Nature. In other words, beautiful forms or colours or power of song among living things have arisen and developed to the extent, and only to the extent, to which females were capable of discriminating the difference in form or colour or song between one male and another. Beauty is on this theory useful only insofar as it influences the choice of females. As the differences between, for instance, the colour scheme of one male pheasant and another, or between the notes of one nightingale and another, can only be most minute, the female in every case is assumed to have a sufficiently delicate and subtle feel for these distinctions to appreciate their difference; her emotional discrimination must therefore be something truly extraordinary, and surpassing any power which the human mind or eye or ear has in that respect. This is the scientific theory of Beauty in organic Nature.

I cannot believe that this is a true account of the whole matter. If organic Beauty has grown only because of its utility in the struggle of existence, in other words, only insofar as each smallest increment of Beauty is dependent for its chance of survival on its discrimination and appreciation by the female, then there is presupposed on the part of the female a power of artistic insight and discrimination so fine and delicate as to be truly unintelligible, if not incredible. The innate artistic sense (in the guise of sexual discrimination and selection) thus implied on the part of the female insect, bird or animal would far surpass anything which the human mind has ever achieved or deemed possible. This does seem to me to place a weight on the theory of Sexual Selection which is more than it can bear. We cannot make the entire efflorescence of Beauty dependent merely on the utility factor. There is a far greater flowering of beauty than the female either calls for or can appreciate in all its marvellous minute detail. In Nature as in human art we must come round to the view that Beauty is not restricted to the useful; that there is more in natural organic Beauty than is seen by the eye or heard by the ear of insect or bird or animal. There is in each case no doubt an element of the useful, a basis of utility which influences and determines the choice of the female. But on that narrow basis of utility a superstructure of Beauty is erected which far transcends all animal faculty and points to deeper factors operative in Nature. To my mind Sexual Selection fails to account for all that wealth and depth and compass of Beauty which is so marked a feature of organic Nature. So much in regard to Beauty in the animal kingdom.

Beauty in the plant kingdom is also explained as due to Natural Selection, the theory being that beautiful and conspicuous flowers and forms help their plants to survive and increase. Insects, birds and animals are attracted by such flowers, and this attraction is supposed to account for all that wealth of Beauty which is associated with the flowering plants. Flowers on this theory arose and were evolved in order to attract the attention of insects and other organisms which were useful for the pollination and reproduction of plants. Flowers which failed to evolve beautiful and attractive colours escaped the attention of pollinating insects, and were therefore weeded out on the principle of Natural Selection. Now this account of the origin of Flowering Plants is probably in a large measure correct. But to go further and to attribute all the beautiful forms and colours which flowers have evolved solely and entirely to the eye of insect or bird is surely absurd. There is more in the Beauty of flowers than the eye or insect or bird has ever beheld or will ever behold. Here again a power of artistic discrimination is attributed to these lower creatures which far transcends all power of mind as we know it. No doubt insects and birds with their undeniable sense of colour have been useful up to a point. But beyond that point there has been a lavish outpouring of Beauty in its inexhaustible riches which must be traced to deeper sources than the perception and appreciation of birds and insects. We have to look deeper for the true explanation of the aesthetic developments in Nature. The button has no doubt been pressed by quite ordinary means. But behind the button there is a great story which Science has not yet discovered.

And the existence of Beauty on so vast and extraordinary a scale both in the animal and plant kingdoms is a challenge to us to look deeper into the nature of things than we have done hitherto under the guidance of current theories and concepts. The fact of Beauty and its profound significance as a principal feature in the universe has not received from scientific thinkers the attention it deserves. We have scarcely begun to scratch the surface of this problem, the importance of which must be apparent even to the most casual inspection. The explanation of Nature must be and remain partial and truncated so long as it largely ignores so important a feature of its total domain. Not only has organic Beauty to be explored much more carefully than has been done hitherto; but beyond it there remains the still more baffling problem of inorganic Beauty which has so far been completely ignored by Science or at best only relegated to the domain of human psychology. All this is most unsatisfactory and tends to make our scientific reading and conception of Nature partial and one-sided. Science has concentrated too much on the aspect of facts in Nature and ignored too much the elements of value which exist in the the universe both inorganic and organic.

It is not possible for me in this place to pursue further the problem of Beauty in Nature. But I may be allowed to add that I have tried a fresh way of approach to it and other cognate problems in my forthcoming book on "Holism and Evolution," to which I beg leave to refer any readers who might be interested in a subject which in itself is most entrancing, and, as leading to further problems lying beyond, most important and illuminating.

J. C. SMUTS.

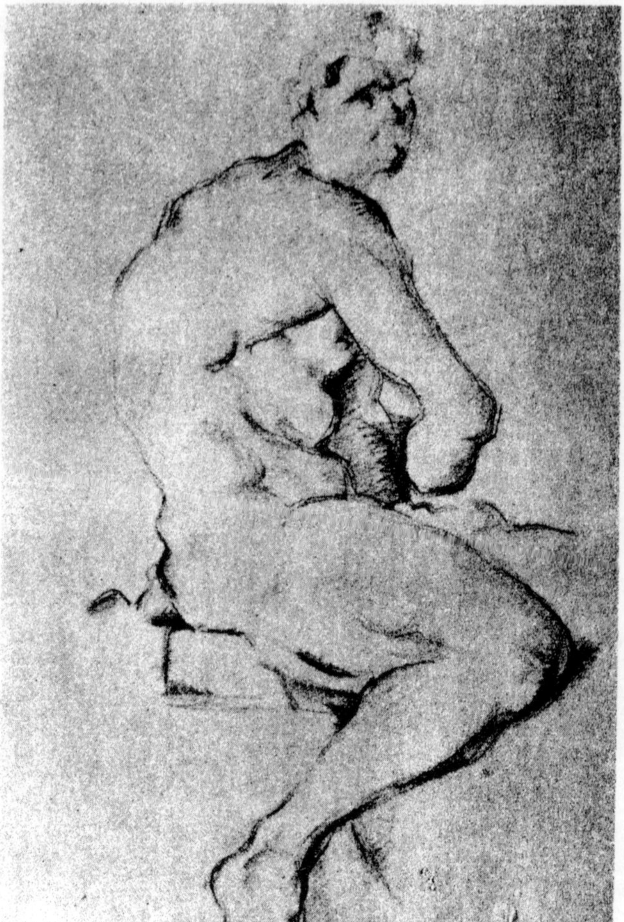

AFTER AN ORIGINAL DRAWING BY CEZANNE

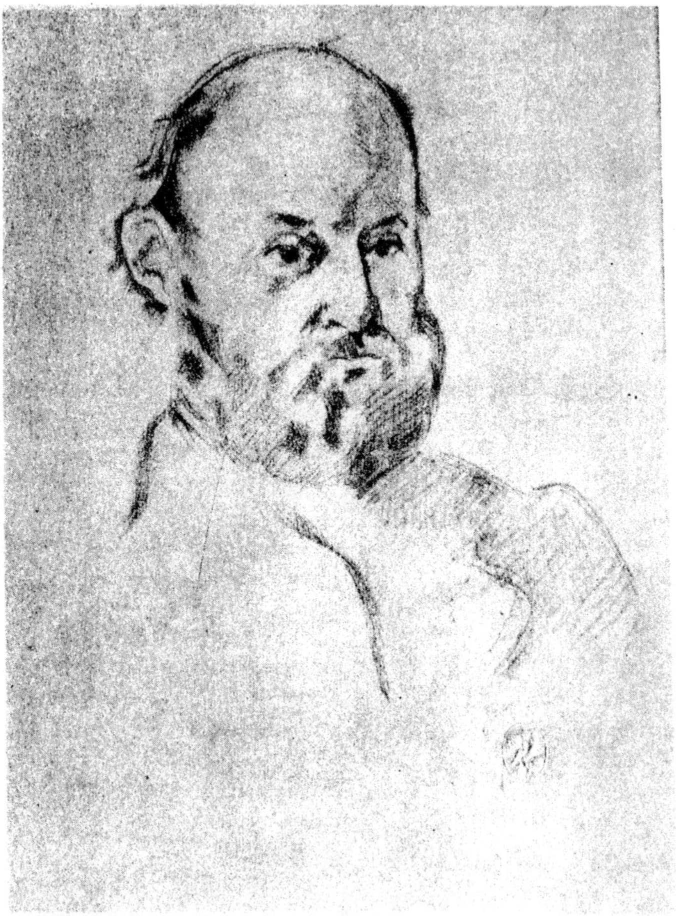

E.P. & C.P. Co., Ltd., DBN.

PORTRAIT OF HIMSELF
Cezanne

Cézanne.

"He had the type, accent and behaviour of a Provencal. In Provence, as in the East, the feeling of class is not very strong nor are the classes very clearly marked. Cézanne had, at the same time something of the bourgeois and the artizan, but with a decency, a dignity and a simple pride very rarely found in those classes. The acuteness of the peasant was combined in him with manners somewhat exaggeratedly polite. He was round-shouldered with a sunburnt complexion, with touches of brick red, a bald forehead, the colour of copper, over which locks of white hair drooped, a large fat Bourbon nose turning purple, little piercing eyes, ferret-like and restless, regarding everything, seeing everything; short drooping moustaches, a tuft of beard in the military style of the Second Empire."

So writes Edmond Jaloux and this is Joachim Gasquet's sketch of the Master of Aix: "A bald skull with long grey hair still abundant on the nape of the neck, a tuft of beard, and the thick moustaches of an old Colonel hiding a sensuous mouth, freshly shaved, coloured complexion, he might have been an old, retired soldier, were it not for the large forehead instinct with genius, of a curve and an admirable fullness, and the dominating bloodshot eyes which fixed you at once and would not let you go." And so it is that we see Cézanne in one of the fine portraits of himself.

In writing first of Cézanne among the modern masters of painting my reasons are as follows: in the first place it is from Cézanne that the most vital influences of modern painting flow, he it was who set out, in his own words, "to make of the art of the Impressionist's something solid and enduring like the art of the Museums." Secondly, there is no man in the history of painting who has shown a more single-minded devotion to his art. Nothing else in the world could divert his attention from those problems of colour and design that occupied his mind from youth to age. Paul Cézanne had no other aim than that of creating harmonies of tone and colour. Every energy was focussed on the attempt to express himself by means of colour and his sole desire in life was to be a painter.

Born in a period of decadence, denied the advantages of working in a living tradition, jeered at and reviled by all the official painters and critics, his work could not but show signs of the intense, lonely struggle through which he at last reached mastery. Not from the despised Cézanne could we expect the golden calm of Titian, the all-embracing perfection of Giorgione, or the superb ease of Tintoretto, for when Cézanne commenced to paint the great tradition was dead and all real teaching had disappeared. All that was worthy he had himself to rediscover. He was the primitive of a new school. We can overlook the minor imperfections and be grateful that in the volume of his life-work he has given us so much of beauty and power. It is perhaps significant that in making comparisons one should think of the great Venetians, for Cézanne inherited Italian blood. Originally his family came from Cesena, they had crossed the Alps and lived in Brianconnais afterwards descending to Provence. The father of Paul Cézanne, Louis Auguste Cézanne was born in the Var. He was in business at Aix as a hatter and there Paul Cézanne was born on the 19th of January, 1839. His mother, Elizabeth Aubert, was said to have had Creole ancestors. Louis Auguste was a flourishing tradesman, but thinking that a bank would be even more profitable he entered into partnership with a Monsieur Cabassol who had been a cashier, and then commenced what soon became a successful concern. He was shortly in a position to buy a fine estate which included a 17th century building and a farm. Paul was then 20 years old and he had been made *Bachelier es lettres* on the completion of his course at the Collège Bourbon. It was there that he became friendly with Emile Zola. Cézanne's father intended Paul to be a lawyer and compelled him to take his first term in law. The painter's vocation had, however, already declared itself, and the father, regarding the painting of little landscapes as an amiable accomplishment in the future lawyer, made the fatal mistake of giving Paul a second-hand box of paints. Zola, now in Paris, wrote enthusiastic letters to his school-friend and the young Cézanne never rested until he got the banker's consent to join him there. This consent, with the help of his mother and sister was at last obtained and the future master found himself in Paris and a candidate for the entrance examination for the Ecole des Beaux-Arts. He failed to pass and for a time returned to Aix. He agreed to work in his father's bank but was more often to be seen with his paint box wandering through the beautiful Aixois country which he and Zola had explored in their schooldays—"a country that Poussin might have adored; with its groups of trees, the expressive line of its hills, its horizons suffused with the sea air;—it is a classic land!"

In 1863 he returned to Paris, this time supported by a monthly allowance of 150 francs whch was doubled by the banker a little later. He now settled in a studio in the Rue Beautreillis near the Bastille and applied himself to the business of learning to paint. He became acquainted with Manet, Renoir, Monet, Degas and Pissarro. It was the last named who had the greatest influence on Cézanne. From Pissarro he took over all the phases of the Impressionist technique;—the effect upon objects of direct sunlight, the visible brush-strokes, and the juxtaposed spots of bright colour. Except for its greater solidity his work at that time had much resemblance to Pissarro's. The earliest work of Cézanne shows the influence of Courbet, Danmier, and Delacroix. The romantic tendency of his mind responded vividly to the stimulus of Delacroix and Danmier. He loved extremes, the thick paint of Courbet became in his hands a revel of sheer pigment, "he literally plastered his canvases; they looked as though they had been done with a trowel and the masses of paint were furrowed with a thousand ravines." Later he developed an enthusiasm for Rubens, Tintoretto, and Signorelli, and at this period he painted the *Léda au Cygne* and the *Tentation de Sainte-Antoine*. It was then also that he commenced the long series of compositions of "Baigneuses"—the theme for whose realisation he strove throughout his life. He lacked models for his female nudes as he expressed extreme fear of women, saying, "they will get their hooks in me." He is known to have employed only one female model and she an ancient char-woman of whom he apparently had no fear for he referred to her as "that good old crow." For his figures he would go to the Louvre and consult Rubens, Poussin, Signorelli, and the great Venetians. Between the years 1869 and 1873 a gradual change took place in his technique.

His violent temperament was becoming more restrained, his vision more deliberate and tenacious; but throughout his life he occasionally returned to the romantic inspiration of his youth. With Pissarro and Monet, Cézanne would only go to a certain point, he acknowledged all that he had gained from them, they had helped him to see the colour of light and they had influenced his actual handling of paint, but his passion for synthesis prevented him from following them in their experiments in analysis. Cézanne's development was towards the expression of the underlying structure of nature—everything was becoming for him a cylinder, cone, or sphere. Already he was embarking upon his life's mission to make of the discoveries of the Impressionists "something solid and enduring." And how completely he achieved his object in the canvases of his maturity—those magnificent pictures whose richness is not only that of superb colour, but a fusion in colour of all the plastic elements, space, mass, line, composition! It was largely this gift of expressing everything by means of colour that made his work appear so unusual to his contemporaries for he did by means of colour what inferior intelligencies did by means of neutral-tinted drawing and in this, after all, he was only following the example of the Venetians. Maurice Denis related the discovery in 1905 in the *Senola di san Rocco* of a fragment of a freize by Tintoretto, which had been folded back against the wall where it was hung because it was too big for the space and which had, so he wrote, retained all its freshness of colour: "There were apples painted in pale green and bright red on a ground of Emerald green leaves. It is all colour. One might say it was a Cézanne."

It was only after several centuries that with the advent of Cézanne the discoveries of the Venetians were completed and extended. He went back to the first principles of art, he attempted to give expression in paint to the grandest and most enduring forms of nature. He sought to realise on the flat surface of the canvas the full volumes of all objects; out of what was passing and transient he wrought things eternal. Many of his subjects are of motionless objects, cups, fruit, flowers and tables. Still-life allowed him to paint with the greatest deliberation—he would hesitate twenty minutes between two touches—colour, form, tone, modelling were all expressed at once, there was no place in his scheme for the happy "accident," the "inspired" improvisation. It is by these pictures of still-life that Cézanne's followers have been most extensively influenced. It is perhaps in his still-life's that his extreme sensitiveness to gradation and contrast has its fullest scope, but also there is nothing in his art more beautiful than those landscapes, many of them of Aixois country, where the master creates living poems of blue, violet, emerald, rose and gold. There is probably no contemporary work which could hang beside these canvases without suffering eclipse. There is nothing in modern art so opulent, so rich. Can we not call him the greatest of our time?

Again, in portraiture, Cézanne has endowed the world with monumental canvases. He considered that the human figure was the painter's greatest task, but he always lacked models and this in view of his extreme unreasonableness was not remarkable. The portrait of Gustave Geoffroy, seated in his library, occupied Cézanne during a whole year; he had eighty sittings for the portrait and in the end it was never finished. The portrait of Vollard remained incomplete after one hundred and fifteen sittings and was finally abandoned with the remark, related by the model, "I am not altogether displeased with the shirt-front." M. Vollard relates what happened in the studio: "When I arrived I saw, in the middle of the studio, a chair on a box which was raised by means of four meagre supports. I looked at this platform not without some misgiving. Cézanne divined my apprehension. 'I fixed up the chair for the pose myself! You need have no fear of falling, M. Vollard, if you will only keep your balance. Besides one does not move when one poses!' Once seated —and with what precautions—I took great care not to make any of those movements known as 'false'; indeed, I remained perfectly motionless but this very stillness induced a drowsiness with which I wrestled triumphantly for a time, but presently my head began to droop on my shoulders, while at the same time, I lost all sense of the outer world; suddenly I lost my balance and chair, platform and myself collapsed on the ground. Cézanne flung himself on me, 'wretched fellow! You have upset the pose! I told you to keep as still as an apple. Does an apple fidget?' After that day before posing, I swallowed a cup of black coffee. What is more, Cézanne kept a strict eye on me and if he thought he saw any sign of fatigue, a precursor of sleep, he gave me such a look that I hastened to resume the pose again like an angel—I almost said like an apple. The sittings used to begin in the mornings at eight o'clock and lasted until half-past eleven. When I arrived Cézanne would close the *Pèlerin* or the *la Croix* which were his favourite reading. The studio in the Rue Hegesippe-Moreau was even more simply decorated than the one at Aix. Reproductions of Forain, cut out of newspapers, formed the basis of the Master's Parisian collection. . . . When the sitting began Cézanne would regard me with fixed and rather hard eyes . . . . . . Cézanne used very supple brushes for painting, rather like the hair of the Marten or the polecat, which he washed after each touch *in a pincelier* full of essence of turpentine. No matter how many brushes he had he dirtied them all during the sitting. His method of working explains the solidity of Cézanne's painting. Not painting in full impasto but putting one layer of colour on top of another, each one as thin as a wash of water colour; the colour dried instantly; there was therefore no fear of changes within the impasto which produce cracks when the upper surface does not dry at the same time as the under painting. I had been told that Cézanne treated his models like slaves; I know it only too well. From the first touch of the brush to the end of the sitting he treated his model as the merest piece of still-life. He was very fond of painting portraits. 'The face is the end and aim of art,' he used to say. If he did not paint more of them, it was because of the difficulty he had in getting models as easy to manage as myself. And so it was that, after painting himself, his wife and some of his more obliging friends many times (in the days when Zola believed in Cézanne, the future novelist consented to pose to him in the nude) he grew to prefer painting apples, and still more, flowers which, in his case, did not perish, as he used artificial ones."

M. Vollard has noted many other interesting remarks. "Just think," Cézanne would say, "I have a feeling, but I don't get as far as expressing it, I am like one who possesses a piece of gold but doesn't know how to make use of it," or again, "painting is decidedly the thing that suits me best. I feel I become much more lucid before nature. Unfortunately I find it extremely difficult to realise my sensations, I cannot express the intensity which I feel with my senses. I cannot get the magnificent richness of colour which animates nature." Cézanne was always striving to achieve perfect harmony. He would not put in a touch which might disturb the general harmony and which would therefore compel him to alter all the rest. M. Vollard tells us that he pointed out towards the end of the interminable sittings that there were still two small patches of bare canvas on the hands. Cézanne explained that he had not yet been able to make up his mind as to the exact tone of these patches, he offered however to attempt the covering of these two bits, but put M. Vollard in a cold sweat by saying, "it will probably mean that all the rest of the portrait will have to be repainted." The unfortunate sitter was careful never to draw the painter's attention to this particular portion of the picture again and these pieces of canvas remain uncovered to this day!

There was surely never in history a great painter who was more reviled and misunderstood during his lifetime than was Cézanne. Though a man capable of strong friendship, his brusque manner, violent temperament, and above all, the difficulty his contemporaries found in understanding his artistic aims, made his life one of almost complete isolation. His sensibility was extreme, and in his work he suffered profound discouragement, he would then give way to violent irritation and in his rage throw away his canvases and tear and burn his water-colours.. Very few people ever saw him at work. To create he had to be alone. He would not put on a single touch until he was sure that he had resolved the tone into its exact relation. The number of sittings he required for a portrait has already been related. He was no more hurried when he painted landscape. He returned to his subjects year after year. The miracle was that after all these innumerable repaintings his picture retained the freshness of a sketch. Towards the end of his life his palette was as follows: brilliant yellow, chrome yellow, naples yellow, yellow ochre, raw sienna, three lakes, vermilion, red ochre, burnt sienna, cobalt, ultramarine, prussian blue, veronese green, emerald green, terra verte, together with white and black. From this simple palette Cézanne made all those subtle and magnificent gradations expressing with delicate yet forcible colour the power and immensity of nature. Cézanne remained from first to last a student of nature, those keen eyes of his were ever piercing deeper into the mysteries of form and colour, but these two he indeed regarded as one, for in his work colour had the unique function of expressing every quality—it was inseparable from form, light, and values. To this task he consecrated his life. In a letter to Emile Bernard, written in 1904, he explains his purpose: "One is neither too scrupulous nor too sincere, nor too submissive to nature; but one is more or less, master of one's model and especially of one's means of expression. . . . . . . I proceed very slowly, nature appearing very complex to me and the progress to be made unending. One must see one's model clearly, and feel truly and express oneself with distinction and force. . . . ." "The Louve is a good book to consult, but it ought only to be the means to an end. Real study is a prodigious undertaking, it is the whole diversity of the panorama of nature."

To the end of his life he persisted in his efforts. In old age he discounted any progress—he feared that he would not be able entirely to express himself before the end. Until the last days he would set up his easel before his beloved Aixois landscape. On September 21st, 1906, he wrote to Emile Bernard: "I am always studying nature and it seems to me that I make slow progress." He was not afraid of the rain and the prospect of a soaking would not keep the old painter within doors. "After having kept up through a shower of rain for two hours," M. Vollard relates, "he tried to get back to his house, but he fainted on the road. A passing laundry cart picked him up and took him to his home." He revived, but all night he was feverish. They say that the following day he wanted to go down to the garden to work on the study of a peasant. But he had a fainting fit and had to go back to bed. He never got up again. He died on the 22nd October, 1906.

EDWARD ROWORTH.

Portraits in the Nude.

TAKHAAR VAN RYN.

MINTA, his wife. OU TANTA MARIA, her great aunt.

FRANS, her eldest son.
DIRK, her second son.
GOLGO, her youngest son. MANDABAZANA, his friend.

CORMORANT, an Englishman.
LILY DU TOIT, a governess.
MR. WINTERHALTER - - } Friends of the family.
MR. AND MRS. OSBOSCH }

SHILLING, a native servant. SARA, his wife.

NOTE.—All the characters in this work are fictitious, and do not refer to any living person.—W.P.

1. A VIEW FROM ABOVE.

The immense plain was misted with a faint bloom. Thirty miles away a grass-fire gave the air a bluish tinge. Fifty miles away the mountains stood miraculous in tones of distance. The house, the sheds and the kraals of Zonnebloem were far below, roofs and walls in a sharp perspective from this height. Further out, the yellow willows and a few silver poplars, with the purple-brown field jutting out beyond that Takhaar was ploughing. There he was, like an ant. The far cries of the Kaffir driver shouting to the oxen, the cracking of a whip, rose small and clear like bubbles in a lovely wine. Over to the right the dam lay bright and tragic, flat and open and serene in the ample afternoon.

---

2. THE COFFEE POT.

The family was sitting round the table. An oil-lamp hung from the ceiling, a lamp wonderful with lustres and brassy scrolls and a painted hood of glass. It threw a strange light on the faces of those present. Mrs. Van Ryn was just putting the tall brass coffee pot on the table.

As it was cold, a fire was burning in the grate. Takhaar, from the plough, was standing at the window. He was looking at the sad light on the mountains. Tanta Maria sat at the side of the fire, her hands folded. Mrs. Van Ryn said:

"You have come in."

Then she went out to the back door to call Golgo.

"Golgo!"

Her voice outside the room, outside the house, sounded unearthly. It was the cold voice of a doll, and yet it vibrated a little with hidden energy and purpose. Some white turkeys near the house gobbled loudly, and all together, each time she called. It was a grotesque chorus.

Lily was looking at her reflection in the coffee pot. It was not the girl she saw in mirrors. Here her reflection was a little distorted.

But she could approve, even in the hatchet-faced miniature, her vivacious elfin air, her oblique eyes and fresh complexion. If this Englishman——

Golgo, who was drinking milk, suddenly upset his cup. Lily saw (reflected in the coffee pot) the white liquid, small and swift, just across the crimson cloth. She turned. Golgo had upset his cup.

"Golgo," said Mrs. Van Ryn.

"O Golgo!" said Lily, "what are you doing?"

Ou Tanta Maria made a curious clucking noise of sympathetic remonstrance, crescendiminuendo. It seemed, on a small scale, like the gobbling of the white turkeys. She who had seen nearly a century of life, terrible and uncertain, warmed suddenly to a swift ineffectual benevolence. She put out her withered claw-like hand and plucked at the boy's sleeve. Golgo wept angrily.

"And what would Mr. Winterhalter say to a little boy who spills his milk?" she muttered relentlessly.

Mr. Winterhalter, a person of vast importance, was coming tomorrow to buy rams.

Golgo rushed out of the room.

---

3. A BUYING OF RAMS.

Cormorant and Dirk, standing on the verandah after breakfast the following morning, began to watch, at a great distance, a small cloud of dust running along the plain before the wind. It was a quarter of an hour before the motor car came along the road between the gum trees and the willows. Whoever was driving the car knew his way. He drove up the hill and stopped at the back of the house. It was a man with a red face and a black moustache.

Although Mr. Winterhalter was a silent man he opened the mouth under his black moustache just wide enough to greet Cormorant. Then he looked heavily round for Takhaar, and followed him into the house.

Nádocsy Winterhalter was the son of a Hungarian count, of a

family of the greatest antiquity and distinction, who had come to these parts, in the course of many wanderings, to augment a diminished fortune. Hereabouts he had lost the little he had left. Being, however, a man of resource, handsome, dashing and romantic, he contrived to live with a local Dutch heiress, of great wealth and ugliness, on her colossal farm. Her coarse and solid heart he enslaved, and on the rare occasions when she faltered he was profuse with promises of marriage. On one occasion, when her doubts mastered her, Count Winterhalter went so far as to change for her the name of her farm from Nord Brabant to Buda-Pesth. For three years he practised the most rigid economies, running the farm like a model, and then departed with most of his lady's money, leaving to her a much improved farm and an infant Nádocsy as a souvenir. To them both he left the memory of his really charming character, a memory that wss all, besides his name and that of the farm, that the younger Nádocsy had to remind him of his paternal origin. From his mother, now long dead, he had the gift of silence and his red face. So that when it came to a buying of rams the Van Ryns had to do the talking.

The sheep were herded in a roomy shed up the hill at the back of the house. It was nearly dark inside, owing to the smallness of the windows. The floor was soft, of dry olive-brown dung, so the sound was muffled of the scampering of the sheep. Winterhalter was deliberate in his choosing. Nobody spoke. Each ram chosen was dragged, unwilling, by the horns, to a gate in the wall, and there let loose into the shed next door. There the selectd could be seen standing, their heads erect, surprised at captivity; their horns curved back low on the shoulder, and then outward, with a round infallible curve; their eyes shining yellow, glassy and lascivious in the light, or large and green and luminous in the dark.

Frans opened the gate in the walls, and they all went into the next shed. Winterhalter only rejected two of the rams he had chosen, and then came back and picked out one he had seen at the beginning. He had bought fourteen rams. This had been a great event.

"Coffee," he said.

There is something, thought Cormorant, between him and Takhaar, some kind of enmity. As they came out of the half-light into the dazzling day Dirk knowingly winked his eye. What does he mean? Cormorant wondered. He felt as if he was taking part in some absurd ballet—Takhaar, very tall and very broad, grizzled; Winterhalter, fat, in a white dustcoat, with a scarlet face and black moustache; what a pair of buffoons! Looking up, one almost expected triangles of paint and large distorted grins to appear on their faces. And no word spoken! And Dirk winked again! Frans had remained with the sheep. It was his function in life to remain with the sheep.

After coffee, when Winterhalter was about to leave, Takhaar was talking, his huge hands holding the side of the car as if it was a toy. Cormorant found himself with Dirk.

"Why did you wink at me?" he asked.

"Mr. Winterhalter and my ma."

"I didn't see anything."

"No. That's just the joke. They were both pretending."

"Pretending what?"

"Don't you know? Hasn't Lily told you yet?"

"A liaison? Why should Lily tell me? Does your father know?"

"Of course he does, though he has never said a word."

"He doesn't mind?"

"No, he doesn't mind."

---

4. A THOUGHT OF DIRK'S.

What a funny kerel this Englishman is, thought Dirk. He never talks about girls and love. Perhaps he knows nothing about them, or perhaps he is one of these dark horses——?

---

5. A THOUGHT OF MRS. VAN RYN'S.

Mr. Cormorant is a very paying guest.

---

6. A THOUGHT OF FRANS'S.

Cormorant's after this Lily. Ja, it's an ewe.

---

7. TWO SERVANTS.

Shilling, a Xosa of light colour, with a reserved but engaging manner, was the chief farm servant. Sara, his wife, worked in the house. At this time the girl, though pregnant, went on with her work as usual. At this moment she was returning from the spring with a bucket of water on her head. Now she stood, hands at hips, talking gravely to Shilling, who was mending a plough.

Suddenly they both laughed.

---

8. AT LESSON TIME.

One morning Cormorant went up into the berg, and Lily watched him going. She was trying at the same time to impress on Golgo (whose mind was at that moment a delightful and inviting playground of a dungheap, haunted by Mandabazana) that H.O.N.D. spells "dog." But there was Cormorant, cold elusive Englishman, going away for a whole day. He would fall over a krans in the mountains and break his neck, and she herself would go and find his body; she would carry it back to Zonnebloem, its neck broken, on her own delicate back—

"Please, Miss du Toit," said Golgo, "why are you looking at Mr. Cormorant?"

"Golgo! Why aren't you looking at your work?"

"I don't like work. I like Mandabazana."

"O, never mind Mandabázana," said Lily. "Remember you're a little white boy, and must learn your lessons. Little Kaffirs belong to playtime."

"He's not a little Kaffir!" Golgo said tearfully, "and I don't want to be a little white boy!"

9. A DEATH.

At six o'clock in the evening Cormorant came down wearily over the last hilltop upon the assembled buildings of Zonnelbloem, almost Egyptian in their solidity and isolation. Although it was nearly dark no light could be seen at any window. The house, with its blocks and angles, loomed bone-grey out of the black earth. A wavering light appeared just below Cormorant's way, as of a lantern held by somebody walking, moving about. It disappeared, but the inside of one of the sheep sheds became illumined with a faint radiance. Cormorant came down to the door and looked in. It was Frans, evidently taking a last look at some sheep. Those that were near the door scampered into the darkness at Cormorant's approach, and Frans, hearing the mild stampede, looked up.

"Who is there?" he asked in his dull way.

"Cormorant."

"You have come back then?"

"Yes, it seems so. What's the time?"

"I don't know the time," said Frans.

"It must be late."

"Ja, it is late," he said slowly.

"Why is the house dark if it's so late? I see no light anywhere."

"My pa will not allow any lights to-night," said Frans. "We are in mourning."

He held up the lantern to show a band of black crape on his sleeve.

"But is somebody dead?" asked Cormorant.

"Ja," said Frans. "Somebody is dead."

"But why don't you tell me?"

"It was Ou Tanta Maria."

"Well, I am sorry," said Cormorant, surprised.

"Are you sorry?" asked Frans incredulously. It was the first time Cormorant had seen him smile. The lights and shadows on his face and beard moved slowly, and took up a fixed position. Frans wore a smile. It took a long time to fade. "Are you sorry? It doesn't trouble me. What was the old ewe to me?"

"Aren't you coming in?" asked Cormorant.

"There is nothing to go in for. There is no supper to-night. My pa says we must fast until to-morrow."

"O nonsense!" said Cormorant, tired and irritated. "I'm going in. Aren't you coming?"

Frans took a long time to answer.

"By and by," he said at last.

He is afraid of Takhaar, thought Cormorant, walking angrily down to the house. He opened the back door. It seemed very dark all of a sudden. He stepped into the passage and bumped into somebody who was muttering.

"My God, who is that?" whispered Mrs. van Ryn, standing stock still. Cormorant could hear her breathing, panting.

"Cormorant," he said aloud.

"Shut up!" she said in a ridiculous stage-whisper. Then she dropped something hard on the floor. It could be heard rolling.

"Damn it," she whispered. "Where has it gone?"

"What is it?" asked Cormorant, groping on the floor. His head touched Mrs. Van Ryn's. He could smell her hair, which tickled his face. He found what felt like a candle. So it was.

"Here it is," he said aloud.

"O, why can't you whisper, Mr. Cormorant? Now we must go out quickly. Come along."

Cormorant was just going to make a scene, but he thought better of it. He would have liked to begin a long oration at the top of his voice about being a paying guest and wanting his supper, but there was so obviously something wrong that he judged it better now to follow Mrs. Van Ryn out into the darkness.

"Can you see?" she asked, groping for the door.

"No," said Cormorant, "I'm going to strike a match." He began feeling for matches in his pocket.

"No, no!" said the stage-whisper, "for God's sake don't! Here, take hold of this. I know the way."

The way, indeed! thought Cormorant. What way? Take hold of this? He put out his hand. Now what on earth's this? It felt like a rope, but silky. It was a thick plait of hair. They made an absurd progress in the dark. Now they seemed to be going through another doorway.

"Let go," said Mrs. Van Ryn, "and give me your matches." Cormorant let go the pigtail and struck a match. She was holding out the candle towards him. He lit the wick with difficulty after striking three matches. Mrs. Van Ryn held up the lighted candle.

"Look at me," she said.

Under the left eye there was a gash in her cheek. The blood was beginning to dry on it, but some had fallen on her dark blouse, staining it darker. In guttering candlelight her face seemed whiter than usual, night darker than ever.

"That is why I didn't want to stay in the house," she said. Yes, her face was haggard.

"But who did that?"

"Mr. Van Ryn."

"Takhaar? Why?"

"You know my Ou Tanta's dead?"

"Yes, I've heard that she's dead. I'm very sorry. But you had better tell me from the beginning. I'm tired and my stomach is empty. I'm not well. If you don't tell me from the beginning I shan't understand anything at all. First let me get some water and wash that cut."

"No no! You mustn't go into the house. Never mind me, I'm all right."

"Very well," said Commorant, "I won't go into the house—yet." He slipped out into the dark, and made his way slowly and blindly down the hill. Twice he stumbled. He meant to get water from the spruit. He knew when he was near the willows: he could see nothing distinctly, but there was a light wind in the branches, and a damp leafish smell. He took off his hat and filled it with water at the spruit. Walking up the bank he caught his foot on a stone, and fell headlong, spilling all the water. It must have been five minutes before he got back to the shed. There was quite a wind blowing. Mrs. Van Ryn thought he was never coming back. Her face had begun to bleed again. She held the brim of Cormorant's hat in her hands. The water looked odd in the candlelight.

"It's quite clean," said Cormorant.

Suddenly a man's voice could be heard laughing very far away, ludicrously, a Kaffir at his kraal, his voice travelling on the wind.

"What is he laughing at?" asked Mrs. Van Ryn.

Cormorant began bathing her face with a silk handkerchief that had been in his pocket.

"The colours in that handkerchief will give me blood-poisoning," she said.

"No they won't," said Cormorant. "I bought it in Regent Street."

"Is that in Capetown?" asked Mrs. Van Ryn.

"No," said Cormorant. "I wish your face would stop bleeding. I've done my best now. You'd better hold the handkerchief over it. Now for God's sake tell me what all this is about."

Mrs. Van Ryn gave a little sob.

"My Ou Tanta was not well this morning," she said hurriedly, shading the candle with her hand. "Ja, she was sick. She wouldn't get up at all. She ate only a little breakfast. Mr. Van Ryn and my sons were out all the morning, and Golgo was doing his lessons with Miss du Toit. At twelve o'clock Dirk came to me for some coffee. He must go to Mr. Winterhalter's, he said, on business. He would not come back to-night, he said to me. He would sleep at Mr. Winterhalter's. I said to him: 'Ou Tanta Maria is very sick. Come back early in the morning in case anything happens.' I don't know why I should have thought that anything would happen. Dirk said to me he would come back early to-morrow morning. After dinner my Ou Tanta seemed much worse. I went to Mr. Van Ryn and told him. 'Ha,' he said to me, 'it is the will of the Almighty.' Then I was frightened. I don't mind if he keeps his religion to Sundays. There is no time in the week for prayers and suchlike. We all have our work to do. 'She is old,' I said. Mr. Van Ryn didn't answer. Now, I thought, if anything happens, my little Golgo must not see it. Why should children see death?"

A wet black stain was spreading through the silk handkerchief. It glistened in the guttering candlelight. The woman took the handkerchief away, and put it back again.

"So I said to Golgo: 'You run out and play with Mandabazana.' Then I went to Miss du Toit. I said to her: 'Lily, if anything happens, my dear, you must help me. I am frightened to be left alone with Mr. Van Ryn.' 'Why?' she said to me. 'He is your husband.' No, but I thought that was a surprising thing to say. I told her here was Mr. Van Ryn beginning to get religious even before my Ou Tanta was dead, and this a Monday too! Indeed, I could hear my poor dear Tanta. She lay breathing with awful difficulty. She has gone a long journey now. O how glad I am that I was with her when she passed away. After a long time I fastened the shutters at the windows and covered up her face. Then I came out and locked the door, hiding the key under my blouse. You see, I was afraid of Mr. Van Ryn. And there he was! He was wearing his dress of sacks. 'Is she dead yet?' he asked. When I told him she was, he went out on to the verandah with that bell of his (his holy bell, he calls it) and began to ring it. This was about four o'clock. He went on ringing and ringing. I went to find Lily, but she was locked in her room and couldn't get out. What could I do? Mr. Van Ryn had the key, and the window of that room doesn't open, so Miss du Toit couldn't get out that way. I thought, when Mr. Van Ryn sees food he will calm down. He must be hungry. Everything will come right. So I went to see about supper. It was getting dark, so I lighted a lamp. By the time I had finished laying the table I had a terrible headache. I thought, now I will go and take my hair down and brush it, then the pain will be soothed. I set the lamp on the dressing table and began to brush my hair. I thought, well Frans isn't here, and even if he came would be no help to me. Dirk is away at Mr. Winterhalter's. Mr. Cormorant is in the berg. My Ou Tanta, my poor Ou Tanta, is dead: Lily is locked in her room. Little Golgo is with the Kaffirs. Whatever shall I do? Mr. Van Ryn will certainly kill me. By gums, he will! He was still ringing that confounded bell. I sat stock-still, looking at myself in the glass. I was very white. The bell stopped ringing. He was coming down the passage. He came in. He came in and shut the door. He said: 'You have been preparing food. How dare you prepare food when there is a dead person in the house?' I didn't answer. I felt quite sick with fear. He took hold of my hair and twisted it round his hand and began to pull it. Ach, that was the most terrible moment of my life. I went as mad as he is. Everything seemed to run from my head. I felt very strong. I took the comb in my hand (it is a heavy silver comb—it was a wedding present) and stood up. He was hurting my hair. I began to hack at his eyes with the comb. He let go my hair. But he picked up something and threw it at me. It must have been that (whatever it was) that cut my face like this. He upset the lamp. I ran out to another room. I got a candle. I ran down the passage. There you were—"

"Listen," said Cormorant, putting out the candle with his finger and thumb. They listened. There was nothing to be heard but the gentle rushing of the wind. Then a voice, an eerie old man's voice, could be heard whining in the darkness:

"O, Minta, Minta, where are you? God Almighty, you have blinded me! O my God, my girl, where are you?" It was the voice of Takhaar.

"Now I shall go to him," said Mrs. Van Ryn earnestly. "He is all right now," she explained, over her shoulder, having already run past Cormorant out into the night.

Now she was soothing Takhaar with her voice, then with her lips and hands. They had gone into the house, those two. Cormorant waited. A light appeared. Then he went down himself.

It was as though the whole house had suddenly sprung to life. It was an awakening from a dream. There was a buzz of voices in several directions. Cormorant arrived in his room, washed, and changed his clothes. Then he came out, apprehensively, but looking perfectly calm, into the passage. In the dining-room the table was now laid for supper. On a very white tablecloth there was food. There was a cheerful fire burning, Frans was standing on the hearth (like a piece of meat roasting itself, thought Cormorant). Takhaar had a bandage over one eye. He was sitting at the head of the table and reading a newspaper with the other eye, fanatical in its isolation.

The liberated Lily came in, with a candle in her hand, and a big childish bow of black ribbon in her hair.

"I have been putting Golgo to bed," she said, as airily as she could. "He asks you to go and say good-night to him, Mr. Van Ryn."

"What! When the air smells of death?" said Takhaar. "O, the little man!"

And he went out.

Mrs. Van Ryn came in with the brass coffee pot. She had two pieces of sticking-plaster on her cheek, under the eye.

Takhaar came in again immediately afterwards, and they all sat down to supper. None of them had had any food since lunch, and they all ate enormously except Lily.

"Miss du Toit isn't eating much," said Takhaar, with heavy facetiousness. "She must be in love."

Nobody answered, but Frans smirked slowly to himself, for the second time in a single day. She must be in love with me, his brain told him, working ponderously. And he looked at Lily with something like, yes, with something almost like interest.

---

10. A BURIAL.

They are burying Ou Tanta Maria in the Zonnebloem burying-place, a grassy kloof. The sky is clouded. A grey sky and a raw wind, so that all those lights and colours that the sun day after day has brought about on this day are not seen, those ochres and yellows and hard shadows on the rocks, those running hues like fire or water in the grass. To-day the kranses, surface and fissure, are grey; so with the grass, the wandering stone-coloured sheep among the stones, the smoke from the kitchen chimney of Zonnebloem, the writhing wind-flowing foliage of the eucalyptuses, and the prospect towards far mountains. Two Kaffirs have dug the grave.

The blue-brown earth lay in a heap at the graveside, bending down with its weight the little hillside herbs. It had been a procession almost brisk from the house to here. Why should one move at a funeral pace? Was there no ploughing to be done? Were there not sheep to be counted? They came to bury the Ou Tanta, not to mourn for her. Now the coffin, a crude coffin, lay in the grave. Dirk and Frans had made it, closed it, and carried it up from the house. Takhaar stood at the foot of the grave, reading from the book of Genesis. The two Kaffirs, with their spades, are at the head. Cormorant finds himself facing Mrs. Van Ryn. A black hat she wears, wreathed with an endless veil of black lawn; a black woollen muffler; her dress is black; she is even wearing black gloves. She still has sticking-plaster on her face. She is agitated.

Takhaar's sonorous voice is carried away on the wind, the same wind that wags his unwilling beard as though it was of as little account as the grass, and eddies of sound reaching the nervous leaf-like ears of the krans-coloured sheep in the stones overhead cause them to lift their heads and hurry away, up higher; while one, far from the others, finding itself alone, bleats loudly lest it should be abandoned.

Takhaar closes the book and lowers his head, praying rapidly in a low voice. He lifts his hand. The two Kaffirs begin to throw earth upon the coffin with their spades.

WILLIAM PLOMER.

(To be Continued.)

The Significance of "Turbott Wolfe."

"TURBOTT WOLFE." By William Plomer: Hogarth Press.; 7/6.

Literary criticism in South Africa is either in its infancy or in its dotage; and the present younger generation who have produced the bulk of that not very bulky growth, South African literature, have had to be patient and forgiving. It seems that political, moral, and theological standpoints are still considered legitimate criteria in reviewing a work of art. Mr. Plomer has probably had to be far more patient and forgiving than anybody else. He has been subjected to the various tests of patriotism, morality and even sportsmanship, and naturally, being a very conscientious artist has failed to pass any of them. To use the jargon of one of his critics, who in his more lucid moments must act as umpire to a local club, "Mr. Plomer has not played cricket." He certainly has not. Any venturesome journalist who opens "Turbott Wolfe" expecting to be bowled to by a popular googlie-expert will be rather taken aback when he finds Mr. Plomer's ten-inch projectile shrieking along towards him.

"When the unconscious of a whole continent and age has made of itself poetry in the nightmare of a single prophetic dreamer, when it has issued in his awful blood-curdling scream, one can of course consider this scream from the point of view of a singing-teacher." To review "Turbott Wolfe" from the point of view of patriotism, theology or cricket is to commit a similar impertinence. To the more serious South Africans who are not content to justify their existence by the mere production of mealie-meal and by the rather noisy form of patriotism of which most of us are victims, "Turbott Wolfe" comes as a timely admonition. It is impossible to refute Mr. Plomer's ferocious indictment in an after-dinner conversation or in a leading article: the only possible reply to "Turbott Wolfe" would be the production of another work of art as significant as Turbott Wolfe—and so far this country has produced nothing approaching it. Olive Schreiner might of course be excepted, but she was of the same genus as Mr. Plomer. Now that she is dead we have forgotten the more uncomfortably prophetic side of her nature and genially accepted her as a bulwark to our middle-class prosperity.

> "Let me have men about me that are fat
> Sleek-headed men and such as sleep o' nights
> Yond Cassius has a lean and hungry look
> He thinks too much; such men are dangerous. . . . ."

These words adequately express what White South Africa will feel towards her first really brilliant satirist. I feel the same. Mr. Plomer is one of those extremely unpleasant individuals who can see further than their own noses. In fact if one were to string the noses of all the politicians and journalists in this country in a line, and if one were to extend this nasal rosary in front of him, it is quite possible that Mr. Plomer's range of vision would reach a good way beyond the longest and remotest of them—even were it that of a Slawkenbergius. For he is probably the first South African, in dealing with the more unpleasant aspects of the native "question," who has been able to realise that it is an emotional "question" and not a political one. He has also realised that it is more of an answer than a "question." We in South Africa have come to regard politics as a sort of religion and political leaders as makers of history! We look on politics as a cause when they are merely a result! On politicians as leaders, when they are merely representatives. Political histories are merely the spoor and dropping of those vast inscrutable impulses, the crowd-emotions, and supply the most convenient formula that we have for tracking them back through time. These impulses are not rational they are generated emotionally and instinctively and they are as primitive as the bison-herd or the wolf-pack. It is these vast submerged emotions that make history; they surge through the minds of nations almost unconsciously; they drive humanity towering upward like an archangel into the triumph of a Renaissance or scuttling down like a rabbit into the anti-climax of a great war; even our civilization is only a furtive attempt to effect a compromise between these vast conflicting emotions and to hold them in a certain amount of stability; but they have had the best of it so far, as Russia and modern Europe can witness; they drag political history in whatever direction they are travelling—like kettles tied to the tail of a tiger. That is why though it is possible to discuss dreadnoughts and drainage in a political light it is idle to try to discuss racial or human questions politically; to discuss them politically is to leave them exactly as they are. Statesmen will go on discussing peace and signing Locarno treaties until the next war; it will also be a "War to end War"; the press will lie as hysterically as before; we will all be engaged in a crusade of right against might; and when its all over and we inquire into the secret history which preceded it, we will hush it all up and prepare for the next "crusade." We will blame it all on the Kaisers and politicians of the world—on anythinng but on our own human nature which is the true culprit.

It is only in the more individualistic walks of life that an outside view can be obtained of those terrific phantoms which mould the destiny of empires and peoples—only in science, art or religion that we can escape far enough away from the collective emotions of humanity to be able to see what they really are. The scientist, the artist and the philosopher see these things productively; but in the humbler and more collective walks of life—in politics, theology, business, journalism or in the martial profession—these things can only be seen relatively and unproductively, through the spectacles of the group to which they belong. If one looks back into history one seldom sees any great thinker afflicted with crowd-emotions—we cannot imagine Einstein brandishing a bayonet in the Great War, or Freud dancing about in a respirator, or Darwin making a recruiting speech. Yet these are names that will be honoured and respected long after the popular idols of the day such as Charlie Chaplin, Foch, Kitchener, Lloyd George, Mary Pickford, etc., "have been relegated to that oblivion which awaits unproductive minds."

Mr. Plomer has escaped just far enough into the serener altitudes to be able to see the great antagonistic race-forces at work but not quite far enough to discard a very strong bias against the white colonist; it is this bias that detracts more considerably from Turbott Wolfe than anything else. Everything Mr. Plomer records is just and true; but he takes a too malicious delight in recording it. He is not content with having produced a large and lively skeleton from our cupboard but he must needs pipe to it and make it dance in front of us, while all we seem to be able to do is to "hold our noses between mentally uncared-for fingers" in a scandalised but futile attempt to repudiate the whole thing. It may not be a good thing from the point of view of the artistic value of the book; but if one regrets this, one can at least be grateful that Mr. Plomer's biting satire has administered an excellent tonic to our self-satisfaction. For as a race we are easily satisfied with ourselves.

What Mr. Plomer has yet to learn is that we in our mental bondage are almost as much the victims of circumstance as the natives in their physical bondage. Since the ancient tribal taboos have been partially destroyed which enveloped the mysteries of the human mind in theological thunders, it has become safer to approach the subject scientifically: and the realm of psychology which save for the occasional incursions of minds such as Shakespeare's and Nietzche's had hitherto been desert roamed over by the wandering speculations of moralists and mystics, is now being opened up by a few scientific pioneers. The work done by Sir James Frazer, Freud, Trotter, Le Bon and others has given us a very different idea of oruselves from that entertained by our ancestors, namely that the white man having ascended from the apes is automatically proceeding, a purely rational creature, by leaps and bounds towards a higher plane of existence. We have been revealed to ourselves in a more tragically heroic but less comfortable, light; individually we see a man as a creature, far more emotional than rational, trying to impose the laws of his reason on the more powerful emotions and lusts which tow him through life; a creature armed with the weapons for his own salvation and destruction but unable to tell which are which: a small and desperate figure warring with the titanic shadows of his own heredity, superstition and imagination. Collectively we see him as an irrational and purely emotional creature: capable of far greater acts of heroism and self-sacrifice: capable too of far more violent inconsistency, panic, cruelty and stupidity—than when considered individually. When a man is plain Mr. So-and-So he may appear to be quite a rational being: but arouse in him the consciousness of the group to which he belongs, whether it be his nationality, colour, church, family or political party and he becomes as primitive as a gorilla.

Mr. Plomer has shown his white characters when acting under the influence of race-feeling, behaving with typical ferocity and injustice. But he fails to let them relax often enough into their individual and comparative decency. He keeps pointing at them all the time and nudging the reader. I have known many farmers who capable of the most callous and criminal behaviour to the blacks, were guileless sons of the soil, as innocent as sleeping babes, with devout souls and sky-blue eyes. Their cruelty and impulsiveness was not even remembered when they relapsed again into their individual rationality. This type is far more normal than the bloodthirsty tpye described by Mr. Plomer, and it confronts one with a far more terrible enigma. If Mr. Plomer had realised this his satire would have been more devastatingly complete and he might have achieved a masterpiece.

Mr. Plomer is at times the victim of his furiously lyrical imagination: he has speculated rather idealistically on the subject of miscegenation. But though standards of convention are easily changed under the pressure of necessity, it does not seem likely that it will ever take place cleanly and openly. The sacred tribal taboos which rule the lower type of white mentality are too strong. It would not tolerate any open or honest violation of these taboos: though it tolerates such violations when they are perpetrated sheepishly and in dark corners. And it is more than likely, if we are eventually to suffer the usual fate of conquering minorities, that our absorbtion will be a long and dismal process. Cases such as that of "Mabel van der Horst" are very rare, though they do exist.

"Turbott Wolfe" is an extremely bold and sincere piece of work. Mr. Plomer has not fought shy of the most disconcerting problems. Only those people who are so unfortunate as to feel anything humiliating or mortifying about sexual questions, only those who believe it is in the interests of morality to keep their eyes shut to the evils that are going on around them, to wit the majority of readers—will be annoyed by it. But if it can make a few people, from time to time, think very hard, it will have achieved a very definite purpose.

I have given the reader no idea of the nervous velocity of the prose of "Turbott Wolfe." Under its bitter and sardonic exterior the book is a very tragic and moving poem: through the whole book one hears the cry of thwarted ideals, of a deep and wounded pity, and of the tragic isolation of a fine and sensitive mind among mentally sordid surroundings. It is not necessary for the intelligent reader to be in agreement with any of the writer's own opinions to realise the significance of this book. What has made "Turbott Wolfe" such a portent is the manner in which Mr. Plomer has seized on the emotional aspects of the colour-situation. By the time we have reached the climax of the story we realise that other forces are at work than those which in their more obvious and shallow operation seem to regulate society: we realise that no amount of political discussion, no policy whether enlightened or benighted has anything to do with the inevitable issue: and the figures that loom largest on the political horizon recede into insignificance like small gesticulating marionettes against a dark and stormy sky.

After having been soundly peppered by Mr. Plomer's withering scorn, with half my self-respect as a white man shot away, I sought refuge in the more slumbrous pages of the daily papers only to be met with two cases of far more unprovoked and despicable cruelty than anything Mr. Plomer records. These cases were "severely reprimanded" and let off with trifling punishments. As no popular indignation has been aroused I take it that Mr. Plomer's savage attack on our mentality is not undeserved. "Turbott Wolfe" however chaotic in structure and anarchistic in outlook it may be, is a very cheerful sign. It shows us that there are some among the younger generation who have ceased to regard empire-building as an end in itself and are searching for some means to justify it. We have got tired of representing ourselves as injured saints staggering under the load of a white man's burden and benevolently studying the interests of the native. We realise that a community which relies for its prestige on such an illusion cannot hope to retain its prestige for long: we wish to be able to rely on other means for our superiority than the mere possession of ammunition and machine guns. The preposterously feudal conditions that circumstances have made nceessary for the time being can only be remedied by discriminate thinking and not by indiscriminate voting. We are beginning to realise that the greater our mental superiority to the natives may be, the more our responsibility towards them increases. South African literature is ceasing to be a playground for domesticated minds: where one may participate in the innocent adventures of some faithful quadruped: or discover some bewilderingly supernatural priestess among conventionally melodramatic surroundings. We are gradually approaching the promised era

When the mute and muzzled stripling
Shall defy the muzzled bore
When the Rudyards cease from Kipling
And the Haggards Ride no more.

To have carried off such a work as "Turbott Wolfe" at the age of twenty is something more than a portent. Mr. Plomer is young but he has lungs which can bellow vociferously: let him bellow while he can: in middle-age we can sing, and in our dotage, croon and chirrup.

ROY CAMPBELL.

NOTE:—An interesting example of the moralipoliticoliterary form of criticism which I have described, has appeared in a leading South African weekly. It is also a review of "Turbott Wolfe." But in view of the honesty of the reviewer who with incredible frankness headed his two bewildering columns "Garbage," I shall refrain from further comment, being unable to think of a more suitable epithet. I wish all reviewers could be as open with their readers.

Tolstoy and Dostoevsky.

To-day when the figure of Dostoevsky looms so largely in the modern consciousness and that of Tolstoy has receded from its former pre-eminence, it is interesting to know in what light the abdicating giant regarded his successor. It may perhaps reveal the petulance of an old and disappointed man. Yet dare one treat with derision, with anything but awe, a personality, an egotism, which was great enough to be able to feel a genuine jealousy for such minds as Goethe's, Shakespeare's, and Dostoevsky's; and to be able to propound a theory of art from which nearly all great names could be excluded save his own?

The following correspondence from which I select the more significant passages was translated by S. S. Koteliansky and appeared in the "Criterion" under the heading of "Extracts from letters exchanged between Leo Nicolayevich Tolstoi and N. N. Strakhov relating to F. M. Dostoevsky." Strakhov, it will be remembered, wrote his reminiscences of Dostoevsky, published in 1883, in the first volume of Dostoevsky's Complete Works. This correspondence extends roughly over a period of three or four years and it is interesting to notice how the cunning hypocrisy of the two old men gradually disintegrated before the more material considerations of jealousy. In an age which has at least as sure a sense of the ridiculous as of the sublime, Tolstoy, the doctrinaire, has been annihilated by Tolstoy, the artist; and the younger generation is apt to treat Tolstoy the doctrinaire with an unwarrantable hilarity. We lose sight of the magnificent extravagance, the superb courage of his gestures, in their ineffectuality. We lose sight of his lonely and very human figure in the clash between his theories and the laws of nature. In his inability to apply these theories to his own life, we are apt to see the laughable failure of a doctrinaire, rather than the tragic defeat of a hero. In him the East and the West came to grips and he could not reconcile his emotional Western temperament to the laws of his oriental mind. It remained for the Eastern people headed by his great disciple Ghandi to give to whatever of his doctrines are likely to survive a dignity and a nobility which they never attained in his own personality and life, nor for that matter in the life of any of his European devotees.

Because he had the courage to rank himself with supermen, we are slow to forgive him for not having come through life with the dignity the steady growth of a Goethe; the cool disinterested suavity of a Shakespeare; or even the tortured epileptic velocity of a Nietzche. Yet there is nothing ignominious in his failure; it is his intense humanity that saves him, and gives to his falure something of a universal human import; something which endears him to us as a type, an Everyman, a Faust; and even at the last, when we realise the stupendousness of the defeat which confronted him, there is something forgivable, and not wholly repulsive in his last senile scramble to share the simplicity of peasants and the innocence of children.

Tolstoy must have been well advanced in his disillusionment when these letters were written for in many of them his art-theories are already militant.

(TOLSTOY TO STRAKHOV, 1880.)

The other day I felt seedy and read the "Dead House" (by Dostoevsky). I had forgotten a great deal of it, I re-read it, and I do not know a better book in the whole of the new literature, including Poushkin. If you see Dostoevsky, tell him I love him.

(STRAKHOV TO TOLSTOY, 1880.)

I saw Dostoevsky and gave him your praise and love. He was very delighted and I had to leave with him the sheet of your letter that contained such dear words. He was a little vexed by your disrespect to Poushkin expressed there (. . . "a better book in the whole new literature, including Poushkin"). "What, *including*?" he asked. I said that you ever were, and now especially you have become, a great "freethinker."

(AFTER DOSTOEVSKY'S DEATH, 1881.)

A feeling of profound emptiness, my dear Leo Nicolayevich, has not left me since the moment I heard of Dostoevsky's death. It is as though half Petersburg had sunk down or a half of literature had died.

This letter rambles on in a broken-hearted strain and is replied to in the same strain by Tolstoy. . . . .

(TOLSTOY TO STRAKHOV.)

How much I should like to be able to say all that I feel about Dosteovsky! You in describing your feelings have expressed part of my own. I never saw the man and never had direct relations with him: and suddenly when he died I realised that he was to me the man nearest most dear and most needed. And it never entered my head to measure myself with him, never! Everything he did was such that the more he would do it, the better for me. Art arouses envy in me, wisdom too, but the work of the heart—only joy. I did consider him as my friend and I thought that we should meet, only that there was no occasion yet, but that it would come. At first I felt lost, but then it became clear to me how dear he was to me and I wept as I weep now. Recently before his death I read his "Humiliated and Insulted" and was deeply moved.

The ensuing correspondence gradually becomes less flattering to Dostoevsky. The two old men feel for each other's confidence and later, in 1883, when most of their reticence has been worn away the repressed jealousies of Tolstoy and the obsequious sensilities of Strakhov rise to a crescendo of malice and hatred.

(STRAKHOV TO TOLSTOY.)

. . . . I cannot consider Dostoevsky either a good man or a happy man (which, in the main, coincide). He was spiteful, envious, lewd, and all his life he spent in such agitations as would have made him pitiable, and would have made him ridiculous, if he had not at the same time been so spiteful and so wise. He himself, like Rousseau considered himself the best of men and the happiest. In connection with the Biography I vividly remembered all these traits.

Here follows an account of various crimes perpetrated by Dostoevsky: the most serious of those which he supports with any evidence is an altercation with a waiter in a Swiss restaurant. But Strakhov is not content with these crimes and exploits the domain of hearsay for monstrous implications and vague suggestions: he continues—

"He was drawn to abominations, and he boasted of them . . . . Note, that for all his animal sensuality, he had no taste whatever, no feeling whatever, for the beauty and charm of woman."

It is instructive at this juncture to compare the respective relationships of Dostoevsky and Tolstoy to their wives; and it would have been even more instructive if their respective wives had ever been able to compare notes. Madame Dostoevsky's reminiscences are not exactly the writings of an insulted or an injured woman.

"A stirring of true kindness, a spark of genuine sincere warmth even a single minute of real repentance could expiate anything. And if I remembered anything like that in Dostoevsky, I would forgive him and be glad for him. But mere exalting oneself into a fine man, mere heady and literary humanity—Lord, how disgusting it is!"

This, it may be remembered, was written about a man who had faced a firing-squad,* four years of Siberia, and penal servitude in a disciplinary battalion after that; a man who had faced death, and worse than death—for his human ideals. And it is amusing to think of Tolstoy well-fed and affluent in his electric-lighted "peasant's hut," with hot water laid on and a private medical attaché: to think of a man who had seldom suffered more in the cause of his ideals than an occasional wetting of rain—endorsing, with sorrowful self-satisfaction, the indictments of Strakhov: and mournfully shaking his head over Dostoevsky's "mere literary humanity."

Tolstoy coquettes lovingly with the idea of Dostoevsky's worthlessness, but at the same time flings a sop to his own conscience.

"I understand you fully, and to my regret, I almost believe you."

* In 1849 Dostoevsky was arrested with a group of other young men who had stood out for liberty of the race. After eight months in prison he was taken out with twenty other young men to be shot. They were bound in threes to stakes. Being the third in the row he concluded he only had a few minutes to live. Suddenly the troops beat a tattoo; they were unbound and informed that His Majesty had spared their lives. The sentence was commuted to hard labour. One of the prisoners, Grigoryev, went mad as soon as he was untied and never regained his sanity. The intense suffering of this experience left a lasting stamp on Dostoevsky's mind. He describes the awful agony of a condemned man and insists on the cruelty of inflicting such agony on human beings. Then followed four years of penal servitude in Siberia with common criminals, and some years of service in a disciplinary battalion.—(These particulars are taken from Constance Garnett's note to the "Brothers Karamazov.")

Then with full confidence in his listener he launches out—

"It seems to me that you have been the victim of a wrong, a false attitude towards Dostoevsky, of his exaggerated—not by you but by all—importance, and of a sort of stereotyped exaggeration of the exaltation into prophet and saint of a man who has died in the most fervent process of a struggle between good and evil. He is moving, interesting, but to put on a pedestal a man who is all struggle—you can't."

Such then was the opinion entertained of an artist who was "all struggle" by a great moral teacher who by that time was nearly all surrender.

He continues—

"There are beautiful horses: race-horses worth a thousand roubles. But suddenly you detect a kink and that beauty and champion of a horse is worth nothing. The more I live the more do I value people without a kink. You say that you have made it up with Tourgenev and I have become very fond of him."

In a former letter Strakhov had remarked and Tolstoy had evidently allowed it, that Dostoevsky had "eclipsed Tourgenev"—an extraordinary conclusion to come to, for no artist can "eclipse" another. Tourgenev's and Tolstoy's work cannot be eclipsed by Dostoevsky's, but like any other work which relies on its artistic qualities for its survival will exist independently and apart, as long as its own merit can preserve it. It was a favourite trick of Tolstoy's in the propounding of his theories to exalt the smaller man at the expense of the greater. It gave him a surer sense of his own supremacy. It began with exalting Tourgenev over Dostoevsky: it ended with exalting the innocent gambols of peasants over the works of Shakespeare and the Greek Dramatists. There was no quality of which Tolstoy was so passionately fond as rustic humility—in others; this quality he admired so much that he was constrained to apply it as a test to all art. Yet he himself with all his simplicity was doomed never to reach the hearts of the masses: and it is disconcerting to one's opinions regarding the value of simplicity in art to see how a writer like Shakespeare in spite of his archaic language, his slightly pedantic style, his cruel and remorseless exaggerations, his utter disrespect for probability, can sway the illiterate audiences that cram the theatres all over Europe and even in the heart of Soviet Russia. It is disconcerting to see a writer who violates all the laws of criticism and literary decorum, not only gripping the hearts of the masses, but exciting the wonder and admiration of the most coldly analytical minds in modern Europe. The new science of psycho-analysis in its preliminary investigations of the unconscious mind has more than once turned a respectful glance on the pages of Shakespeare and Dostoevsky and Nietzche where it has used the work of most other great writers merely as material for diagnosing the various—what Tolstoy would call—" kinks " in their mentality. Tolstoy himself has more than once been approached as a pathological subject, with very interesting results.

Tolstoy in his anxiety to demolish Dostoevsky is reduced after his mention of Tourgenev to searching for " kinks " in Dostoevsky : he does not inform us as to what is the kink he has discovered : but continues his metaphorical allusion to the race-horse.

" It is amusing, we prefer Tourgenev just because he is without a kink and will take us there : and here you have a race-horse, but it won't take you anywhere. Lucky if it does not land you in a ditch. Both Pressensé and Dostoevsky have a kink. In the case of the former all his scholarship and in the case of the latter all his wisdom and heart, were wasted. Tourgenev will outlive Dostoevsky and not for his artistry, but because he was without a kink."

The only " kink " that seems to have presented itself to Tolstoy's point of view was Dostoevsky's honesty as an artist : a quality which, even though his characters only seem really to differ in their degree of pride or humility renders them more distinct and living than those of almost any other writer.

Tolstoy on the other hand even though he is more grandly objective in his conception of character always warps the actions of his characters in accordance with his moral bias. Even in his most triumphant moments as an artist he is never far from being a preacher : and even the most finely conceived of his characters is liable at any moment to become a megaphone for his doctrines.

Herein lies his difference from writers like Dostoevsky and

Shakespeare through whose minds the whole unconscious spirit of the human race seems to rise and make poetry of itself. They are impersonal, they stand away from the canvas and trust the characters they create to move of their own volition.

Tolstoy's "kink" is fairly obvious. As a young man he rioted himself sick. He gave way to his lusts and thoroughly gluttonised himself with the result that his constitution suffered. At the age of thirty he was bald and toothless. What was there left for him to do but to become a moralist. He fled to the arms of middle-class respectability for protection. Surfeited to sickness, his whole attitude to the joys of physical existence was soured and warped. He was irritated by the physical paradise which he could no longer enjoy and turned his face away in a doleful scrutiny of the soul. He became the trumpet of the philistines.

Dostoevsky was as deeply involved in his physical existence as in his spiritual existence. Through Dostoevsky the whole tragic spirit of his age, his race, his species flared up like a volcano: that is why he has such a hold on the consciousness of the youth of modern Europe who are struggling so desperately to rebuild something out of the chaos which the political activities of their "elders and betters" have left them to inherit.

MARY ANN HUGHES.

The Strandloopers,

Strandloopers? Quite the lowest form of man!
We ought to be ashamed to think how we began!

Professor Pimp, who lectures on them, tells
They left no culture—only oyster shells,

He says that they went naked on their rambles,
And where they squatted always left a shambles.

Isn't it shocking to repeat these facts?
And so suggestive of disgusting acts!

Professor Pimp says they're our ancestors!
Of course no sense of decency occurs.

To scientists or highbrows as a rule,
Professor Pimp's a Bolshevik, a fool!
To think a man like that's allowed to teach a school!

Strandloopers? They were just wild brutes!
They had no stays or stockings, spectacles or boots!
Nothing to smoke, not even cheap cheroots!

No bioscopes or beer or guns or daily press!
No ships or trams or aeroplanes, much less
Euphonious radio, sweet symbol of progress!

From cold sea-slime to port and a cigar,
From shell-fish to shell-factories we follow a bright star.

Professor Pimp's a highbrow—I'd like to see him shot.
Had they no culture? We have quite a lot.

PAMELA WILLMORE.

Dr. Leys and the Colour Question

What is the colour question? It is to ask what attitude ought to be taken up by races of Nordic origin towards the races whose skins are not white. It is safe to say Nordic instead of European because the colour problem, as Dr. Leys has pointed out* in his monumental work, "does not exist outside Protestant Europe and America, and it is only in our Empire and the United States that is exists in any dangerous form. The emotion from which it arises is felt neither in France, nor in Southern Europe, nor in Spanish and Portuguese America." The work of Dr. Leys can hardy be too highly praised or too freely quoted. He was written, with the utmost restraint, a complete history of an experiment in Imperialism, a frankly disgusting experiment. Dr. Leys has approached the colour question with unusual detachment and commented on it with unusual perception. One by one he clears away falsehoods and hypocrisies, rank weeds of our civilisation, and at last leaves this colour question in clear outline in broad daylight. His book ought to be widely read in South Africa, and extracts from it could be taught with advantage in schools. One only suggests this because one has enough faith in our own country to believe that its white inhabitants have a great character. However badly natives may be treated here, however falsely they may be regarded, we have still time to avoid some of the systematic humbug and injustice which held up English methods in Kenya as a disgrace to the name, the honour, and the civilisation of England. The policy in Kenya has been the economic exploitation of the native for the benefit of the European settlers. All principles of justice, Christianity and humanity have been set aside in order that a few whites may make fortunes. To take the matter of land, "we get the extraordinary contrast of 10,000 square miles alienated to Europeans and populated by 1,893 Europeans, with 5,000 square miles reserved, somewhat precariously, to nearly 2,000,000 Africans. And this, be it remembered, in a country. . . . which we occupied with the professed object of protecting its inhabitants."

* "Kenya," by Norman Leys (The Hogarth Press, 15.-.)

However, it is less to the purpose here to follow all Dr. Leys' disclosures, than to admire his conclusions. He does away completely, for instance, with the idea that the African races are inferior to ourselves. There are those who think that the African races are in most ways superior. There are those who cannot believe in the colour bar. Those who do believe in it, says Dr. Leys, "believe, not because they have been convinced by economic considerations or by ethnological researches, but because they feel they are right in so believing. And that belief is held passionately by millions." Their arguments "have simply been invented to prove what was already an article of faith." And in a footnote we see the first British Governor in Capetown worshipping in Church in the same pew with his African servants.

The author's next achievement is to state concisely the undeniable failure, with the possible exceptions of the Society of Friends and the Church of Rome, of historical Christianity in matters of colour. Dr. Leys, presiding at a Scottish reunion one St. Andrew's Eve in Mombasa many years ago, cleverly pointed out that "if St. Andrew himself, or his Master, had arrived at Mombasa that very day he would not have been allowed to land unless he had a sum of money which no wandering apostle would be likely to have, and certainly his Master never had; that if he were allowed to land, a Syrian Jew would be allowed to do no work but a labourer's; that he would be refused admittance to the dinner held in his honour; and that most of those who were partaking of it would refuse to take him by the hand."

It seems at last that there are only two solutions of the colour problem. One is thorough economic exploitation (which violates all possible principles of any permanent value) and the other is complete social equality (which violates nothing but an illusion). The choice of these two alternatives would seem startling to most white South Africans, but sooner or later they will have to choose. If they choose exploitation they will sooner or later be damned and overwhelmed. If they choose equality they will sooner or later be saved. Dr. Leys points out how, when the power of the Roman Empire "was at its height, and during those generations when, in the judgment of Gibbon, its subjects were happier and more prosperous than in any earlier or later society, race feeling can hardly have existed at all. The highest posts of the empire were open to, and not seldom filled by, the children of men as barbarous as Masai and Zulu." Further, "our ancestors . . . . treated Asiatics and Africans as ordinary men and women. In the eighteenth century a quarter of the seamen in the British Navy were coloured. Race feeling in our country, as distinct from ordinary dislike of foreigners, seems to have arisen about the time the slave trade was abolished."

In this country, more perhaps than in any other in the world, these lessons must be taken to heart. We hear a great talk about "preserving white civilisation for our children." What does Dr. Leys say? He refers to "that system of industrial autocracy, and ruthless competition and ambition for profit, from which men of every school of thought in Europe are seeking to escape." Let every school of thought in South Africa learn to seek escape, and we shall be saved. White civilisation is in many ways a dirty business.

General Hertzog has pointed out that our Dutch compatriots are Socialist by nature, by religion, and by tradition. So are the natives. So all professing Christians should be. What then is to hinder a common unity? How much longer is the colour of a man's skin to influence his rights as a man? It will not be enough to elevate the Cape Coloured people to an equal status with Europeans. It will be necessary to learn to recognise every man's human qualities as a contribution to the building up of an indestructible future, to judge every man by the colour of his soul and not by the colour of his skin. Otherwise the coloured races of the world will rise and take by force what is denied them now by a comparatively few muddle-headed money-grubbers.

WILLIAM PLOMER.

A Contemporary View of Van Gogh.

We are indebted for the following particulars to Mr. E. J. Horniman, who was a fellow-student with Van Gogh at the Académie des Beaux Arts in Antwerp during the winter 1885-1886. Of this period Meier-Graefe says in his biography :[1]

"Towards the end of November in 1885, Van Gogh went to Antwerp for a few months. . . . He worked at the Academy in order to get cheap models. Once again he was so short of money that he had not enough even to buy dry bread, and he began to feel the effects of this monotonous diet, together with acute mental exertion. The fear of an early grave, which never left him, increased his passion for work, and his furious labours only brought the danger nearer. In Antwerp Vincent had, of course, made enemies of all the professors and students at the Academy . . . He suffered from fever."

Such, then, was the position of Van Gogh when the following sentences were inspired :

"His eyes were green-blue," says Van Gogh's fellow-student. "He was very lined, owing to his habit of making faces all the time he worked. He wore peasant's clothes (much affected by Dutch and Belgian artists then) and sabots, with, I remember, grey knitted socks to keep his feet warm in winter, the studio being stone-paved. We worked sitting on boxes or stools, using drawing boards with two adjustable legs, a third one at back; he used to crouch over his, making strange faces and noises. He was subject to violent passion, and seldom spoke. He worked very rapidly in charcoal, looking steadfastly at the plaster cast of an antique figure and then at a great pace making a strong black drawing of, say, a landscape with peasant figures in a storm. The visiting master used to be very annoyed, but I think recognised his talent. We thought him mad and were in awe of him —his work was so strange that in those days, when even Whistler was hardly accepted, few conceived that a new school was already in

1 "Vincent Van Gogh," 2 Vols., The Medici Society.

being. Ludovici,[2] who never saw him, is wrong in believing he could be thought good-looking—he was ungainly and gave the idea of red earth—short hair; red, wiry beard; morose and repellent in manner and expression. I am surprised he was so well educated. He appeared more like a typical peasant, but then he never talked much to me nor I think to the other students.

"My friend H—— knew Van Gogh in Paris and much wished he had been able to help him then by buying drawings at 5 francs each!"

2 Ludovici wrote the preface to the English translation of the "Letters." (Constable 1911).

Marginalia.

It is rumoured that a new edition of George Moore's works is about to be published. It is difficult perhaps for the younger generation to attach any significance to the event, but among those of our grandfathers who survive it may arouse pleasant memories. George Moore certainly did great work in demolishing the false idols of his day, but he has been predeceased by many of the idols he set in their place and it is doubtful whether much of his work will survive. Most of his works were written in collaboration with the other half of his dual personality—Miss George Moore, a querulous and irritable spinster. Unfortunately her work preponderates and may seriously interfere with the survival of Mr. George Moore who has written some amusing pages. It seems astounding that George Moore can ever have been considered as a dangerous and wicked iconoclast, for we survey him to-day as a respectable institution, as blameless and comfortable as the Y.M.C.A. Yet the period in which he lived seems to be remoter from us somehow, than the eighteenth century: a period in which amorous intrigues were still considered daring enough to be indulged in for their own sake and exciting enough to be recorded in memoirs. We miss in George Moore the physical zest, the tremendous vitality, and the freedom from sentimentality, which render the work of his eighteenth century predecessors in the art of reminiscences so readable. To re-read "Avowals" or the "Confessions of a Young Man" is to enter an antediluvian world peopled by such almost antediluvian monsters as Gustav Khan, Catulle Mondes, and Walter Pater. However, we must revere his clean and sincere appreciation of the Russians and of such men as Corot and Baudelaire. But though we may forgive him his rather treacly taste in poetry, his pure and watery prose and his petulant jealousy of his contemporaries, we are afraid that it will be difficult for the younger generation to take very seriously the enthusiastic little figure that could dance such assiduous attendance on the dandy Manet in the Café Guerbois, while the great painters of the period, Cézanne, Van Gogh and Renoir, sailed daily but almost unnoticed over his head, like thunderclouds over the head of a sparrow. George Moore is an interesting example of a man who was able to subject his whole life, his works and his undeniable gifts, to a narrow and rather spinsterish sense of "correctness"; and he became impatient with other novelists who violated his sense of literary decorum. Yet when we look back to his generation for stimulation of any kind it is only in the less meticulously correct novelists and writers—in Doughty Conrad, Cunninghame Graham, Hardy and Hudson—that we can find work that lives with any organic vitality of its own.

PAMELA WILLMORE.

The collected works of T. S. Eliot are now obtainable at a reasonable price (Faber and Guire, 7/6.) Few writers have raised such a storm of conflicting criticism: yet it was evident to the discerning from the first, that his work had come to stay: for it is only a powerful mind that can stir the reviewers into columns of vituperative bombast. Since the appearance of "Prufrock" in 1915, these fulminations and thunders have perceptibly decreased and have in many cases begun to groan forth a plaintive enthusiasm. The chief reason for all this wrath seems to have been the fact that Mr. Eliot's outlook is one of utter hopelessness and disillusionment—a reason which if it were valid would disqualify some of the best work of Shakespeare and Dostoevsky.

More than any other modern artist Mr. Eliot has captured the brooding restlessness of the age: he has captured the gloomy introspection and bitter disillusionment of the youth of Europe. His irony cuts like a knife: his tremendous emotional tension, his powerful and sombre imagination challenge comparison with the finest of the Elizabethans.

The publication of the "Waste Land" marks a new era in English Poetry. It is one of the most relentlessly honest works of the age. For in it the spirit of historical culture is made to recognise its futility: the soul of man shrinks horrified from the gulf to which it has been advancing so unconsciously with flags and banners for the last two hundred years. Mr. Eliot's enormous erudition and imagiative power concentrate with a horrified and hypnotised glare on the naked spectre of the truth. One hears the crash of falling ruins, the querulous expostulation of the old ideals and idols against the powers of a new and inscrutable darkness. High over the sleepy self-satisfaction of middle-age one hears again and again the agonised searching question of youth now rising into a hoarse shout and then breaking off into an exasperated hyena-like chuckle—mocking, blasphemous, unanswerable.

Mr. Eliot has invented a new form in which he aptly captures the rhythms, the bewildering kaleidoscopic movement, of modern life. The sordid drifting of industrialised herds, the obscenity of the sham ideals of the crowd, the mental non-existence of the man in the street, the huge unwieldy paralysis of the gods, are flung before one in their grim reality: insisted on with a terrible mechanical reiteration: until one feels sick and giddy and shuts the book.

Mr. Eliot writes with the restraint of despair, a quality which has often been called cynicism: time and again he crosses over the boundary of anguish and comes to the breaking point where pain turns to a shrill hysterical laughter.

> O O O O that Shakespeherian Rag—
> It's so elegant
> So intelligent.

There are passages of extreme pathos, wild buffoonery and almost classical beauty. It is the closeness and logical sequence of these passages in Mr. Eliot's poem that make it such a true picture of modern life.

A woman drew her long black hair out tight
And fiddled whisper music on those strings;
And bats with baby faces in the violet light
Whistled and beat their wings,
And crawled head downward down a blackened wall,
And upside down in air were towers
Tolling reminiscent bells that kept the hours,
And voices singing out of empty cisterns and exhausted wells.

There is something significant in his attempt to readjust old tags to modern life.

When lovely woman stoops to folly and
Paces about her room again alone,
She smoothes her hair with automatic hand
And puts a record on the gramophone.

Here is an amusing readjustment of lines by Marvell and Day:

But at my back from time to time I hear
The sound of horns and motors which shall bring
Sweeney to Mrs. Porter in the spring.
O the moon shines bright on Mrs. Porter
And on her daughter.
They wash their feet in soda water.

These lines are more than a mere playing with words. They show how foolish it is for us to pretend that there is any longer any connection between the culture and education on which we pride ourselves so much, and the dirty little money grubbing existence we lead.

Yet there the nightingale
Filled all the desert with inviolable voice,
And still she cries (and still the world pursues)
"Jug, Jug" to dirty ears.

Mr. Eliot's poetry is stunted, tortured, twisted. It is unpleasant, like dry clotted blood. Yet it is all the more valuable in that it is the blood of a human heart. There are enough of the hedge-songster school of poets to fill a large asylum, people who have the time to kindle with kindly warmth over daisies and buttercups when the world is rocking on precarious hinges. A little unpleasantness is an excellent tonic if it can wake a few middle-aged reviewers from their benevolent snoring and infuriate them for a moment or two.

Mr. Eliot is probably known to the South African public better by his cool and stately prose than by his crabbed and vehement poetry. Mr. Eliot, it will be remembered, has a dual personality, and his book of criticism, "The Sacred Wood," ranks with the criticism of Dryden and Arnold as the finest in our literature.

To read Mr. Eliot's poems is to realise the necessity for new values in modern life. There must be a great destruction in the human consciousness: we must gibe, sneer and ridicule our venerable reviewers into epileptic fits: we have plenty of muck to clear out of the way before we can start the great work of reconstruction.

ROY CAMPBELL.

THE WORSHIP OF NATURE, by Sir James George Frazer; Macmillan; Vol. I., 25s.

It is only comparatively recently that anthropology has been dignified to the rank of a great and inspiring science. In the days of Darwin and Huxley it was a cul-de-sac: the scientists of the Victorian era were disconcerted by the less comprehensible phenomena of the human mind and trumpeted abroad their belief that there were no mental happenings which could not be expressed in material terms. Ten years after Charcot had shown that bodily diseases can be generated mentally—they were still trumpeting their belief. Darwin himself was easily irritated by anything that savoured of the supernormal and once stubbonly refused to witness a demonstration in hypnotism in which he scornfully refused to believe. Since then the theories of Freud have come to us and along with them the greatest intellectual feast of the century, Sir James Frazer's "Golden Bough." The works of these two scientists have mutually contributed to one another, and grown side by side until they have thrown their reflection over the whole of modern thought.

Again we have spread before us one of the most magnificent feasts that learning, industry and wit can provide.

Time has long gone by, thanks to Sir James Frazer and his fellow workers, when the beliefs of the ancient and existing pagan world could be dismissed as foolish and mischievous superstitions; for amid much that is crude and abominable there remains always something of moral and spiritual value, some germ from which has sprung the science and philosophy of other times. The study of comparative religion might well be encouraged in a country like ours in which the laws are based still on the white man's mental superiority to the native—a superstition which was exploded by science ten years ago and by Christianity two thousand years before. And to those of our tribal medicine-men, the politicians, who can read or know how to use a dictionary the study of such books cannot be too strongly recommended. The fact that we as a nation are three hundred years behind modern Europe and five hundred years behind modern art and science is no excuse. I use Olive Schreiner's figures, lenient as they are. We have no excuse for our parasitism on the native and the sooner we realise it the safer for our future. We are as a race without thinkers, without leaders, without even a physical aristocracy working on the land.

The study of modern anthropology should be encouraged as it would give us a better sense of our position in the family tree of Homo Sapiens—which is among the lower branches: and it might even rouse us to assert ourselves in some less ignoble way than reclining blissfully in a grocer's paradise and feeding on the labour of the natives.

ROY CAMPBELL.

THE WHITE MAN'S BURDEN.

Anybody can write one good novel.—(*The Cape Times*).

WARNING!

——— & Sons, Undertakers, etc., beg to notify all persons who are Members of our Burial Society that Mr. ——— and Mrs. ——— have no authority whatsoever to canvass for or collect monies on behalf of our Society known as "———'s Burial Society" (Pink Book).

FURTHER.

We have no responsibility for and are entirely unconnected with the Society known as "The ——— Friendly and Burial Society" (Green Book) on which our name appears other than as Burial Contractors to that Society.

——— & SONS. (*Recent advertisement*).

I have never missed an opportunity of raising my voice against this imposter (Van Gogh).—(*Natal Mercury*).

Blue bells! Blue bells!
Nodding, bobbing in the breeze, etc., etc.—(*The South African Nation*).

It is rather Shakespeare's characters (in King Lear) who are puppets . . . . (*Same paper*).

"A LITTLE BIT OF 'OLD ENGLAND' IN OUDTSHOORN."

We were "Polly" tourists. That is, it was the long slinky blue car of the world-famous Polytechnic. Touring Association that had brought us many hundreds of miles from the grim blue face of Table Mountain . . . to this widespread town of crystal clear air and radiant blue rain-washed skies into which leaped pointedly thick slender tapering yews. . . . . I shall never forget the yews of Oudtshoorn—probably pines, but very like yews.—(*The South African Nation*).

Chapman's humour and Jonson's gentle didacticism.—(*The South African Quarterly*).

VOORSLAG

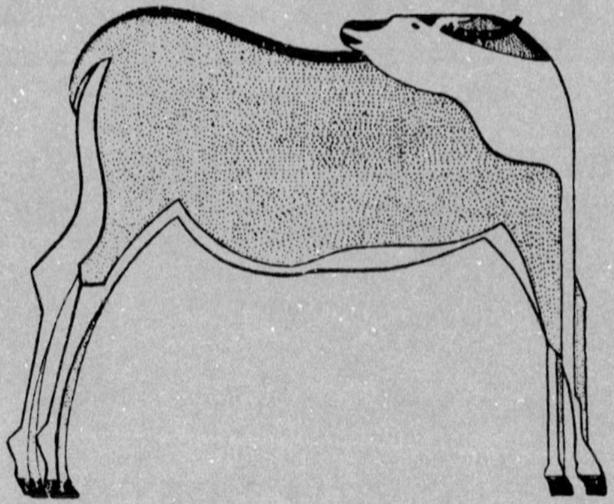

Vol. I JULY 1926 No. 2

Two Shillings and Sixpence

VOORSLAG

A MAGAZINE OF SOUTH AFRICAN LIFE AND ART.

Published by A. C. Braby, Durban.

MSS. and all communications should be addressed to Box 731, Durban.

Vol. I. July, 1926. No. 2.

Contents

VOORSLAG

Vol. 1 JULY 1926 No. 2

Fetish Worship in South Africa.

A SKIRMISH ON THE BORDERS OF POPULAR OPINION.

AT one of Théophile Gautier's parties where Baudelaire was a guest, a young man picked up a hideous little African idol which stood on one of the tables. "What an obscene and hideous little monster," he exclaimed with a horrified shudder. "Take care what you are saying," the sombre voice of Baudelaire interrupted him. "How do you know that you are not insulting the True God?" This is not an idea which can be dismissed with a laugh: Baudelaire was not joking: his was not a mind which indulged in flippancies. He spoke from a deep and bitter experience of the ways of God and Man. Fortunately for most of us we have not the intellectual stamina to face such an idea: we have to drug ourselves with more comfortable beliefs. A prominent German scientist after exhaustive researches recently came to the conclusion that out of every million individuals only one is really conscious. The others are entirely submerged in the mass-consciousness. Now this mass-consciousness as far as the average human being goes is Omnipotence, the True God—*Vox Populi, vox Dei.* It makes no difference in what name we worship it whether it be in the name of Jesus or Mumbo Jumbo: what matters is that we obey it: and when we investigate it closely we find that it bears a considerable resemblance to the pot-bellied little idol that stood on Gautier's table and none at all to the Man who died on the Cross. The inspired and fiery logic of Christ has been too much for humanity.

Yet it has seized our imaginations so powerfully that we have been unable to shake it off for two thousand years. It has given us a vision, an ideal—of how we would like others to behave towards us. We could not kill the wisdom of such a great poet as Christ. What was to be done? Why, use it for ones own ends: make it a paying concern: float a company: and the result is "Christianity." "Christianity" is the most ingenious device that we have been able to invent to combat the influence of Christ: it acts as a buffer and softens the impact of His teaching. We can still go on worshipping Mumbo Jumbo as long as we give him a respectable name. Anatole France pointed out that the success of "Christianity" was due to the fact that it could reconcile itself to any policy. It has reconciled itself in turn to the Crusades, the slave-trade, the Inquisition, the War and the Colour Bar. The few real Christians who have objected to these things have always been looked upon as cranks and have been accordingly either knocked on the head or otherwise insulted. There would be nothing regrettable in this were it not that true Christianity is a very good policy in itself and were it accepted as a racial system would be one of the surest means of self-preservation and one of the pleasantest means of self-assertion that one could imagine. It is one of the cleanest ways of preserving one's own individuality with the minimum of interference with other people's business—more especially in the racial and political sense than in the personal sense. True it has not yet been tested racially or politically: but if we examine any of the great catastrophies in history we can find few that were not solely brought about by Mumbo Jumboism and still fewer that could not have been averted by a certain amount of tolerance and courtesy, which are, in the main, ingredients of Christianity. Mumbo Jumboism concentrates on compassing its own immediately material ends: it does not make any provision for the slow but inevitable retaliations of Nature. Both Christ and Nietzche in formulating their two in many ways similar systems took into account the laws of Nature and either of their systems would be preferable to Mumbo Jumboism. But both these philosophers overestimated the intelligence of humanity. Their systems can only be put into practice by fearless individualists and they are both of them far above the scope of mass-consciousness. An investigation into history shows that the mass-consciousness or *Vox Populi* has been responsible for nearly all the catastrophes that have ever happened while the few noble and lasting things that have been produced by humanity have been the work of individuals. Crowds and communities are actuated solely by the most primitive instincts: panic, suspicion, race-feeling, colour-prejudice, ferocity and patriotism. Yet if one were to tell the average respectable citizen that he was one of the bloodthirstiest, most intolerant and barbarous savages that ever lived on the earth—he would think one was joking with him. His own superstitions, taboos and witch-rituals are so natural to him that he uses them even as standards by which to gauge the barbarity of others.

What the mass-consciousness clamours for is a leader who obeys it: it always selects a victim from its own ranks whom it can saddle with its responsibilities and on whom it can wreak its disappointment when its commands are frustrated. The mass-leader only leads the mass in that he goes in front of it—between the shafts. He doesn't know where he is going—he leaves it to the mass· The mass don't know where they are going—they leave it to the leader. What the mass-conscious really needs is a driver not a leader: but whenever it finds one it becomes panic stricken and either nails him to a Cross or poisons him as it did Socrates or drives him mad as it did Nietzsche In herds of animals and in savage tribes the "leader" is really more of a driver—he rises to his place by active competition. But it is a long time since this has ceased to be true of us Europeans. Our leaders compete with each other in mediocrity: the leader who can make the greatest compromise with popular opinion is the one who gets most power: he becomes the incarnation of average mentality. Now there is no more reason why popular opinion should be right in regard to politics or sociology than it is in regard to art, music, or literature. In these three arts popular opinion only has a taste for what is ephemeral and trashy. The intellectual power of a community is not increased by numbers, for all the more individualistic elements in a crowd conflict and neutralise one another: it is only the emotional power which is increased by numbers, for emotions are contagious. It is disconcerting therefore in trying to assess what is represented by the *Vox Populi,* or in other words the *Vox Dei,* to have to come to the conclusion that the mental power of a high and respectable state in its collective functions is little more than the mental power of a moron or even a criminal lunatic, and it is even more disconcerting to realise that this mental power is backed up by tremendous physical and emotional resources.

The first and eternal demand of every community of human beings is for its bogey-men or tribal medicine-men. Superstition has always been inseparable from mass-life. In savage tribes the business of the bogey-man or witch-doctor is controlled and organised with a certain amount of consideration for public freedom and safety. But in what we call civilization superstition reigns supreme and governs everything. It is no use trying to destroy it: superstition is the most necessary of all emotional nourishments. When Lenin put his foot through the hierarchical machinery of Russia he thought he had done a service to humanity: he imagined he had hit Mumbo Jumbo very hard on the head. But Mumbo Jumbo did not worry. He did not live in the churches but in the hearts of the people. The monger of pseudo-scientific platitudes stepped into the shoes of the priest, and things went on as usual. The bogey-man is as eternal as the human race, and in modern civilization he wields more power than in the primitive tribe.

READER: Whom do you refer to as witch-doctors and bogey-men?

WRITER: I refer to priests, politicians, journalists and military commanders.

READER: They seem to fulfil their purposes all right. What have you got against them? I can't imagine them throwing bones, telling fortunes or smelling out victims.

WRITER: No. They jingle medals, wave flags, make fatuous prophesies, and as for smelling out—hounding out is more like it. The mob gets excited: they don't know what it's about. Then the journalist invents a few lies for them to make them feel sure that their indignation is righteous. Then the politician orders mobilization. Then the priest comes along and blesses the guns and breaks bottles of champagne on the backsides of dreadnoughts. Then the recruiting sergeant begins smelling out victims and the old general comes and rounds them up like cattle into a sausage-factory. Smelling out, you say? There is something intelligible in the smelling out of savages: there is usually some personal spite or some other human motive to account for it, and in any case a primitive witch-doctor selects rather than collects his victims. If he were not cautious in his selection the tribe would knock him over the head. But the more we are hounded out by witch-doctors the more we love, honour and obey them. Mind you, I don't blame the witch-doctors—they aren't responsible for it; we keep them for the very purpose of officiating in our emotional debauches—they are merely doing their duty. Imagine what would be the fate of a journalist or a politician who did not say exactly what the public wanted him to say.

READER: Do you think then that there was no cause for us to step into this last war to save civilization?

WRITER: If you were able to inform me as to who were the aggressors, what were the causes, and what was the object of it all, I might try to reply to this question. As for saving civilization, it had nothing to do with civilization. The Germans were "saving civilization," everybody was "saving civilization," and when we woke up five years later we found we had all been helping to destroy civilization. Any way, what was worth saving about it? A civilization which could not assimilate the tremendous scientific resources at its command for any better purpose than to make guns and torpedoes deserves to have been blown to pieces by them.

READER: But surely you cannot see anything in going against the ways of your kind. Has the ideal of service never appealed to you? What can there be productive or creative in sailing against the stream?

WRITER: There is nothing productive in making oneself part of a great human sausage machine which has neither rhyme nor reason. As for the ideal of service, it depends whether you mean service to mass-opinion or service to the clear intuition which nature has lit in every human being but which nearly every human being manages to extinguish in himself, either by means of drink, or middle-class education, or any other drug which is handy. As for there being anything creative or productive in my attitude, how do you imagine that man could ever have risen from the monkeys, if it were not for the few individualists that had the courage to step over the silly little boundaries of ape-life, and lead others after them.

READER: Then you object to war on conscientious grounds?

WRITER: Not at all. I have no conscience. I can think of no better way of disposing of an enemy than of blotting him out of existence. I would not be at all annoyed if killing were legitimised in civil life. But to glorify this extremely dull, mechanical, unreasonable killing is absurd. As long as people kill without reason they are heroes: but if any one has a motive or a reason for killing—then he is a criminal. The more justifiable a homicide is the more we deplore it: the more unreasonable it is the more we admire it.

READER: Come, come, you are only playing with words.

WRITER: That is what you older people always say when you are at a loss for an arugment. I am dealing scientifically—with facts.

READER: You are flippant, impertinent and insolent· You think it amusing to be so. I forgive you because you are young. I used to have the same ideas myself. You will come to think differently. Ha, ha, ha, my boy: you are young, very young.

WRITER: You may not be aware that the remarks you have just made have been thoroughly dealt with by anthropologists. The epithets of youth, insolence, and impertinence, when used in the place of arguments are the last resort of mental impotence. (See Trotter's "Instincts of the Herd in Peace and War.") The fact that you are no longer young does not invalidate the opinions you once held: and the insolence or unpleasantness of a statement is no disproof of its truth.

READER: You are very dogmatic to-day. What's the matter? Swelled head?

WRITER: Yes: since I have returned to my native land my head has swelled considerably· Everything tends to expand in a vacuum.

READER: Well, what have you got against this country—more grievances?

WRITER: None at all. Life in this country is absolutely unconscious. There is nothing to quarrel with. South Africa mentally is merely an irresponsible foetus of a country: an interesting subject to study biologically but not to get angry with. But I will diagnose it later. Meanwhile if you listen attentively I shall give you some very interesting examples of Fetish Worship as it exists in our country. When we have finished with these we shall make our final deductions. I have selected these examples with great care and as they will illuminate my arguments I beg that you will keep your mouth shut and not interrupt unless you can think of something worth saying. Remember that epithets are not arguments and that you are never too old to learn. There was a religious celebration of Trafalgar Day a year or two ago. As I was anxious in my benighted Paganism to see in what way Christianity reconciled itself to Imperialism, I attended. The speakers were all clergymen. They inspired one with the belief that God Almighty was strongly imbued with British sentiments—this was evidently a guarantee of his fitness to occupy so responsible and exalted a position. One received the impression that heaven was a British Institution and that the Almighty was an Omnipotent edition of Jellicoe and Kitchener rolled in one: and in the end I was troubled with visions of the same august Personage in Boy-Scout's uniform hoisting the Union Jack at the new base at Singapore. On the other hand in Dutch churches I have collected much evidence to the contrary and I understand that the Almighty is Dutch, a real old Afrikander. I think this evidence is supported by Blake's drawings of him and I am far more credulous of this point of view. Man made God after his own image. Perhaps the most memorable example of Fetish worship that I ever met was at a prize-giving at school, some years ago. A famous and rubicund general who presided over the ceremony after assuring us that man was a "fighting animal" exhorted us to play games and drill well so that we should one day be prepared to participate in the joyful triumphs of war. His moustachios coruscated with rapture: his decorations bounced on his paunch as he inculcated his divine wisdom into the susceptible minds of the children. We all loved him: he was a fine fat jovial old fellow. But I remember being assailed with this doubt. "Man is also a procreative animal: what would people say if he gave as glowing an account of the joys of concupiscence as he does of the joys of bloodshed?" And it has since puzzled me very often why we should exalt with drums and trumpets the unnecessary and boring process of exterminating one's species while we speak with shame and humiliation (or ribaldry, which is the same thing) of the most innocent and enjoyable pastime of which the species is capable—that of increasing itself. Cinderella has to skulk round corners under the various names of Adultery and Fornication while the big fat Ogre swaggers down the streets under the titles of Honour and Glory, covered with decorations and buttons.

READER: He jests at scars who never felt a wound!

WRITER: I don't jest at scars—I object to them. But that does not prevent me from treating with derision, surely the most antiseptic of sentiments, a class of men who can make an honourable living out of receiving and inflicting them. Now there are two examples of what is going on every day all round us. They show how deeply we are submerged in the unconscious rigmarole of mass-life. Nobody in the audiences in either case was the least bit inclined to scoff and the two functions were splendid successes. Never has the mentality of White South Africa been revealed to me more clearly than when I sat in the gallery in the House of Assembly. A heated discussion was in progress. Few speakers spoke at any length who did not contrive to contradict themselves once or twice before the end of their speeches—not obviously, perhaps, but in such a manner that a few simple mental deductions would have neutralised the purport of each speech. These self contradictions were either taken for granted or not noticed. It was purely a battle of group-sentiments: reason only functioned in a curious inconsequent manner as it does in dreams. All those who spoke were entirely submerged in and only actuated by the dream-consciousness of the crowd. It caused me a certain amount of uneasiness that instead of using arguments the opponents regularly and almost automatically sought for low and selfish motives to which to impute each other's sayings and actions. I do not contend that this revealed anything shifty or uneasy in the general conscience, for we are not concerned with the moral part of it here. It was the psychological interest that held me almost spell-bound. The speakers were charged with a fierce elemental electricity. I have never been more impressed in my life. I experienced something of the same sensation as a child when I attended a Spiritualistic séance: only this was more ghostly and there was no trickery about it. The mental atmosphere was as of some strange moonlight, into which arose the phantasmal emanations of the race-consciousness—the ghosts of ideas: agitations in glaucous depths: faintly phosphorescent expostulations: the quicksilvery sheen, the fusion and rarefication of ever-changing mental shapes—all hankering up towards consciousness. It was as if the ghosts of things that had died in the womb before they had attained any definite shape were emerging in some ineffectual attempt to realise themselves. The question under discussion was one which would have puzzled a commission of anthropologists. Yet these gallant agriculturalists, business-men and martial veterans sailed into it as boldly as if it had been a question of turnips, stocks and shares, or strategy: and they spoke with a fervour, an assurance, a conviction that would have been denied to more sophisticated intelligences. One felt that the race-antagonism between the English and the Dutch was nothing: that the mentality of the opposing parties was so inseparably one that the existence of an opposition was only an accident: one felt that an Act of Union had been consummated psychologically as far back as 1850 and that the backbiting and haggling was merely an attempt to generate enough friction to set up that vague current of emotional electricity with which they all were charged. I repeat that as a race we are unconscious, utterly unconscious. There is only the race-mind, the mob-soul. In the vast and ancient communities of Europe where society rotates round many different axes, where there is a conflict between equally opposed forces and where these forces have had time to gather impetus through hundreds of years—there you find a certain amount of consciousness: for the average consciousness of the individual varies in proportion to the diversity of the activities of the community. It is possible in considering any large and highly organised community to treat it as a conscious body whose cells differ in their functions. One can point to the scientists as its brain: to its artists as its procreative organs: to its workmen as its heart: to its business-men as its stomach: to its journalists and politicians as its posterior. But take a small community like ours which has isolated itself from the only possible competition that it can hope for. There is no circulation, no nerve-telegraphy. One aching stomach and that is all. The cells cohere in some sort of slipshod fashion but they all function in the same way. Mentally we have just arrived at the protozoic stage. If you want any further proof of this read our newspapers and political speeches, go about in clubs and other places and if you hear one remark or read one sentence which is not a platitude or an echo of something else you will be very lucky.

Now let us come to the more cheerful side of things. Here I have a photograph of a gentleman who belongs to an old, a very old South African family.

READER: I say, what a fine head! This face quite belies all your evidence as to the unintelligence of South Africans. The only interesting face I have seen for three or four years.

WRITER: Yes, he belongs to an old South African Family—the Wildebeestes. This is a fine old bull Wildebeeste. You know what I like about him? Why, in the first place, he is self-contained and sufficient. He never goes about trying to inflict his language, his point of view, or the laws of his existence on anybody else. He never has a grievance, he never whines for protection or tries to restrict anybody else's liberty. He doesn't grumble or talk politics. If you try to make him swot up English or Afrikaans he simply kicks up his heels and scampers off. Whenever he wants to say anything he says "Kngrarhr!" He always says the same thing, like a politician, but he doesn't contradict himself and he is more concise. He hasn't got any colour-prejudice or race-feeling. He doesn't care a hang for fences, taboos and restrictions he just bounces gracefully over them, but he doesn't entangle himself with them or try to break them. He just sails over them and lands the other side. He is one of the few individualists in this country, one of the few who are not tied up with some dirty political institution, colour prejudice, or race feeling. He is about the only creature in South Africa who has any vestige of aristocracy or breeding about him. He is a true Nietzschean, and I uphold him as an example to South Africa. Follow the Wildebeeste! His outlook is scientific and artistic. If we had nine or ten individuals such as he is among our human population South Africa would be a different country.

READER: What makes you say that?

WRITER : Because we need a few Wildebeestes to jump over the fences, prejudices and tribal taboos that hem us in on every side. Once they started jumping others would follow. And South Africa would be turned from being an archeological curiosity into a gymnasium of athletic personalities. Your old fogeys whenever anything puzzles you about our country, begin discussing politics. You start blaming things on General Smuts and Hertzog or on Mr. Tielman Roos, who are no more responsible for our national belly-ache than you or me. They are all very fine men : and they are very conscientiously serving the communities they represent. They are quite innocent of any sinister motives or thoughts : why, they are all so busy they don't get any time to think at all.

READER : But don't you think a measure like the Colour Bar means anything?

WRITER : Not at all. It is only an official recognition of something that has always existed. It removes a certain amount of ambiguity : and it is therefore a very honest measure. The colour bar has always existed socially and in the minds of the white races. It is not General Hertzog who made the Colour Bar. It is the people. I don't blame General Hertzog, and I don't blame the people. It is inevitable. When the white people came out here they gave the native the Bible and the native in exchange gave the white man a great black fetish to worship. It is this fetish that rules the country—Colour-prejudice. The Colour Bar will never be broken down by invoking the spirit of Christianity or Justice. Justice does not play very much part in inter-human relationships. The Colour Bar will be an excellent hurdle for the individualists, whether white or black, to amuse themselves by jumping over. Once it is jumped over socially (which is not illegal) it will be easily negotiable legally. Literature and science have always worked hand in hand and popular opinion usually trudges on about fifty years behind hand. But satire and ridicule have knocked more obsolete institutions to pieces than all the long-range guns that ever existed.

READER : But does the ideal of a White South Africa not appeal to you?

WRITER : Why all this mania for tabulation—White South Africa,

Black South Africa, Yellow South Africa? It is quite unnecessary: it is only the result of middle-class education: the mob is terrified of any thought or idea that is not tied to a label; this mania forces us to tie tickets on to things before they exist. It is all the outcome of fear the strongest of all mob emotions, and it forces us into all sorts of necessary tyrannies. We are so afraid of liberty ourselves that we absolutely rely on discipline and love it better than anything on earth: this makes us suspicious of others who do not need the same amount of outward discipline. We forget that we are probably the most rapacious savages on the face of the globe, and that what we are pleased to call culture is little more than a vast array of instruments of destruction which we have had to invent for keeping each other in order. The native is emotionally reserved and for that reason has not had to invent guns or trousers: but compare the average native's conversation with any of our parliamentary orators' speeches and one might be excused for doubting whether the former is not more refined, cultured or intelligent. It certainly shows a greater capacity for formulating and expressing ideas and a greater freedom from platitudes.

Now fear and suspicion are the two emotions most easily generated in mass-consciousness, and wherever there is the slightest motive for these emotions they take possession of everything. The crowd is always terrified of leaving anything in the balance and must always have some wretched ideal to tie its nose to. "White South Africa" is one of these ideals. It is just vague and mystical enough to appeal to sentimentalists: and sentimentality is the chief quality of the South African character. Apart from the Victoria Falls, which is another mist-covered South African institution, "White South Africa" has given rise to more bad rhetoric than anything else. It has just enough haze round it to produce an effective rainbow—and to second-rate intelligence there is nothing more attractive than a rainbow. One of our bards has acknowledged that as a child he wept because he couldn't catch a rainbow. But he acknowledges that when he was older and had ceased to try to catch it, he was able to experience what must have been a curious and extremely pleasant sensation, with his feet.

"And o'er my feet the rosy radiance crept."

Perhaps if we remove the rainbows from our brains we may one day experience the delightfully ticklish sensation of feeling them creeping over our feet. A study of South African Poetry will show that on the whole we are more sensitive with our feet than with our heads :

> . . . . . "upon thy footsteps ope
> The fount of light that gleans from skyey cope."

It is dangerous therefore that we should trust too much to our heads : let us rather trust to our feet and practise jumping : let us jump the mean little fences we have put up around us : even if we are a pure and soulful race, surely we can find something better to do than to sit in colourless spinsterish seclusion and dream about rainbows. It takes more colours than one to make a rainbow. I cannot see that the world would benefit much by a White South Africa which would only mean an extension and multiplication of that mental obesity for which we are already world-famous. "White South Africa" only conjured up before me a vision of an enormous Gents' Outfitting Establishment. But why worry about it? The Colour Bar is the first official recognition of the mental equality of the races : the second can only be the removal of the Colour Bar, or rather its natural and peaceful demise.

If we could only realise, as a race, that politics are of secondary importance : that a staff of intelligent and friendly clerks could probably rule the country better than a collection of quarrelsome old gentlemen : we should get a long way further. We make our politicians too self-conscious; we impute all sorts of sinister motives to them, and yet when we open the door on them, there they all are like a lot of fussy little tailors discussing the cut of a National flag. Everyone knows that it doesn't matter one little damn what our national flag is like. A fashionable dress designer could stitch one up in a few minutes. All the suggestions put forward are moderately sensible, and yet they haggle like a crowd of superannuated spinsters at a bun-fight. Why, sirs, if you are all so keen on your own suggestions why don't you all design private flags of your own : go home and get your wives to sow them across the seats of your trousers and then we shall all know what good taste you have! But metaphorically speaking, that is the place where

I shall wear my national flag until we have justified our existence as a nation by something more substantial than the mere production of mealy-meal and the restriction of the liberty of the natives—which is the utmost we can claim to have done so far. The fact that this flag question has stirred up more indignation than the passing of the Colour Bar shows what a miserable lot of fetish-worshippers we are.

READER : That's right, foul your own nest.

WRITER : I am not fouling my nest, I am trying to clean it : if the dirt falls on you, get out of the way.

READER : There is too much of the clever young man about you.

WRITER : And there is too much of the stupid old gentleman about you. You have about as much sense of human nature as a cabinet minister—

READER : I will not be insulted.

WRITER : You will, as long as you can't see any farther than your own nose. If you find the truth insulting don't go on reading this. Go and buy one of the political papers. Go and drown your last vestige of commonsense and decency in some stagnant puddle of race or party feeling. I know you mob-people only too well. If Colonel Creswell says anything unintelligent you say that he says it because he is an Englishman. If Generals Smuts or Hertzog say anything unintelligent you suggest that it is because they are Dutch. You don't take into account that any of them may be congenitally unintelligent, or even that they might be intelligent. It takes quite a clever man to be able to make a fool of himself : most people are such fools already that they can't. Why, you mob-people even try to translate science and art into terms of politics, race or colour. I have seen these two holiest of the muses publicly strumpeted, raped and mutilated in the newspapers of all three political parties—either in attempts to distort the former into political evidence or to dissuade the latter from living amongst us at all. You people get an ideal like "White South Africa" tied to your noses and then you can't see anything else. You consider White South Africa to be more important than South Africa itself. It is all the fault of that dear old colour-fetish. It is the incarnation of all that is superstitious, uneasy, grudging and dishonest in our natures. Individually taken, we are all very nice people, a little pudding-headed, but that is all. But we are all afraid of our individual decency: we have to submerge it in respectability. The mob consciousness rules everything. It puts the cart before the horse: and worships Mumbo Jumbo in the name of Jesus, and it worships the Colour Bar in the name of White South Africa.

READER: But how do you propose to kill this Colour Fetish.?

WRITER: It can only be killed by the individual in himself That means it will never be killed at all. Britons and Boers have found it easy enough in the past to jump over the colour-bar to gratify themselves sensually. But they would never do it to gratify their consciences as by this they would endanger the most sensitive part of human anatomy—their pockets. It is this fond marsupial consideration that keeps us fenced in so carefully. No policy has ever been productive that has not accepted, encouraged and fertilised the utmost physical and mental resources that it can command: and probably the end will be that we shall break down the colour-fence ourselves out of sheer boredom and starvation of ideas. We shall soon get tired of playing Robinson Crusoe. Nature is a capricious goddess: she loves emulation, competition: she only pays interest on what is invested: she will not be wooed by an old-fashioned figure sitting inside a fence and ogling her with rhetoric about White South Africa. We shall merely be putting on fat while the native puts on muscle.

READER: You seem to be theorising rather wildly.

WRITER: I am not theorising. I speak from a sound knowledge of the herd instincts in men and animals.

READER: You are merely amusing yourself with youthful flippancies; you respect nothing, you believe in nothing.

WRITER: I do not believe in nothing. I am a deeply religious young man.

READER: Well, what do you believe?

WRITER: I believe that the power behind the universe is something better than an omnipotent old parson or predikant with a colour prejudice and a dirty puritanical mind. I believe that it is genius, the genius of Leonardo, Christ, and Goethe rolled in one and multiplied by infinity, a genius eternally striving towards some unattainable perfection, eternally coming short of it, and eternally striving towards it again.

What little of this power can be realised in human nature can only be realised in the individual himself. It cannot be realised in submerging oneself in the sleepy rigmarole of mob-life which is only the first primitive hankering upward of matter for consciousness: a hesitation between life and death. The death-instincts in the mob are quite as strong as the life-instincts. No one can be clean and sane who submerges himself in the nightmares and dreams of the mob-psyche—for they are all dreams, illusions, nightmares—your wars and colour questions. The crowd rushes about actuated by hideous fears and suspicions, it makes a noise and then it comes up against the iron will of a single individual like Ghandi, and what are all your Union Jacks and machine-guns worth then? They are powerless. One little Indian gentleman can stand up unarmed and paralyse the whole thing. It's no use trying to kill him, his personality will persist. The mob passes: the individual remains. The human soul is not a thing that can be sat on by Governments or officials: why the whole of history is simply a list of different cases in which officials have tried to sit on the human soul—and been bucked off every time. The mob knows it has no life of its own: so it has to invent an after life to believe in. I have no belief in after-life, but I have a fervent belief in this one. I don't believe in progress or evolution as far as humanity goes, for we have long ceased to progress mentally and physically. "I love the world of centuries and vast ages—mammoth worlds beyond our day and mankind, so wonderful in his distances, his history that has no beginning, yet always the pomp and the magnificence of human splendour unfolding through the earth's changing periods. Floods and fire convulsions and ice-arrest intervene between his civilisations. But nothing will ever quench humanity or human potentiality to evolve something new out of a renewed chaos. I do not believe in evolution, but in the strangeness and rainbow-change of ever-renewed creative civilisations. The soul must take the hint from the relics our scientists have gathered out of the forgotten past and from the hint develop a new living utterance. The spark is from dead wisdom, but fire is life."

I do not believe there is anything creative in the white man's sitting inertly on his little island and humbly worshipping a Colour Fetish. So far it is the Colour Fetish who have ruled this country—nobody else has had a word to say in South African affairs: every political party that has been in power has assiduously licked the boots of the Colour Fetish: and the boot-polish is so sour that there is no more intelligent expression in our faces than a sour puritanical grimace.

Once when I was under gas at the dentists I heard, through my coma, a tremendous voice reverberating across the universe and reiterating with terrible hypnotic concentration the idiotic syllable—"OM. OM. OM. OM." If ever I wake up in the night and think about the future of South Africa and wonder in whose hands the destiny of the white and black races has been placed, I see in my mind's eye a great spookish, impersonal, featureless spectre looming over the land; it is about as high as forty skyscrapers, and its mouth, gorping with the rhythmic precision of a fish, utters the same monotonous idiotic syllables, "OM. OM. OM. OM." Every day he grows taller his mouth opens wider and his voice grows louder. That is a faithful portrait of your Colour Fetish—*Vox Populi, vox Dei.*

READER: Then what do you think is the solution of the white question in South Africa?

WRITER: OM! OM! OM! OM! OM!

R.C.

Gauguin.

ON the island of Atuana, one of the Marquesas, just twenty-three years ago, there died in circumstances of the greatest misery and distress one of the most forceful and romantic personalities of his time. A painter of powerful originality, a sculptor, a distinguished worker in ceramics, a writer on art of the first rank and a martyr in the cause of a just treatment of the natives, Gauguin's career has in it all the elements of romance and, indeed, little known though the facts of his remarkable career are to the great majority of people, there has already been a novel and a play founded more or less upon his life.

Here was the paradox of a man who made money with the greatest ease, in fact a few years after entering business as a stock-broker he was making an income of 40,000 francs a year, who threw up his business and lived a life of almost constant poverty and want; a man who in Paris mixed as an equal with the most brilliant and distinguished men of his age, yet left it all to live the life of a savage among the Polynesian natives in a hut that he built with his own hands.

It must be remembered that there was nothing in the way of popular advertisement to be obtained in those days from adopting the native outlook in art and life. The fashion for negro art and jazz music had not yet swept over Europe, and as the upshot proved, he was to sustain nothing but loss and degradation by his association with the natives, and it is not even certain that posterity will rank his Polynesian work as high as the Brittany studies done before his departure for the South Seas. But Gauguin appeared to be possessed by some demon of unrest which drove him ever onwards toward some ideal of unattainable happiness.

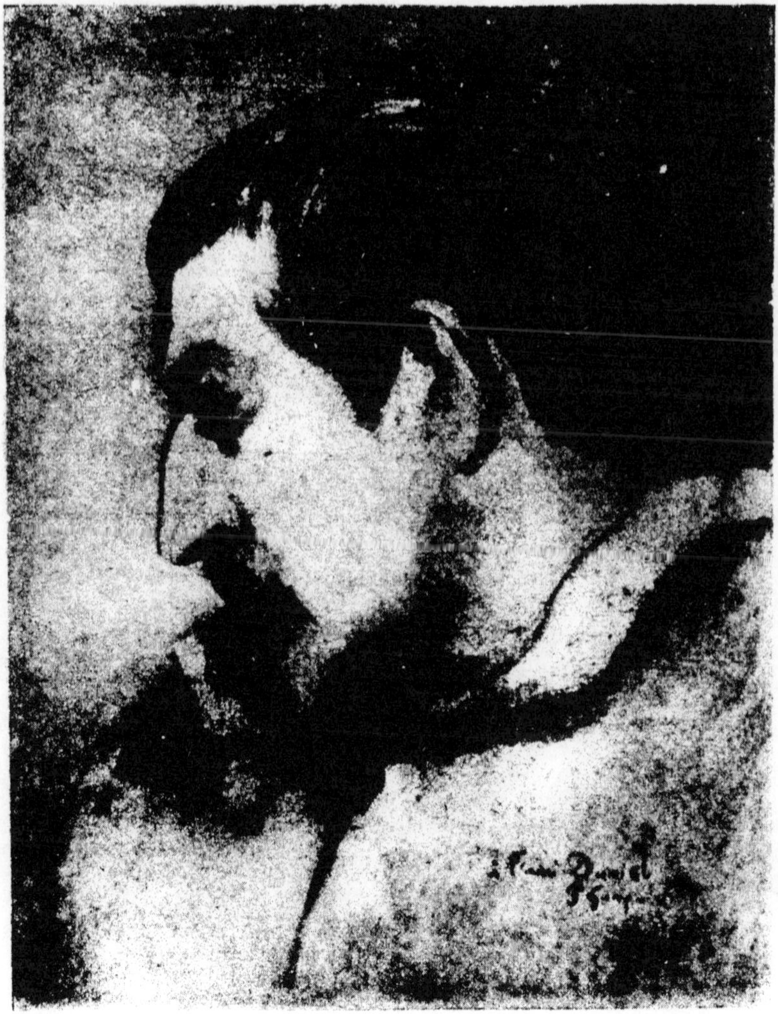

SELF PORTRAIT, GAUGUIN

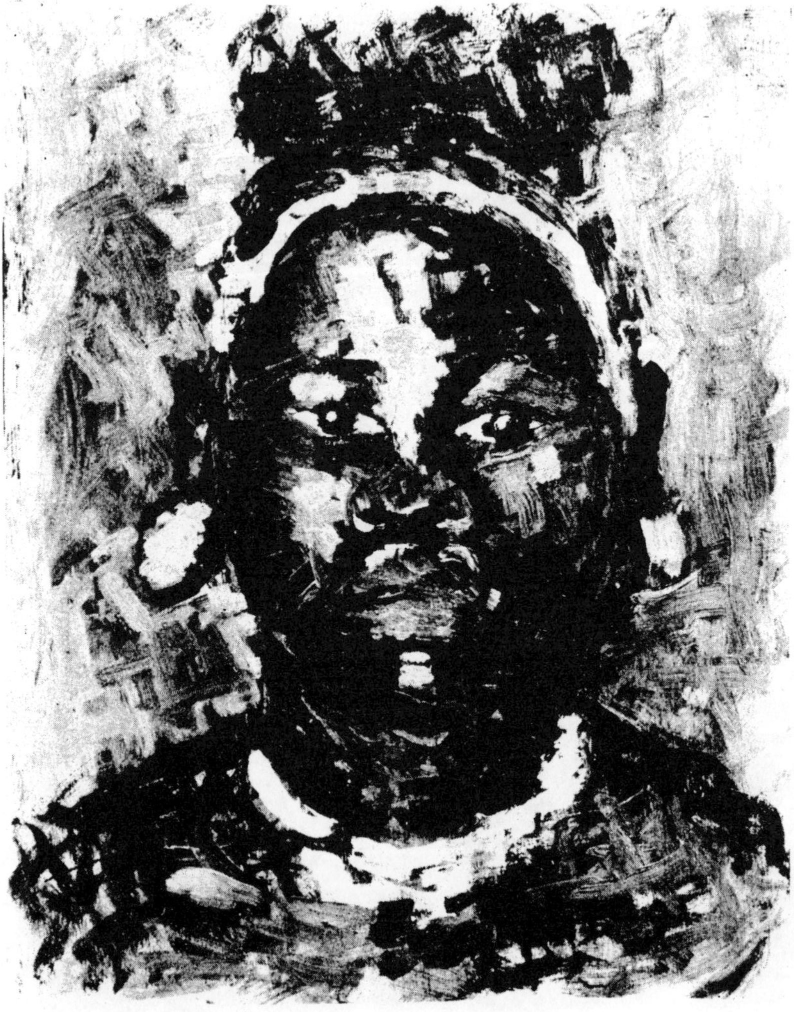

E.P. & C.P. Co., Ltd., Durban

HEAD OF NATIVE GIRL
BY
ANNA DE SCHUBERT.

Paul Gauguin was born in Paris on June 8th, 1848—those "June Days" of "48," during which Paris was filled with tumult and the sound of guns. His father, Clovis Gauguin, was editor of the "National." Madame Gauguin was the daughter of a Monsieur Chazal, of whom little or nothing can be recorded, but her mother, Flora Tristran, was a lady who had enjoyed a brief literary and revolutionary vogue and who had been born in Peru in 1803. She had been through exciting times at the close of Louis-Philippe's reign, and in 1836 turned Saint-Simonist and a militant advocate of humanitarian theories. With the suppression of the revolt of June, 1848, and especially after Decceber 2, 1851, the political situation of the Editor of the "National" became somewhat unsafe, so he decided to take ship, with his wife and his two children, Paul and Mary, for Peru. Unfortunately Clovis Gauguin died during the long voyage of heart failure, and so the young widow and the two small children arrived alone at Lima.

There is no doubt that the scenes and influences of the early years coloured Gauguin's whole life, for always he felt the call of the wide seas, of far-away tropic isles, of the skies and colour of the South. Perhaps his revolt against Europe commenced when as a little seven-year-old boy he was sent to a boarding school at Orleans. He spoke nothing but Spanish when he arrived in the chilly north and apparently made little progress with his studies. At eleven years of age he was a student at the little Seminary and afterwards at the Lycée where he began studying for his degree. He wanted to become a naval officer but was not able to pass the necessary examinations, so at the age of seventeen he shipped as navigating cadet aboard the "Lusitano," sailing between Havre and Rio de Janeiro. Gauguin wrote of his Captain, Tombarel, as "a delightful fatherly quadroon," he also tells of how he was enthralled with the beauty of the harbour of Rio and also of the stories of the wonderland of Oceania related to him by the second mate who had been, when a cabin boy, stranded upon some little Eden in the Archipelago and whose life there had been like a fairy tale come true. He left the "Lusitano" before he was twenty, enrolled in the National navy, and shipped as a third-class hand and stoker on board the "Jerome Napoleon." Within the next three months his mother had died and he obtained ten months renewable leave and left the ship.

The two children had been entrusted to the guardianship of a friend of the family, Gustave Arosa, who was the means of getting Paul started on a brilliant financial career. He obtained a position for him as a clerk at Bertins, Stockbrokers, of The Rue Lafitte. There he remained for eleven consecutive years giving proof of financial abilities of a high order. He quickly mastered the technique of Stock Exchange operations, was astute and far-seeing in his speculations and soon became the possessor of undoubted wealth. He had at this time a yearly income of forty thousand francs, which sum, in the "seventies" of last century meant a large degree of wealth. In 1873 he had married Miss Mette Sophie-Gad, a lady of Danish birth whose family was living in very easy circumstances in Copenhagen and enjoyed a high reputation· One of Miss Sophie-Gad's sisters became the wife of the celebrated painter Fritz Thalour.

So far there was nothing in Gauguin's life to indicate the fantastic destiny that fate had designed for him. He apparently led the life of any prosperous business man the world over, he surrounded his wife and young family with every comfort and had not the direction of his life been handed over to some mocking genie of Art he might have lived and died surrounded by ease and luxury with the Legion of Honour in his button-hole, and an expensive tombstone to mark his last resting place. One wonders if any glimpse of the shadowy, incredible future ever troubled the eyes of the prosperous sharebroker?

Gauguin at this time was a man of great physical strength, he was famous as a fencer, and skilled in all forms of sport. What psychology is profound enough to explain the transformation of this strong, sane, capable business man, not to be distinguished from millions of others who have lived and carried on their businesses and died universally respected, into the revolutionary artist, the man who not only struck the bourgeoise in the face but even despised and trampled on his fellow revolutionaries and finally abjured the whole of the white races of mankind and lived and died among the natives.

His career as an artist only extended over some sixteen years, but in this brief period his ideas influenced a considerable body of modern European painters. It is useless to speculate upon how he first became a prey to that passion for art that was to part him from his wife and family, ruin his business, and lead him finally, outcast, broken, and penniless, to his lonely death on that far Pacific island. We know that he somehow became acquainted with Camille Pissarro, who was then making a heroic fight as a leader of that new spirit in Art—the "Impressionist" movement. Pissarro, who was born in the Danish West Indies may perhaps have been acquainted with the family of Madame Gauguin. Anyway we know that in order to fill up his spare time Gauguin bought canvas and paints and brushes and commenced to paint on Sundays.

Soon after in 1876, Gauguin, through his friend Camille Pissarro, was in touch with several revolutionary Impressionists. More and more is he obsessed with the problems of painting. He meets Manet, the cultured accomplished man of the world, who encourages him; he has long talks with Cézanne and Guillaumin. His enthusiasm grows. He buys fifteen thousand francs' worth of paintings by Manet, Daumier, Jongkind, Claude Monet, Cézanne, Pissarro, Guillaumin, and Sisley. He leaves his house and settles in another one which is provided with a large studio. Gauguin now began to show works at exhibitions of the Impressionist group. In 1880, 1881, and 1882 work by him received favourable notice from the critics. By this time the unfortunate business man was completely in the power of his genie, it is true that he was still making large sums of money, but he could no longer bear to be dragged from his easel at the call of business, so in January, 1883, he made the cruel, heroic resolve to sacrifice all to his art, he gave up his business, he turned his back upon the Stock Exchange. He would devote himself to his art and to art only —I wonder if somewhere there was heard a chuckle of immortal laughter?

At a considerable loss he sold his collection of paintings. Like so many who pursue the phantom of art he believed himself to be a practical man. He removed his family to Rouen because he understood that living was cheaper there. He gave up a business worth forty thousand francs a year, but he made it a matter of vital importance to live in some place where bread and meat were a penny a pound cheaper than elsewhere! Throughout his life he placed the greatest hope and confidence in his "economical" spirit. The means of life became so difficult to obtain at Rouen that Gauguin determined to go with his family to Copenhagen, where his wife's family were in easy circumstances. Apparently, Gauguin the successful, genial, business man, was far better as a husband and a father than Gauguin, the iconoclast painter; anyway, after considerable trouble had ensued, life together became too burdensome and Paul Gauguin and his wife separated in June, 1885, never to meet again.

Now alone, Gauguin returned to Paris and rented a small studio, he was soon in real want and the man who thirty months before was turning over big money on the Stock Exchange was now working as a bill-poster, at a pay of three francs fifty centimes a day. In a little note-book which he later dedicated to his daughter Aline, he says: "I have known the depths of want: to be hungry and all that this means. It is nothing or almost nothing: one gets used to it, and, with the exercise of the will, one ends by making sport of it. But what is terrible is the bar to work, to the development of intellectual faculties. It is true on the other hand, that suffering sharpens genius, but you must not have too much of that suffering, else it kills you."

In spite of everything, Gauguin managed to paint nineteen pictures which he sent to the eighth Impressionist Exhibition in 1886.

The hardships of daily life drove Gauguin from Paris and he took refuge at Pont-Aven in Brittany, and again it seemed that fate had guided his footsteps, for it was the rigid, bare outlines of the Breton landscape that formed the first backgrounds to his inward dreams, indeed, as I have said, his Breton pictures will probably be ranked eventually above any of his subsequent work.

Gauguin returned to Paris and then may have come to him recollections of his childhood in the South, and of his youth at sea. He remembers the West Indies, gets excited at the cheapness of living there, says Martinique is even cheaper than Pont-Aven and so decides to go to Martinique. He persuades a very youthful and earnest Impressionist, Charles Laval, to accompany him, sells his last possessions and he and Laval sail for Martinique in 1887. Gauguin revels in the colour and light, his palette takes on the full range of pure vivid pigment and the coloured people commenced to exercise that singular attraction for him that was to persist until the end. In January, 1888, Gauguin and Laval were back in Paris, fever and dysentery had driven them from that deadly paradise.

Gauguin again went to Brittany and later in the year, Theo van Gogh, the brother of Vincent van Gogh, who was manager for the firm of Boussod and Valadon, organised Gauguin's first private exhibition in the firm's premises in the Boulevard Montmartre. The exhibition filled two small rooms and included pottery. Gauguin sold very few pictures. Vincent van Gogh, that great simple spirit, had made a little home in Arles and was filled with the idea of founding a brotherhood of painters. He heard that Gauguin was still suffering from the effects of the Martinique climate and begged him again and again he share his home in the pure air and beneath the brilliant skies of Provence. The letters to Theo in which Vincent tells of all that he expects Arles to do for Gauguin are very beautiful, and in view of the tragic sequel, deeply affecting. Surely no two beings were ever more unsuited to be together. On the one hand Vincent, simple, transparently sincere, of a childlike ingenuousness, and imbued with the spirit of Christ, who painted as a humble servant of humanity; and on the other hand Gauguin, hunted from land to land by an unappeasable restlessness, cynical, capable, and confident of his powers, with a bitter, clever tongue and a delight in making either friend or foe look ridiculous. The tragical outcome of it was that the cynical taunts and ironic laughter of Gauguin deranged Vincent's mind, already possibly in a state to be effected by reason by his custom of working at his easel bareheaded beneath the direct noonday rays of the brilliant Provençal sun.

Gauguin again returns to Brittany and this time a group of disciples gather around him and they became known as the School of Pont-Aven, although it really was at Pouldu that Gaugin this time made his headquarters. His divorce from all the practice and theories of the Impressionists was now complete. So far did he diverge from the paths of his early friends that he could write of them in these terms—"They are the conventionals of to-morrow, and worse than those of yesterday. . . . The art of the latter if carried to its end, produced and will yet produce masterpieces, whilst the conventionals of to-morrow are in a tossing, ill-steered and unfinished craft. When they talk of their art, what is it? Purely superficial, coquettish, materialistic art, wherein thought resides not."

Amongst the better known younger men who gathered around Gauguin were Emile Bernard, Sérusier, Filiger and De Hann, a diminutive Dutchman who admired Gauguin fervently and kept his accounts, that is to say, paid his board for him. M. Ch. Chassé has told in detail the life led by the group in 1889 at Pouldu, while Armand Seguin published in "L' Occident," in 1903, an amusing description of the inn at Pouldu as adorned by Gauguin and his friends, the walls covered with arabesques and designs, window panes painted and turned into stained glass and lintels adorned with encouraging or arrogant phrases. Here Gauguin carved eloborately his celebrated pair of wooden clogs, which he painted and gilded and afterwards wore upon the Parisian boulevards.

It was during the Pouldu period that Gauguin was heard to exclaim, on commencing a new canvas, "Now to produce a Cézanne." This must have meant, that some qualities in Cézanne's work had been an inspiration to Gauguin, in fact it may have been some formal resemblance to his work which made Cézanne say that Gauguin had stolen from him his "little sensation" in order to cart it round in every tramp steamer! But the Master of Aix made no claim to have evolved a painter out of Gauguin—on the contrary Cézanne said, "He never understood me . . . I never have agreed and never will agree to the absence of modelling or gradation: that is nonsense. Gauguin is not a painter: he has only turned out fantastic figures." It is indeed difficult to rebuild the artistic reputation of one who has received such a shattering blow from the paw of the old Aixois Lion. The truth of Cézanne's devastating verdict becomes more evident as time goes on; for Gauguin is to-day regarded as a remarkable innovator, a decorative artist who brought back into modern art factors of design and linear composition rather than as a painter of the first rank.

In the celebrated wooden clogs, a fisherman's blue cap, a woollen jersey and a Breton cape, but with little or no money in his pocket Gauguin returned to Paris at the end of 1889. He was homeless, but a friend took him in and provided him with shelter, but at the end of a year Gauguin has had enough of Paris. He happens upon a book telling of Tahiti; all his restlessness becomes crystalised into a resolve to leave his fellow white men forever and live a new idyllic life among the Polynesians. He makes a selection of thirty of his pictures and offers them for sale at the Hotel Drouot. The sale realised 9,860 francs. Before he sailed Gauguin was granted by the Ministry of Public Instruction a purely honorary title—he had the right to put after his signature "entrusted with an Art Mission"!

It must not be supposed that because it was difficult to find purchasers for his canvases that therefore Gauguin was unknown and neglected, on the contrary he was regarded as the leader and inspirer of the new school of Synthetists who had inaugurated a campaign against the Impressionists. Before he left Paris his friends gave him a farewell dinner at the Café Voltaire, and a few days later the Theâtre d'Art arranged a benefit performance at the Vaudeville for Gauguin and Verlaine.

Gauguin landed in Tahiti on June 8, 1891. The local authorities were impressed with his "mission" and the painter was well received by the white community. It was no doubt a narrow life that was led by these officials and Gauguin soon tired of it. We know much of his life from day to day. He wrote constantly to his friend Daniel de Mondfreid and he also wrote a curious journal which he entitled *Noa-Noa*. We learn that he left Papeete, the seat of government and settled down twenty-eight miles away in the district of Mataïea. He lives like the natives, going barefoot and nude to the waist. For a time peace filled his heart, but it was short-lived; soon his letters to his friend expressed bitterness and unrest. He marries a native girl called Téhoura and fully intends to settle down to savage life.

But Gauguin's work was not selling as well in Paris as he had expected. In his letters to De Mondfreid he talks of nothing but money. In December he has only one hundred and fifty francs and he asks to be helped back to France, the months pass and his letters get more insistent, he declares that his friends are not doing their best for him. At last De Mondfreid gets a letter from Marseilles in which Gauguin says "got here to-day, Wednesday noon, with four francs in my pocket." Then a stroke of luck befell him, an uncle died and left Gauguin 13,000 francs, he at once hurried to Paris and arranged an exhibition of the paintings he had brought back with him. This exhibition of forty-six paintings and sculptures, owing partly to the exotic character of the work and partly to the romantic personality of the artist created something of a sensation but only eleven of the pictures found purchasers.

But Gauguin was busy spending the 13,000 francs left by the uncle who died so opportunely. He furnished a studio in the rue Vercingétorix about which many stories are told, it is described as follows by Rotonchamp, who was an intimate friend: "Many a painter, many a writer has visited it. Every one remembers the small door, the panes of which adorned with paintings by the Master, showed this characteristic motto: *Here faruru*: Here one makes love. On the left of the entrance was a small room, with a fireplace and a camp-bed, which was used as a bedroom. At the farther end of the antechamber was the studio, the door of which was masked by a San Germano tapestry. The room itself was fairly large, and painted all over in light yellow—light chrome—and at once impressed one with a sense of unexpectedness and strangeness. On the walls, together with barbarian paintings were hung trophies of military weapons: knobkerries boomerangs, hatchets, pikes and lances, all of foreign woods, red, orange, black. On the matelpiece stood shells and mineralogical specimens. When sounded faintly a primitive door-bell the visitor saw approaching him a splendid Mulatto woman with shining eyes, whom Gauguin had come across in Paris and who had come from Java. A shivering monkey cowered among the easels, and in this setting, which recalled at once the temporary lodging of the naval man and the occasional home of the explorer, one felt tremendously far from Paris. There came and went incessantly a stream of friends and idlers. Gauguin, now a swell, had a day on which he received visitors, just like a candidate for the medal of honour. He gave parties, had tea served and cakes passed round with silent dignity by the sombre rival of Téhoura."

Gauguin himself wore a singular costume during these days of ease and magnificence; a long frock-coat of light blue cloth, fitting close at the waist with mother of pearl buttons; a waistcoat—blue also—buttoning down the side, and with a collar embroidered in yellow and green silk· A pair of yellowish trousers, a grey felt hat adorned with a broad bright blue ribbon. White gloves; a walking stick carved by himself and at the top of which was set a pearl. In this get-up, looking like something which had strayed from a revue, he called at the Colonial Office to apply for the post of Administrator in Oceania. His request was apparently not taken very seriously in official circles.

Gauguin again tired of Paris. He went down to Pont-Aven, taking with him the Javanese favourite. There he became involved in a row with some drunken sailors, one of whom kicked Gauguin, breaking his ankle. Gauguin was taken to hospital, and the ungrateful Javanese hurried back to Paris, looted the absurd studio and vanished. Gauguin's ankle was never completely healed. The 13,000 francs having disappeared Gauguin determined to sell up everything and return to Tahiti. A sale was arranged and took place on February 18, 1895, and comprised 49 pictures most of which had been shown at the exhibition held nearly two years before· The sale realised a fairly large sum and he now left Paris for ever.

He landed this time in Tahiti under very different circumstances. No longer invested with "an Art Mission" he was ignored by the white community. His manner of life had ruined his health and until his death he suffered greatly from his broken ankle and from open sores on his legs. He was soon in want and he borrowed a thousand francs from the Tahiti Agricultural Bank. He writes on September 10, 1895: "I can see nothing but death that can free me; I owe eighteen hundred francs this month and I have no longer credit . . . ." and he ends: "A wild but sad and wretched adventure my coming to Tahiti." In the early weeks of 1895 Gauguin tried to commit suicide. He collected arsenic and swallowed it. It was, however, too large a dose and his life was saved. He managed to secure a delay of payment of his debt to the Agricultural Bank and had to ask for employment as a clerk in a government office on a salary of six francs a day. At this period he sent to Vollard, the picture dealer, nine canvases which were sold and the proceeds enabled Gauguin to pay his debts and leave Papeete.

Nothing now can save him, he is soon again plunged into hopeless misery; his health becomes worse and there is no money to pay even for the simplest wants. But his friend De Mondfreid is looking after his interests in Paris, patrons are becoming more numerous and, financially, the worst is over.

In June, 1901, Ganguin decides that living is too dear in Tahiti. He writes: "I think that in the Marquesas, in view of the facilities for procuring models (which becomes more and more difficult in Tahiti) and with open landscapes—in short with new and more primitive elements, I shall accomplish great things. Here my imagination is beginning to cool." In March, 1902, he tells of his life on Atuana and it sounds fairly happy. In a letter to De Mondfreid he says: "I have begun to settle down seriously to work, though I am still ill. No one can have any idea of the quiet life I lead here in my solitary home, quite alone, embowered in foliage. It is restful and I needed that, away from all those officials in Tahiti."

Then came the end. Gauguin conceived it to be his duty to protect the natives from certain arbitary acts on the part of a white official. He denounces this official and Gauguin is arrested for defamation and sentenced to three months' imprisonment and a fine of one thousand francs. Gauguin appeals from the sentence. He writes at the end of April: "These worries are killing me." On May 8, 1903, Gauguin died. At the request of De Mondfreid, the Rev. V., who lived in the Marquesas, supplied the following interesting information: "All the time during which I knew M. Paul Gauguin he was ill and almost helpless. Rarely leaving his house, he produced a painful effect upon one when, for a wonder one met him in the Atuana Vale, with difficulty dragging himself along, his legs bandaged and wearing only the very primitive native costume; on his head a flat schoolboy's cap of green cloth with a silver ball on one side. A very amiable man, extremely gentle and unassuming in his intercourse with natives who were equally so towards him. And when your friend died I heard several natives utter a cry of regret: 'Gauguin is dead! We are done for!' Alluding to the services Gauguin had many a time done them by taking them out of the hands of the police, who are often very hard and unjust towards the natives.

Very generous and chivalrous, Gauguin had taken on himself to protect the natives. Many are the instances given of his kindness to them."

EDWARD ROWORTH.

For the extract from the letter of the Rev. V. and for much of the data of the foregoing article, I am indebted to the monograph by M. Robert Rey in the *Maitres de l'Art Moderne*."—E.R.

"Eunuch Arden" and "Kynoch Arden."

(TWO TENDENCIES IN MODERN LITERATURE).

THE genius of the English race has never fully expressed itself in any of the arts save poetry. We have very few, if any, great novelists, painters or musicians. Yet through its poetry alone English literature ranks second only to that of the Greeks as having exerted the widest influence over the great writers of other countries. Voltaire, Goethe, Poushkin, Dostoevsky, Nietzsche and Baudelaire have all admitted their debt to English poetry. In the Soviet theatres of Moscow, Shakespeare still holds a firmer place than ever he did on his own native stage. In France and Germany he reigns supreme. In the struggle of India for freedom, Shelley is as active as Ghandi—in fact as one of the leading Indian patriots has said, the struggle of India for emancipation dates from the introduction of English poetry. Our intellectual empire is a wider and less destructible one than our geographical empire—a fact of which only foreigners seem to be conscious—and it is in many places undermining the latter.

The rapid sequence of our great writers is something phenomenal in the history of literature—Chaucer, Skelton, Spencer, Marlowe, Shakespeare, Milton, Dryden, Swift, Burns, Blake, Byron, Shelley. Though we omit a host of almost equally important names, such a fusillade has never been fired off in such rapid succession by any other nation. Yet when we come to the end of the romantic period we come to the end of English literature. After the death of Byron we descend almost vertiginously through the later Wordsworth, Tennyson, Swinburne, Marris and Wilde till we land in the puddle of Georgian poetry.

A hundred years ago all Europe was looking to English literature for those revitalising influences which were to eventuate in the work of Nietzsche, Baudelaire and Rimbaud. While Victor Hugo and Nietzsche were looking to the English romantics for inspiration, their English contemporaries, the Victorians, were looking to the public for instruction. England is the only country in which art and literature have ever become industrialised into trades. The public has a sweet tooth. Poetry became a form of confectionery and so it has remained for nearly a hundred years. The very word "poet" has come to have a ludicrous meaning in England—and deservedly.

The sluggish stream of Victorian poetry flowed out of the Lake school of poetry and ended in the Marsh school of poetry.

The Lily of Malud
Was born in secret mud

we are informed by one of the cheerful batrachians of this morass of toffee, which is gradually congealing as the interest of the public grows cooler. Even the public can get tired of sweet things. They could stand the Victorians who were mildly sugared: but they are getting tired of the concentrated saccharine of the "Georgians" who are only distinguished from the Victorians by name and extra sweetness. The poetical fondants of Mr. De la Mare, the Marsh mallows of Mr. Squire, and the Turkish Delight (made in Cambridge) of the late Mr. Flecker, have outsweetened anything in the literature of the world. Even the ghost of Wilde is left gasping: and Dowson's misty Cynara becomes flesh and blood when we compare her to the gaseous muses of Mr. De la Mare.

Before the war English poetry, with the exception of Doughty and Hardy, who are Victorians, was a vast bath of treacle, to which Rupert Brooke added the faint sting of peppermint. There was something faintly challenging in his poetry like the sound of a Boy-Scout's bugle, for which we must be grateful. The war brought us one good poem, one might almost call it a great poem, Wilfred Owen's "Strange Meeting": and it brought also some healthy satire, "Counter Attack," by Siegfried Sassoon, and "Wheels," the first attempt of English poetry to get in line with the great traditions of European literature for a hundred years. The contributors to "Wheels" were young but they were fearless and sincere: with unerring instinct they searched European literature for plunder and they returned even to the traditions of English literature itself. Pope and Dryden, who were considered by the Victorians to be mere versifiers are beginning to be read again. Marlowe and other Elizabethans are being acted. We are beginning as a nation to be faintly conscious of the fact that we have a literature behind us: once we are conscious of this the Victorian débacle will be complete. A few of the earlier Victorians will survive along with Hardy and Doughty but without their lustre.

To-day all English artists and writers who are doing anything worth while have their eyes on Europe. We have been mentally inbreeding for a hundred years with the result that we can produce nothing but bon-bons.

Mr. Osbert Sitwell, a useful satirist, has formally buried the spirit of the Marsh school of poetry under the name of "Eunuch Arden" in an amusing pamphlet entitled "Who Killed Cock Robin?" He has shown how easy it is to write "nature" poetry which is still acclaimed by many old-fashioned papers. Osbert Sitwell's "nature" poem eclipses any of the "nature" poems of the Georgian school. I remember only the last two lines.

"The hedgehog by his reedy ghylls
Curls up and rolls—the bloody fool!"

This at any rate registers a definite action and a definite attitude on the part of the author towards it, which is more than most Georgian poems can do. Osbert Sitwell then proceeds to quote slabs of Georgian poetry among which is the notorious "Rugger Match," the funniest serious poem in the language, which covers many pages and ends with the climax

"And now I think I'll go home and open a bottle of port."

The cruellest thing one can do to Georgian poetry is to quote it. But before we go any further it would be unfair not to acknowledge Robert Nichols who, though a Georgian, has written some very fine lines and one fine poem the "Deliverer." A man who can write such a line as

"The star's one glimmer, daggered in wet sands,"

shows that he has the eye and the nerves of a poet. Compared with the Oscar Ashe Melodrama of Flecker

"We have rose-candy, we have spikenard,
Mastic and terebinth and oil and spice,
An such sweet jams meticulously jarred
As God's own Prophet eats in Paradise."

or this unmeaning bombast reminiscent at its best of Kipling:

"We storm at the ivory gate, pale kings of the sunset, beware!"

The work of Nichols shows a power and manliness which is not common even among the most hearty of his rugger-playing colleagues. If Mr. Nichols had enough sense of humour to check him from such emotional debauches as the "Assault" and several other of his war poems he would be a force to reckon with. At any rate Mr. Nichols is free from the innocent and infantile bubbling of such poets as Mr. W. H. Davies, Mr. De la Mare or Mr. Hodgson, whose attitude to life may be summed up thus:

"What were life, if full of care,
We had no time to stand and stare?"

or thus:

"O what a clatter when
Titmouse and Jenny Wren
Saw him successful and
Taking his leave!
How the birds rated him;
How they all hated him!
How they all pitied
Poor motherless Eve!

This false naivete was imported into English literature by the later Wordsworth and Tennyson. It is still fashionable. Blake could do that sort of thing without being sentimental; even his poems to babies are clean and free from mucus. But no one else has been able to do it since. Swinburne also needed a bib when he wrote about babies. No wonder the average healthy Philistine laughs when he hears the word poet. These things sin against the dignity of the species, if it has any dignity at all. Where did all those vital impulses which manifested themselves in England during the romantic period find outlet? Although Goethe and Pushkin were greater than any individual writer among English romantics, yet the movement manifested itself in England so vigorously, and in so many ways, that England remained the central power-station of the movement. Even minor writers like Scott exerted an external influence and, incredible as it may seem, contributed to the making of such writers as Balzac and Flaubert. Continental literature derived far more from our romantics than we did. Victorian poetry was merely a continuation of the old age of Wordsworth; in Georgian poetry, though embalmed in all the eastern spices of Mr. Flecker, the spirit of Victorianism is already beginning to disintegrate.

But the symbolists and parnassians were directly in the stream of tradition and their successors, the futurists, are the direct descendants of the romantics. Shelley may be said to have been the first forerunner of the futurists. He often resembles Marinetti:

> "The rocks are cloven and through the purple night
> I see cars drawn by rainbow-winged steeds
> Which trample the dim winds: in each there stands
> A wild-eyed charioteer urging their flight.
> Some look behind, as fiends pursued them there,
> And yet I see no shapes but the keen stars.
> Others with burning eyes lean forth and drink
> With eager lips the wind of their own speed.

This has all the speed and movement of Marinetti's "Monoplane." Hugo was the first poet to absorb the spirit of the romantic movement after the death of Goethe. He had an almost titanic grasp of language and a wonderful power of using it, but he had a common mind and was no explorer. However, he vastly improved the machinery of French poetry. Baudelaire did a great deal to bring poetry into touch with modern life. While the other parnassians were producing beautiful and interesting but not vital work, Baudelaire explored the darkest abysms of human consciousness, every now and then soaring forth like an archangel in such poems as "La Benediction," and then returning to brood over his own infernal universe. But Baudelaire was no innovator of literary forms. He packed the parnassian form so full of meaning and emotion that it became as massive as an iron bell through the sullen clang of which one could just discern the shrill vibration of its silver alloy. It remained for Nietzsche to voice the whole subconscious spirit of the age in "Zarathustra" the greatest poem, next to "Faust," of the last century. Nietzsche sprang from Goethe but he was profoundly influenced by Shelley, and like Goethe, by Marlowe. Like Marlowe he innovated a wonderful new form and through it he was able to pour out some of the profoundest thoughts that ever stirred the human consciousness. Though a saint and almost an ascetic in his life, he was looked upon by his contemporaries more as a monster: they were terrified of him. Every time he uttered a thought it was regarded as an earthquake.

Still another star was to rise in the French firmament, Arthur Rimbaud, one of the most phenomenal writers in history. He began writing at the age of fifteen and left off at the age of nineteen. Never since Marlowe has a poet dazed us with such stupendous impetus. He electrified the old form with a new velocity and galloped it to its death. In the "Bateau Ivre" one hears the back of Rimbaud's charger crack and break through sheer exertion. At the age of nineteen he had crammed into two volumes more reality, more poetry, and more experience than Hugo or even Baudelaire did into their complete works. "We were suddenly amazed to find," said Anatole France, "that a new Villon had risen amongst us." At the age of nineteen he had realised that he would be driven mad if he gave way to the full scope of his thought. Instead of taking the risk like Nietzsche, he ceased writing and spent the rest of his life trying to kill the maddening intensity of his imagination. He became one of the most prominent

French explorers, penetrated the Sahara, and lived the rest of his life in Abyssinia. He never could bear to hear his poetry mentioned: and flew into a paroxysm of rage when he heard that he had become famous. Only when he returned dying and delirious to France did any further poetry escape him. He pretended to be unconscious of what he was saying, but even his sister, a country woman, who looked on his writings as wicked and unmentionable, said "Il l'a fait expres."

Rimbaud, the greatest French poet of the last century, is the father of modern poetry. Futurism was merely a manoeuvre to get into line with Rimbaud. It was incoherent and it lacked stamina intellectually. But it was a gesture in the right direction and it was an excellent instrument of destruction. The dynamite of Marinetti has done its work. Kynoch Arden has supplanted Eunuch Arden.

It is doubtful whether, with the exception of D. H. Lawrence and Hardy, there is any English poet who is read on the Continent; one can think of very few who would not pale into insignificance beside Paul Valery, Pellerin, Toulet or Marinetti. But the younger generation are coming on, and with such a vigorous forerunner as D. H. Lawrence there should be no fear for the future.

LEWIS MARSTON.

(Next month "Voorslag" will publish several translations from Rimbaud and Baudelaire.)

Kuns Ontwikkeling in Afrikaans.

DIT is jammer dat die taalkwessie in Suid-Afrika vir so lang as uitsluitend 'n Taalkwessie beskou was. Daardeur is 'n baie algemene begrip veroorsaak dat Afrikaans slegs 'n politieke en nie 'n letterkundige betekenis het nie. Selfs van die weinige letterkundige werke wat verskyn het is 'n politieke vraagstuk gemaak. Beide die opponente en voorstanders van Afrikaans het heirdie fout gemaak om Afrikaanse letterkunde van 'n politieke standpunt te kritiseer. Aan die een kant het hulle dit sonder feil afgekeur en die ander weer het dit verheerlik en bo die wolke verhef. Vir die voorstander van Afrikaans was dit waarskynlik 'n heeltemaal natuurlike houding; dit was in elk geval in die begin 'n uiters nodige houding. In die stryd wat hy gevoer het om Afrikaans as 'n skryftaal vas te stel, was die pen een van sy magtigste wapens. Die beste geskrifte wat Afrikaans in die begin voortgebring het, was in sy oë, kragtige ammuniesie teen die vyand; die slegste miskien niks meer as 'n klip nie, maar tog ammuniesie. En as ammuniesie het hy alles wat in Afrikaans geskrywe was aangemoedig en verwelkom. Gelukkig is daar op die oomblik, wanneer die taalstryd so te sê afgeloop is, kentekens van 'n suiwerer beskouing van Afrikaans. Ook is daar tekens dat die tyd wanneer Afrikaanse Letterkunde sal bewonder word vir wat daarin skoon is en vercordeel sal word vir haar gebreke en wanneer Afrikaanse kultuur in die regte perspektief—in vergelyking met die kultuur van die Buiteland—sal gesien word, vinnig nader kom. Maar dit neem egter nie weg van die feit nie dat die ontwikkeling van 'n eie Afrikaanse Letterkunde tot nou nog toe selde behoorlik raak gesien is.

Die Afrikaanse Letterkunde het met die begin van die Patriot-beweging ontstaan. Daar het wel enkel geskrifte voorheen verskyn, maar geen poging met enige erns om Afrikaans as 'n skryftaal vas te stel was voor dié beweging gemaak nie. Verskillende onvermydelike omstandighede het veroorsaak dat die letterkundige opbrengs van die Patriotte, en hul kuns ontwikkeling, gering was. Die eerste Afrikaanse skrywers het nie geskrywe ter wille van hul kuns nie. Hulle begeerte was alleenlik om die taalstryd aan te help en om op vaster grond te kom in die stryd teen Engels, wat gedreig het om Afrikaans te oorrompel. Hulle werk was voortrekkerswerk. Tussen al die vreemde invloede wat dwing om hulle kultuur te ondermyn, moes hulle 'n weg baan. "Die Afrikaners, veral die jeug, het nou 'n afkeur gekry teen vreemde tale en sede, veral teen Engels, en daar is 'n ambiesie opgewek vir ons eie volk en eie taal" verklaar "Di Patriot" in die eerste jare van sy bestaan. Elkeen was vir die oomblik entoesiasties en wou wys dat by Afrikaans kon skrywe. Dit was 'n "nou-rmy-ons-lekker" periode. Elkeen van die wyle Generaal Piet Joubert tot die skaapwagter het probeer rym. Meeste van die rymelaars het nie die flouste besef van poësie gehad nie. Nog minder het geskrywe om 'n innerlike onweerstaanbare dwang. Die dryfveer van die hele beweging was 'n sug om nasionale eer, en die inspirasie van die rymelaars in groot alleenstaande feite uit die geskiendenis, wat in die woorde van Preller "'n nuwe sukkel-moet slaan op die gelittekende pionierras." Dieselfde skrywer sê: "Op nasionaal sowel as letterkundig gebied was dit vir die Afrikaners 'n Tydperk van soeke en rondtastende onbewustheid." Dit was ook 'n tydperk waarin die gevoel van die rymelaars en skrywers nie diep en ernstig genoeg nie en te ligsinnig was om hulle tot digterlike hoogtes te verhef. Sentiment om Vaderland en Moedertaal deurtrek die letterkunde van die Partiot-beweging, maar sentiment van dié aard het nog nooit die groot letterkunde van die Wêrde gekenmerk nie. Nou en dan, egter, verskyn daar 'n skrywer wat deur die forsheid van sy taal, sy eenvoud en kinkerlik-grote geloof in egte lieriese geroep bo die versiesmakery van sy tyd styg. Maar oor die algemeen openbaar die versies 'n gebrek aan gevoel vir maat en ritme, neem 'n grappige trant aan en vertoon dikwels 'n vrolike onbekooktheid. Die grootste woorde van die letterkunde van die Patriot-beweging lê waarskynlik in die definitiewe afwyking wat dit van Nederlands gemaak het en in soverre as wat dit gehelp het om 'n volksbewussyn te kweek. Suiwer kunswaarde het dit egter min gehad en na die verklaring van oorlog in 1899 het die beweging gou doodgekwyn.

In die oorlogsjare wat daarop volg ontwaak Afrikaners oorals tot 'n voller volksbewussyn. Die kentekens daarvan was al in die tyd van van der Stel te bespeur, maar dit is as of op die oorlogsveld, in die konsentrasie-kamp en in tydelike ballingskap menige Afrikaner tot 'n dieper besinning kom. "En na Vereeniging" skryf Preller, "is dit oopgegaan, saggies-seer, en beginne drup-drup, soos bloed-trane uit die geheuge drup." Die vrolike gees van ligte dilettantisme van die Patriotte het deurgeslaan in 'n dieper, ernstiger en gevoelvoller noot. In die plek van die rym van vroeër het daar stadig aan hoër attribute van poësie gekom. Dit gloei eers flou in die woorde van die balling wat "die soeklig van die wagskip" sien skyn op sy tent in die nag en "droef oor huis en makkers en die speel-tyd van weleer"; en later met die "Winternag" van Eugene Marais vlam dit sterker. Die digter in Afrikaans het nie meer alleen gesing nie maar diep in die siel van die nasie het sy verse 'n weerklank gevind. Eindelik kon die voorstanders van die nuwe beweging roep "'t is ons ernst."

Die taalstryd het nou weer met meer vasberadenheid en erns begin. In die letterkundige voortbrengsels van die periode, sit daar ongetwyfeld sterk militante elemente. Schoonees verklaar dit deur te sê: "die letterkunde van alle volke is 'n weerspieëling van die geestlike strominge wat die volksiel diep gerôer het. Vir tientalle van jare voer ons al 'n taalstryd—'n stryd wat feitlik elke indiwidu dwing om grondig na te dink oor allerhande taalkwessies." Boeke het 'n kragtige wapen in die stryd geword. Die geroep van die teenstanders van Afrikaans wat hulle op die eeuoue letterkunde van Holland beroep het, dat Afrikaans nie 'n letterkunde gehad het nie, het baie in 'n gloed van entoesiasme, tot skrywe gedryf. Die kunstenaar het nie die tyd gehad om uiting aan sy kuns te gee nie. Hy moes sy kuns opoffer om in die stryd te help. "Ons bloed is nog aldag te veel in beweging, jaag ons aan, ons het te veel om te doen; ons moet gou klaar wees; het nie tyd om veel te droom of te peuter nie," roep Celliers uit. Daar was 'n groot bevolking by wie 'n leeslus moes gekweek word. Dit het veroorsâak dat baie skrywers, veral in prosa, soos de Waal en Langehoven hulle daarop toelê om leeslus aan te moedig. Skrywers het die Engelse ontspanningsroman gevolg en hulle meer op "handelinge en vermenigvuldiging van gebeurtinisse aangelê as op karakterstudie van 'n persoon of versameling van persone." Vir 'n tydlang is 'n groot deel van die letterkunde in 'n rigting van awontuur en isolasie van vreemde invloede ontwikkel Die ontwikkeling het skrywers en digters gedryf om hulle agtergrond in die verlede te soek, meesal in periodes waar daar ook tekens van die gestadige ontwaking van 'n nasionale selfbewussyn voorkom. Die Anglo-Boere Oorlog, die Groot Trek, die van der Stel Periode, selfs die opstand van 1914 het stof vir talryke geskrifte opgelewer. Maar oor die algemeen slaan skrywers in dié rigting die bal mis. In die woorde van Celliers is die resultaat van hulle werke "meestal nie veel meer dan 'n gekleurde historieprent nie." Ook op taalgebied sukkel meeste skrywers maar swaar voort. Hulle taal het hulle eers gister leer skryf en met groot onsekerheid tas hulle rond vir 'n juister vorm. "Ander weer soos Preller, skryf al in 1906 'n gekultiveerde taal, klankvol, wegdeinend op bevallige ritme en telkens verassend deur oorspronklike beeldespraak ontleen aan Afrikaanse Volk en Bodem."

Maar dit is op die gebied van poësie waar 'n ontwakende geesteslewe e die skoonste uiting vind. Dit blyk dat die digters van die Twede Taalbeweging meermaal daarin slaag om hulle uit die koorsagtige en woelende atmosfeer van die taalstryd te verhef en van die afgesonderde hoogtes van suiwere kuns, waar die geroep van benede slegs flou weerklink, te skrywe. Dit gebeur dikwels met Celliers waar hy in gevoelvolle uitbeelding sing van die natuur. Ons tref dit in die stille droefheid waarin Totius sy gedagte skep, soos die atmosfeer van 'n kalm en donker winternag. Ons voel dit in die gedigte waar Leipoldt skryf soos 'n man "wat in verbysterde wanhoop 'n onvergeetlike smart wil verdrink in 'n roes van vergeetlikheid; wat jou aanroep met 'n stem wat geen geluid wil gee nie, en aankyk met oë wat geen trane het nie," ook waar die digter tussen die trane 'n ondeunde glimlag om die mond het en in die kleur, lewe en beweging van sy poësie is daar suiwer kunsgevoel te bespeur. Maar ook by die digters vind die reeks van gebeurtenisse wat op die volksiel "'n merk vir die eeue gebrand het" 'n weerklank, en is 'n suiwer kunsuiting net in 'n paar afgesonderde stansas en lyne aanwesig.

Die letterkunde van die twede Afrikaanse Taalbeweging tot dusver besit geen buitegewone kunswaarde nie. Vir die Afrikaners het dit 'n baie groot kultureele waarde. Maar in vergelyking met die eeuoue werk van die Buiteland is ons letterkundige oes baie middelslag. Die tekens is daar dat van ons jongere digters stadig oorgaan tot die "uitbeelding van 'n dieper menslikheid" en al hoe meer skrywe omdat hulle moet, "omdat daarbinne iets woel wat uiting soek." Nogtans bewys die Afrikaans letterkunde tot so ver alleen dat die regte gevoel daar is en dat "Afrikaans in smydigheid, in seggingskrag en klank, alleen 'n kunstenaar nodig het om tot sy reg te kom."

LAURENS VAN DER POST.

Portraits in the Nude (continued)

II. A JOURNEY.

Lily went away for a holiday, and soon afterwards it was time for the family to leave Zonnebloem for nagmaal at Rooi Rivier.

Just before the wagon's departure, on a cold, calm evening at sunset, Mrs. Van Ryn walked down the hill to where Cormorant was standing. She was dressed for travelling in a new black sunbonnet and a black dress. She wore, at the waist, a bunch of faded artificial violets. Her face was slightly flushed with excitement, and its usual white looked bluish-pink in the light of this tranquil evening. She was dabbing at her eyes with a black handkerchief.

"You are good to me always, Mr. Cormorant," she declared, with an excited sentimental sigh.

"I hope so," said Cormorant, very slightly embarrassed.

"I don't know, I don't know!" she said wildly. "I like to go to nagmaal—yes very much—but my dear Ou Tanta Maria cannot come with us, and Lily cannot come with us—Miss du Toit, that is—and I wonder if everything will be all right."

The sun had set, and the sky near the horizon was tinted an icy pink.

Dirk came down from the house with Frans. Golgo ran after them, and finally came Takhaar, like a primitive Christian saint, but not like an old man, though his face was very lined under a great grey hat. He was carrying his bell.

"But you are not bringing your bell!" Mrs. Van Ryn exclaimed in a shrill voice.

Takhaar looked angrily and deliberately at his wife.

"Ja," he said slowly, "I shall want it."

She didn't answer, but a very curious smile made itself shown on her face.

"Aren't there any church-bells at Rooi Rivier, daddy?" Golgo asked ingenuously.

Takaar slapped the child savagely, twice, on the cheek. Golgo was too frightened to cry. His face was white in the half-light and his eyes were very bright. His cheek stung, but he was proud that he had been able to provoke his father, to whom he was devoted.

"Here's a fine way to start for nagmaal," said Mrs. Van Ryn, enraged. "Leave the child alone!"

"Silence, vrouw!" thundered Takhaar.

They all climbed up into the tented waggon. Takhaar sat in front.

"Loop!" he ordered in a loud voice.

Shilling cracked his whip and shouted to the oxen. The voorlooper's head could just be seen through a forest of horns. The waggon lumbered away under the first few stars.

"Ma," said Golgo, "could Mandabazana come with us next time we go to nagmaal?"

But Mrs. Van Ryn didn't answer. That peculiar smile was at her lips again, though nobody could see it in the dark.

The waggon had been outspanned, and after supper Cormorant wandered along the road with Dirk. When they came back the others were beginning to compose themselves for sleep under the hood of the waggon. They had a lantern in there, and from it a faint radiance shone through the thick covering, outlining darkly the hood's framework like curved ribs, under which moved dimly the shadows of those within, moving shadows. Jonah and his family, thought Cormorant, in the belly of a whale.

He and Dirk slept on the ground under the waggon, sheltered by a bucksail. Early in the morning he woke up, when the wind rose and began to flap the sail against the wheels. Shilling, outside in the grey murk, was kindling a fire. The boy had gone after the oxen. Overhead the Van Ryns were astir. The sail began to flap violently in the wind. From where Cormorant lay he could see that the whole sky was overcast with a thick fleece of racing clouds. It was very cold. Dirk sat up.

"It will snow to-day," he said, "before we get to Rooi

Rivier." They all breakfasted bleakly round the fire roaring in the open gale, which couldn't tear away fast enough the flames and shreds of flying smoke. Afterwards they trekked, rolling slowly, cumbrously, over the long monotonous road. As the day went on it got darker.

After they had been outspanned for some time at midday the wind seemed to go down a little. It was all at once warmer.

"The snow is coming," said Takhaar. "Loop!"

The waggon wheels rolled forward. At the same moment snow began to fall.

It became a weary journey. The travellers were all crowded together under the hood in an atmosphere at once cold and stuffy. The snow could be seen falling thickly before black walls of mountainous rock on both sides of the road. As they progressed through the long afternoon the tracks of the waggon, at first blackish in the thin covering of snow on the road, became white as the snow got thicker. Shilling now was oftener cracking his whip and shouting to the oxen. If they didn't get to Rooi Rivier soon after nightfall and if the snow continued, they might get into difficulties. But the snow stopped. The sky was very black. And at last there was hardly any wind.

Takhaar put his head out and then said:

"I think we are nearly there. As soon as we are outspanned we shall go to Mr. Osbosch. And what is Mr Cormorant going to do? You can come, if you like, to Mr. Osbosch's. He will find you part of a bed, a corner somewhere. Or, if you will, stay with the waggon."

Cormorant said he would rather stay with the waggon—no doubt Mr. Osbosch wouldn't have room for any extra person in his house.

"He wouldn't have room for an Englishman in his house," said Dirk, with a hard laugh.

"O Dirk!" said his mother, defending Cormorant. "I don't think he would mind even an Englishman on a night like this."

"I won't trouble him," said Cormorant. "No doubt I can get on just as well without Mr. Oddsfish as Mr. Oddsfish can without me."

"Osbosch," said Dirk.

"To tell you the truth," said Cormorant, "I don't care tuppence what his name is."

The waggon was going over rough ground. It came to a halt.

"Here we are," said Takhaar.

They all climbed out, very elaborately. A short figure in a heavy overcoat came forward out of the gloom with a lantern.

"Good evening, Takhaar," said Mr. Osbosch.

"Here is Mr. Osbosch," said Takhaar in a loud voice.

The Van Ryns went off in great feather with this individual, who said they were quite right to leave the rooinek with the Kaffirs, and laughed unpleasantly with a bitterness which he had jockeyed himself, not without reason, into feeling for anybody who wasn't Dutch.

Just as Cormorant was going to sleep in the waggon he heard somebody say in a dirty voice:

"This is the last time we come in to nagmaal with a ——— waggon! A fine ——— nagmaal this is! We'll have a ——— motor-car next time!"

This speech provoked a quantity of laughter, high, low, and boozy, together with an inaudible but evidently very humorous repartee.

Cormorant was soon asleep. So was Mr. Osbosch. He was snoring. His elbow was in his wife's ear. She grunted uneasily. Takhaar and his wife and Dirk and Golgo were all asleep in one double bed, for the Osbosches had only a small house.

12. PORTRAIT OF A FARMER

WHO WAS AT ROOI RIVIER FOR NAGMAAL.

A blood-faced hell-handed witless loveless many-acred stone-squeezing leather-bellied blockhead.

13. NAGMAAL.

The next morning was Sunday. Cormorant and Shilling breakfasted at an open fire while the snow was thawing under a dazzling winter sun. Everywhere flames and smoke were pleasantly dancing, many fires being kindled round about. Over the tops of the waggons could be seen the little town of Rooi Rivier, the walls of whose houses were of stone and stucco, whose only trees were storm-twisted evergreens, and whose roofs of corrugated iron, unpainted, shone like silver in the sun, while snow-water gurgled in the gutters.

At a quarter to eleven Cormorant came round a corner to find himself right before the Dutch church, the glory and pride of Rooi Rivier. It was a great church of stone, very new, with a solid shining spire, the whole building in machine-made Gothic. A number of loud cheap bells began to jangle harshly in the tower. They were protesting, no doubt, at a certain rate of interest, because they had not yet been paid for. A few pigeons fluttered on the roof, where they had already been able to leave little marks of disapproval.

Cormorant approached a gateway in a dusty hedge, entered, and knocked at the front door of Mr. Osbosch. It was opened by Dirk. They went in. There was a strong smell of nutmeg, hot air, cold air, dust, stale food, camphor, and dirty clothes.

"We are waiting in the sitting room," said Dirk, "for Mrs. Osbosch. She is getting ready for church."

There they all were—Takhaar, gaunt, silent and austere, in a black suit; Golgo, with a lace collar, looking like a fish out of water; Mr. Osbosch, swarthy and assured, with hard shiny black boots and hard shiny black eyes. The photographed heads of his father and mother, double-life-size, glowered on the wall. Mrs. Van Ryn, a trifle overdressed, seemed to-day a different woman. She was almost lively in her manner. She gave you an impression to-day of rosy cheeks and laughing eyes. You forgot the hard lines of her face because her mouth pouted a little, her mouth that was always set in lines of reticence, not a sensitive but a secretive reticence.

"Is Tossie nearly ready, Mr. Osbosch?" she asked coyly. "Here's Mr. Cormorant, and the bells are ringing." A tune uprose in Cormorant's memory:

"The bells are ring-ing
For me and my gal——"

At that moment the door opened and in came Mrs. Osbosch

with a disapproving look at him and a great rustling of cheap silk.

"Tossie, this is Mr. Cormorant," said Mrs. Van Ryn.

"Is it," said Mrs. Osbosch rudely. "Good morning."

"I am ready," she added, stuffily, for she had a pug nose. Poor Mrs. Osbosch! She was by heredity, by birth, education, taste and desire, a killjoy. A stranger to happiness herself, she must needs play the preacher to reduce, to try and abolish the happiness of other people. How is it that everybody preaches, and how is it that most people preach the most iniquitous doctrines? The bells were silent, and through the window people could be seen arriving for the service. Mrs. Osbosch led the way out of the house and into the church, which was nearly full. As they went up the aisle Cormorant detected a strong smell of self-righteousness. He was stared at, especially by fat meisjes here and there, flappers with matronly figures, imitation daisies in their hats, meaty complexions, and an air of boorish perplexed heartiness. They nudged each other and giggled. One of them dropped a prayer book: being sternly reproved by an angular parent, she blushed as though her life depended on it. The party still led by Mrs. Osbosch, found their way into a pew on the right hand side of the nave near the front. Fancy allowing one's self, thought Cormorant, to be led by Mrs. Osbosch. She was followed by her husband, then Takhaar, Golgo, Mrs. Van Ryn. Dirk insisted on taking the outermost pew, because there was somebody he wanted to make eyes at, so Cormorant found himself sitting between Dirk and Mrs. Van Ryn. He looked about. Before him there were broad rough-hewn backs, behind him there were broad rough-hewn faces. The old looked solemn and the young looked old. Each lot of new arrivals provoked an excited whispering of personal remarks. The final peal of bells vomited a cacophonic warning through the roof. The service began. The Lord's House, the Lord's Day, the Lord's Table, the Lord's Supper, the Lord's Flock of Sheep, and the Lord's People's Pastor! The predikant, among his elders, was engaged in a long prayer which he was making up out of his head. He wasn't fluent, so when his thoughts jammed he repeated his last phrase in a voice twice as loud. In any case it was an aggressive voice.

The service was very dull. Now the congregation is standing

and singing a supposed hymn of praise in the same way that it would sing a funeral hymn. It is a desolating tune, a narcotic noise. Now there is nearly silence, now there are prayers. Now we are all kneeling and now we are all standing and now we are all sitting— it is a kind of symbolic dance. Now we are almost at the culminating point of this nagmaal. They are preparing the Sacrifice of the Lamb.

Cormorant became aware of a slight commotion to his right. Takhaar, the large-bodied, was trying to get out of the aisle. He looked not at all at ease in his high celluloid collar and little black tie. His face was working convulsively. His coarse nose seemed to miss the mountain air. His monstrous hands (the destructive-constructive hands of Europe) would grip more contentedly the handles of a plough than that silly varnished chair-rail by which he strove to steady his swaying bulk in its awkward progress. Before he reached the aisle he scraped a chair, stumbled over a hassock, knocked a prayer book out of Golgo's hand, and kicked Dirk on the shin. Mrs. Osbosch blinked, Mr. Osbosch stared, Golgo asked a question in a stage-whisper about the state of his father's bowels, but Mrs. Van Ryn cared for none of these things; she was looking straight before her under heavy intoxicated eyelids, she was smiling dreamily.

Nearly the whole congregation turned to watch Takhaar going out, his black coat hanging awkwardly from his shoulders, swinging awkwardly. Mrs. Osbosch leaned over and tapped Mrs. Van Ryn on the knee.

"Is he sick?" she asked.

"I don't know," said Mrs. Van Ryn.

"Shall you go out and see?" Mrs. Osbosch demanded.

"He may come back. If he doesn't, perhaps I'll go."

"No, it's better for you to go now. You must go now," Mrs. Osbosch ordered. "Shall I come with you?"

Mrs. Van Ryn seemed suddenly to recollect herself.

"No, no, Tossie," she answered. "It's all right. I'll go *now*. Don't you come."

She got up and moved into the aisle, and stood a moment (the congregation breathless with interest) to pat her hair with her hand. In the face of the mob her face looked determined again, yet charming, unusually charming. She didn't make for the main door at the back where Takhaar had gone out. She turned towards the chancel and then to the left down the narrow passage between the front row of people and the chancel step. She didn't hurry. All eyes followed her. She came to the side door. How her heart was beating! The door had a heavy latch . As she stepped out she turned once more towards the congregation, but her eyes were looking over their heads at the place she had left. She smiled. It was a womanly affectionate smile. It seemed to Cormorant that it was intended specially for him.

"What has come over Minta? Mrs. Osbosch asked her husband. "What is she laughing at? Why didn't she go out at the proper main door?"

The same questions were being asked at the same time all over the church. The predikant raised his voice in prayer: he hoped to regain a little attention.

"Man, you'd better go out and see what's up," Mrs. Osbosch whispered to her husband.

"Shut up, vrouw," was the answer she got. "Can't you see they're doing the Lord's Supper?"

They took their places in the slow, shuffling queue that extended up the aisle in the direction of the Lord's Table. The odours of cheap scent and boot polish rose up continually instead of incense. Dirk had timed his departure for the Lord's Table to coincide with that of the girl he was interested in: he was even bold enough to whisper to her. Mrs. Osbosch, now some way ahead, stared indignantly at a female hat just before her nose, a hat which set a seal of triumph on the summit of the person who wore it. It was a remarkable hat, too romantic for nagmaal, more suitable, perhaps, for a harvest festival. Where did she get it? Mrs. Osbosch wondered. How much did she give for it? How dare she wear it? Even Cormorant, from where he sat, could hear a faint click-clacking of millinery grapes. No wonder Mrs. Osbosch disapproved.

It was an interminable service. The faces of those returning to their pews seemed to say: "Now we have patronised the Lord. We have done our duty." Now the last row of communicants was kneeling before the predikant. Cormorant wondered why Takhaar had gone out, and more why he hadn't come back. Perhaps he was ill.

"Do you know why your father hasn't come back? he asked Dirk in a whisper.

At that instant a bell began to ring somewhere near at hand, just outside the church. No, it was not one of those bells in the roof. It was on a level with one's ears. Cormorant suddenly remembered that Takhaar had brought his bell on the waggon. The ringing grew much louder, and then stopped. Nobody seemed to have noticed it much. But the side door was opening, where Mrs. Van Ryn had gone out.

Enter a man, stark naked.

Good God, it's Takhaar. Who else could it be? Only one or two saw him as he came in. They were too flabbergasted to speak. The silence was almost complete. The last communicants were coming solemnly down the chancel. By now Takhaar was walking swiftly in the narrow passage between the front row of the congregation and the chancel step. Many had seen him now, and an angry murmur arose, that bestial voice of a crowd that knows what it wants and doesn't know why. Everybody craned their necks at what was certainly an unusual sight—the nude figure of a strapping bearded giant, a figure from Michael Angelo, carrying a copper bell, and walking like a prophet through the Lord's House, his eyes rapt.

"Ja, it's that mad Takhaar Van Ryn," said a comfortable matronly voice, quite loud, behind Cormorant. "Magtig! but he's a strong man!"

There was already confusion. Somebody screamed. Two children howled. A woman fainted. Five others pretended to faint. Everybody was talking. All the fat maidens nudged each other frantically, blushed purple, nearly burst themselves with suppressed laughter. An elder in a frock coat approached Takhaar with a firm step: he hoped that afterwards people would comment favourably on his presence of mind. Others began to follow him. Takhaar held his head high. He didn't utter a sound. But all at once, unexpectedly, every muscle in his body seemed to send up his arm, straight up, his hand grasping the bell, which came down in a noisy clangorous flash on the elder's head, who fell to the floor. Takhaar began to swing his bang-roaring bell up and down before him like a censer, but in an instant he was lost to sight in a swarming mob of black-coated Christians. The aisle was full of people—some were hurrying out, some were hurrying forward to be in at the kill. Everybody was talking and protesting. Mrs. Osbosch had fled. Osbosch was in the fray. Golgo hid his face in Cormorant's coat and wept. Dirk had disappeared. Takhaar was hustled out by the mob, and some order was restored. The predikant addressed the people. Cormorant made for the side door.

There were not many people just outside the church, because Takhaar had already been taken over to the Osbosch's. It was now high noon. In the clear sunshine, in the open air, the black coats seemed to have lost their blackness. Here at the Osbosch's a pretty scene was in progress. At the front door of the house, before a considerable number of people, Osbosch was arguing with his wife. She was red with anger. She trembled all over. Even the bow of ribbon in her hat was quaking.

"How can I ever have him back in my house?" she demanded, with angry tears. "How can you all ask me to take him in? Can't you see that he has disgraced the church, he has disgraced us, us all——" The words stuck in her throat.

"No, no, wife," Osbosch protested, "you can't hold up the whole service just for our sake. We all know it's a disgrace, but the harm's done now. Let them bring him in now, quick, just for a time."

On the steps of the verandah Takhaar lay prostrate, held down by the elders, rural inquisitors. His eyes, because they had looked for God, were bound with a black tie: they had bound his wrists with a pair of braces: and his nakedness had been covered with an unwilling frock coat. The copper bell had been set down on the verandah. Even the shape of it was ludicrous. It sat there, with its squat curves, the laughably innocent tool of fervour.

Takhaar (in a kind of trance) was carried in by five of the righteous: it took five of them to carry him in. His heavy muscular body was like the vast corpse of a rat being removed by ants. Those who had remained outside, all talking excitedly together, returned to the church. Dirk appeared. Then those emerged who had carried in the saint. They, too, returned to the Lord's House, but as they passed Cormorant they regarded him suspiciously.

"That ——— Englishman," said one to another, "I shouldn't be surprised if he's at the bottom of this trouble. Man, fancy the girls seeing Van Ryn like that, eh?"

The other did not laugh quite so boisterously as he felt inclined. Was it not the Sabbath Day?

Takhaar had been locked in his room, and the window shutters had been fastened on the outside. Meanwhile Mrs. Osbosch was having a bedroom scene with her husband on the subject of their guest. She could be heard sniffing more earnestly than ever. She didn't like to see any show of independence on the part of any of her family, her guests, her servants, or her friends. She was convinced that she herself was the hub round which her little universe was supposed to revolve. Her own children, three in number, had left her at the earliest opportunity, and although she was remotely fond of them she only regarded them as three manifestations of her own decorous personality. Of such a character, she had disliked Cormorant from the first, because he made no attempt to meet her on her own ground: so now with Takhaar, he had soared up and away like a rocket from the narrow and decent bounds of osboschity. He was out of reach, out of control, so therefore he was out of favour.

"But what can have happened to Minta?" she said. "What a worry! It is very inconsiderate of her to disappear like this." And she peeped in at the sitting room door as if she expected that Minta, at her words, would be bound to materialise.

"It's no good worrying," said Osbosch.

"No good worrying! It is for Minta to worry! Takhaar will have to pay damages! Poor Mr. Pfaff that he knocked down with his ridiculous bell! His head must be very sore. And an elder, too! Just when I want to talk to Minta about it—tsha! she's nowhere at all to be found."

Cormorant noticed a letter on the mantelpiece in the sitting room. He didn't remember having seen it there before, so he went nearer to look at it. It was addressed: *To my Husband Takhaar.*

"Here's a letter," he said, "that might have something to say about Mrs. Van Ryn."

"Where? What?" said Mrs. Osbosch, dashing forward.

"But surely you're not going to open it?" said Cormorant: "It's addressed to Takhaar."

Somehow it seemed to him a much greater sacrilege that Mrs. Osbosch should touch Takhaar's letter than that Takhaar should have behaved as he had in the church.

"Ja, ja, we must open it," said Mrs. Osbosch. "Takhaar's not fit to read letters now."

It was a hobby, a favourite hobby, of Mrs. Osbosch's to tear open other people's letters, but it was a hobby in which she couldn't indulge. Now in a perfect frenzy (she was convinced that Minta Van Ryn was plotting against her) she tore open this envelope, and read the letter aloud:

"Takhaar, I am going to Mr. Winterhalter for a time, as I told you. I won't be away very long. Don't forget that the key of the sugar-cupboard is hidden in my stocking under the mattress on our bed—I didn't like to leave it with Frans, he's so fond of sugar.

Your loving Minta."

"But what is Minta doing?" Mrs. Osbosch almost screamed, in a shrill horror-struck voice, and looked wildly round her." Are they all mad, these people? Who is it she has gone to?

"Winterhalter," said Dirk.

"And your pa knows?"

"O yes, he knows all right. It has been plain for a long time," said Dirk, grinning.

"Listen to this! And he laughs—the boy—he laughs!"

A loud knocking was heard. Takhaar was shaking his door.

"Ach, don't let him out!" Mrs. Osbosch clamoured, her hands clutching her breasts. But her husband rebelled. He went out of the room.

"Yes, what is it, Takhaar?" he could be heard saying.

"Don't let him out!" Mrs. Osbosch repeated in an agonised whisper from the sitting room door.

"He'll break the door if I don't," said Osbosch.

It was the only clever thing he ever said.

Mrs. Osbosch ran into her bedroom and locked the door, but she didn't lose interest in what was going on.

"You want to come out?" Osbosch was saying. "Have you got all your clothes on? Will you come out quietly? Are you sure you'll come quietly?"

Osbosch opened the door and then led out Takhaar firmly by the arm.

"Here you are, man, sit down," he said when they reached the sitting room.

Takhaar sat down.

"Now where is my holy bell?" he asked casually.

"Why, you don't want it now!" said Osbosch quickly.

"It's quite safe here, in the house," said Cormorant.

"I thank you, Mr. Cormorant," said Takhaar.

As for Mrs. Osbosch, in the next room, she had pressed her ear to the wall. She had wrinkled up her nose. She foresaw, in a beatific vision, the impression she would be able to make with her gossip about the Van Ryns. She would be, for once, the cynosure of Rooi Rivier. The Takhaar episode was the finest copy that had ever come her way. She hugged herself, in a fever of fear, excitement and righteous indignation.

"Ja, we shall be trekking to-morrow," Takhaar was saying.

Mrs. Osbosch couldn't hear him plainly, so, in order to be ready for his next word, she rapidly picked her ear with a hairpin. Why, he might say anything, he might do anything, a wild man like that! I never knew he was so wild, she thought. I do hope Mr. Osbosch will be able to grapple with him if he gets out of hand—now Takhaar was speaking again:

"Ja, but I'm hungry. It must be time for dinner, Mr. Osbosch?"

Mrs. Osbosch had no sense of humour. Now I must run quickly and get the dinner, she thought. That'll take his thoughts off. A few minutes later she and her husband could hardly believe their eyes—here was Takhaar calmly feeding his face as though nothing had happened! But Dirk and Cormorant were unmoved: they didn't even notice Mr. and Mrs. Osbosch exchanging glances.

"Ja, I'm very fond of Minta," Takhaar remarked at last, "and she is very fond of me. When she wakes up in the morning she likes to stroke my head. She's gone to Winterhalter's, you know. You know that white coat he always wears? She went with him in his car this morning. He always gets his rams from us, you know. I should like a little more beef, if you please, Mr. Osbosch."

Takhaar handed his plate. Osbosch began to carve the beef with an unsteady hand. This time it was his ears he couldn't believe.

---

14. DIRK.

The next morning it was discovered, when one had to get ready to return to Zonnebloem, that Dirk was extremely drunk. When this news was brought to Takhaar he was not vindictive.

"Dirk must be thirsty," was all he said. "We shall not wait for him. We must go back to-day to the farm and he can come back when he is ready."

Takhaar, Golgo and Cormorant, the only remaining members of the party of five that had set out for nagmaal, were almost as glad to leave the Osbosches as the Osbosches were to get rid of them. No sooner had they left the house than Mrs. Osbosch clapped on a bonnet and took her tongue out calling, to such effect that before the day was out Takhaar and his family and Cormorant had become dragons, portentous mythological figures, breathers of fire. On their way to the waggon these three, not yet fully anathematised, had called in at the post office, where Takhaar had sent a telegram for the recall of Lily (who must keep house at Zonnebloem until the return, at an unknown date, of Mrs. Van Ryn), and the girl behind the counter had looked at them all, especially at Takhaar, in a way that left no doubt in their minds of the impression he had made. In the streets they were stared at by the outraged bourgeoisie.

The waggon retreated over the plains and between the mountains. It moved with dignity. Very little was said by the travellers. Sweet was the desert air.

Dirk, meanwhile, was at the house of his fantastic friends the Fitzmichaels, the most disreputable and the most engaging family at Rooi Rivier. The first South African Fitzmichael, deserter from an

Irish regiment, was the doubtful son of an Irish Peer (who was really an Englishman, but whose mother was half-Danish and half-Spanish) and a gipsy. He married a black woman, who was so fat that the wedding ring on her finger became invisible, and who presented him with a son. He died of quenching his thirst. Meanwhile the son grew up and married the daughter of a half-caste Dutchman, whose wife's father might or might not have been an Anglo-Esthonian Jew. The family consisted at present of this second Mrs. Fitzmichael, who looked like an Italian, and her fourteen children, most of whom spoke only Afrikaans. It was one of the daughters who attracted Dirk, and it was with two of the sons that he had been drinking. The whole family lived in two rooms.

At the actual moment when Takhaar's waggon was leaving the outspan, Mrs. Fitzmichael was saying, in a fruity voice, to most of her children :

"——, you, —— ——'s ! When shall you learn not to leave your —— friends about just where I'm walking ? Who is this ——?"

She had nearly tripped over the body of Dirk, prone on the floor. He was still remarkably intoxicated. The girl was going through his pockets, where she found three shillings and sevenpence, a pipe, a box of matches, tobacco, and a button. She kept the money and the button, and divided the rest between a number of her brothers, one of whom was thoughtfully, solemnly, dropping the ashes of a cigarette into Dirk's ear, an occupation that he abandoned on the entry of another of his sisters, to whom he called out, very loudly on account of the screaming of a child on the other side of the room :

"Been after your—— black boy again, eh ?"

"What if I have ?" said the girl, sticking out her tongue. "It's my —— business, isn't it ?"

"Well, don't you bring no more —— niggers in here, my girl."

"I shall if I —— well like," said the girl, and so, no doubt, she would, if she —— well liked.

Three large cockroaches ran across Dirk's face, one after the other, and a baby began to chew his bootlaces.

15. DIRK AND SARA.

Takhaar, having temporarily no woman in the house, had arranged that Sara, the wife of Shilling, should come in from the kraal and do such housekeeping as was necessary. Her child had been born while her masters were away at nagmaal. She wasn't very greatly concerned over the agonies of child-birth and the responsibilities of motherhood, but she enjoyed being able to wear the child outside instead of inside. She carried it now on her back, swaddled in a blanket, and solaced herself, as was her custom, with fumes of the strongest tobacco through a long-stemmed pipe decorated with blue and white beads. As for Shilling, he was active and agile, as he had always been; he had very little to say and a great deal to do, the ideal servant.

The day after Dirk came back Sara entered the kitchen at half-past three in the afternoon to make coffee. She came in leisurely, pipe before, baby behind, eyes downcast. It was a cold afternoon. The sun was bright but gave no warmth. For once the Kaffir woman took the baby off her back, and laid it down on the floor, in a dark corner under a cupboard, where it would be safe. She thought it might be cold, so she covered it with a sack. Then she added some more fuel to the fire, and went out to fetch water.

For some time there was no sound in the bare sunny kitchen but the breathing of the fire, and the wind hurrying on the roof. Dirk came in to get something out of the cupboard. He trod by mistake on the baby, which began to cry tinily under the sack. He swore. Sara came in again.

"Hau," she muttered, putting down her buckets and running forward to the baby. But she ran unexpectedly into the open arms of Dirk. The stem of the pipe between her teeth got snapped in half. She nearly became an unwilling lover. The baby's small and wailing voice rose as in muffled protest. The Kaffir woman bit the lobe of Dirk's ear and got away to the kraal, where she was reproved by her great-grandmother, who said, taking snuff:

"You're a fool, child of the child of my child. When a white man loves you it's easy to steal his money."

Sara ran back to her baby. She put it on her back again, and carefully wrapped in its blanket the fragments of her pipe. When Takhaar and the stolid Frans came in from the everlasting plough they found their coffee ready. Dirk sat with them at the table, and began to smirk like a satyr at Sara as soon as she set the coffee pot on the table, but she, in terror and loathing, never looked at him. Golgo was out with Mandabazana: now that his mother was away nobody remembered to call him in to coffee.

When Shilling heard about Dirk he shrugged his shoulders.

16. A BLACK CHRIST.

When Lily came back Cormorant had gone away on business. A few mornings after her return she got up confused by an acute headache. She would willingly have stayed in bed, but if she allowed herself to be ill who would look after the house and its inhabitants? Men are such fools, she thought, they can't look after themselves, and if I don't get up they'll waste the food, and start eating new things before they've finished the old. What would Mrs. Van Ryn say, who is so fond of her house?

When breakfast was over, and the men were all out in the fields, she looked at herself in the glass. You go out for a walk, she told her image, and leave the precious housework to-day. She pressed her cold hands against her temples. How her head ached! Something must be going to happen, she told herself. This pain is a sign—it's like the thunder before the rain—oh, nonsense—now I'll go out. She went up into the berg.

Half-an-hour later Dirk came in to fetch his pipe, which he had forgotten when he went out. He was in a savage humour that morning, and he became no gentler when he couldn't find the missing pipe.

"Sara," he called, "have you seen my pipe?"

Sara was washing up in the kitchen, and didn't hear him call.

"Sara!" he called.

And still she didn't answer. He could hear a splashing of water, and the noise of plates being moved, so he knew what the woman was doing. Why didn't she answer? He felt a cold and terrible resentment at her silence. He went into the kitchen and seized her by the wrist. The wretched woman was beside herself with fear.

"What are you doing?" she cried.

She had never seen a face so hard, so set, so cruel. Dirk's eyes were wide and staring, and there was no colour in his cheeks. Of all things he laughed.

"Why will you not answer me when I call you?" he said bitterly.

"Au, baas, I didn't hear you," she pleaded hoarsely.

"You liar," said Dirk. "You black bitch."

Sara wrenched her arm free from his grasp and fled out of the house. The white man made as if to pursue her, and then turned and went out of another door. If you had seen him come out you would have noticed that he carried a sjambok. He mounted a horse, and rode at an even pace, without haste, for a distance of about two miles, until he came to his brother Frans, who was sowing rye in an enormous field. Frans turned and watched without any interest his brother's approach. Dirk leaned down and whispered something, and within a few minutes they were riding together, without haste, to the house. When they reached the house everything they did was done deliberately and with accord. First of all they released the two horses in a paddock. The two saddles, with the two bridles, remained side by side on the ground. The two brothers turned away, each retaining his sjambok in his hand. They walked over to the kraal, where Shilling was working in the sun. He was mending the wall, filling up gaps with stones.

"When is your Sara going to learn her manners?" Dirk asked, menacingly.

"I don't know, baas," said Shilling, in his mild, almost shrill voice, with a gentle smile which didn't hide the fear in his eyes. He waited to hear what Sara had done.

"You don't know, you swine?" said Dirk. "You think you can cheek your baas, do you?"

Frans's whole face began to light up, as his father's did in moments of religious ecstasy.

"No, baas," said Shilling.

WILLIAM PLOMER.

(To be continued.)

To a Young Man with Pink Eyes.

INDIGENOUS to realms unreal
Where those necessities are free
Which only through our wounds we feel
And only through our tears may see,

Through the fair garden of your mind
Whistles the blue flight of the dove:
A sound of bees pervades the wind
And vegetables making love.

Narcissus of what lilied pool,
In what fair Eden do you sigh?
Out of its mirror clear and cool
What bullfrog ogles you to die?

What guarantee do you embody
O ace of automatic hearts,
O patent soul, asbestos body,
Immune to all inflaming arts?

In tepid sentiment you plunge
The rosy flannel of your sight
And with boracic vision sponge
The irritation of the light.

How sweet with you by waters flowing
To suck contentment to the dregs
To hear the shrill bananas growing
And breakfast on the angels' eggs.

While the soft jujube of your eye
  Cohesive to all beauty stays,
Mine like a lighthouse round the sky
  Swivels its fierce tormented rays:

And while those flagging fins, your ears,
  Flounder you gently down the scale,
My own among the whirling spheres
  Propel me like an angry whale.

Into my paradise whose bound,
  A ridge of rocks without a tree,
By fiery clouds is circled round
  And washed with thunder by the sea.

Experience, warding the grey gates,
  A gorgon with erected crest,
Admits the cold infernal hates
  Whose company I love the best.

Unguarded by the sword of Michael
  The fruit of knowledge tempts the tooth,
And on their tyres of moonlight cycle
  The hissing cobras of the truth.

Each to himself a holy book
  How vainly we mythologise,
When but a difference in the look
  Corrects a difference in the eyes:

For though our glances, steel to pork,
  Impinge, O man of little guile,
Why is it I with pain who squawk
  And you unfeelingly who smile?

ROY CAMPBELL.

Marginalia.

I WAS recently comparing two anthologies of South African poetry, one in Afrikaans and the other in English. There is much that our poets could learn from the Dutch. I was especially struck by "Die Vlakte," by Celliers. He writes naively, sometimes echoing Shelley and then suddenly switching off into the hefty and vigorous metaphors which are so aptly suited to his language. Who, for instance, among our poets, in describing a hailstorm would haye been capable of this?

"Soos 'n perde-kommande wat dreun oor die lande."

That is the sort of stuff we would like to see our poets producing instead of trying to fillet the language of all its bones.

Even when we compare the two anthologies at their worst, we have more sympathy for the emotion which gave rise to the following outburst:

Hoera vir die Vrystaat, hoera vir Transvaal!
Hoera vir ons groot Kommandant-General!

than for that ornithological elation which burst into this cheerful strain

Sing, Singoingetje, sing, sing, sing,
Sing the song of the sun!

or this address of the "Bulbul" (locally known to schoolboys as the Toppie) to his mate:

"Sweet, why did you? Speak, speak, Sweet why did you?
Why did you? Speak, speak, speak, why did you?

It is high time that our wild birds were protected. The S.P.C.A. would find many culprits among South African poets.

The main fault with both schools of poetry is that they are too fond of diminutives. They love to attribute to natural phenomena sneaky and furtive little motions. Stars always "wink, peep, or peer." Winds always "creep or whisper." Streams "steal"; so do shadows. If it be true that art is the humanisation of nature, it is a poor look out for humanity in South Africa. It is curious that our country, so rugged and massive, should have produced such a polite, meagre, peeping, creeping, stealing style of poetry. The bushveld and the Karroo are no place for garden-rollers: and a young husky brutal type of town like Johannesburg is more in need of pile-drivers than of millinery. When one reads the English anthology, one ceases to wonder that Shakespeare shocks some South Africans, so much so that one venerable old gentleman wrote a letter to a leading South African weekly to ease his outraged feelings after reading "Lear." Judging from the poetry written by English South Africans the general attitude to poetry is that it should be something genteel, quiet, touching or otherwise soporific: and it is natural that there should be expostulations, when genteel old gentlemen stumble inadvertently on the real article. But true poetry has no connection with drawing-rooms or drawing-room modesty. "The soul of the poet," says Nietzche, "is pride, the pride of the peacock. The poet would spread himself out and glitter like the sea, even if it were only to daze the bloodshot eyes of buffaloes." Very few of our poets are anything but modest.

As a backward student of Afrikaans, the more I learn of it the more I realise that it is a language of great possibilities. It is a forcible and weighty language and one regrets that it should be tortured to fit such diminutive and flowery thoughts. Celliers has shown that it is capable of being made to pound along like a commando of horses. Dr. Leipoldt has shown that it is capable of subtler uses. It is just the language for a new Whitman to use. Many of the younger Dutch writers seem to have suffered from their contact with English Victorian poetry. But the younger Dutch painters have discovered for themselves the most vital influences in modern painting: the works of Van Gogh, Cezanne and the moderns are quite familiar to them. Why should not the younger Dutch writers acquaint themselves with those in modern literature. There is something in Whitman (who is the equivalent of Van Gogh in literature and who was partly Dutch) that would give a vital impetus to Afrikaans poetry: Whitman voices the birth of a new race; he lived when America was in much the same state as South Africa is to-day: he had also a civil war and a colour question to deal with. He was by far the most important English-writing poet since the Romantics, and has had a great influence on French, German and Italian literature. Nietzsche and Rimbaud with their tremendous zest and vigour would do much to relieve the emancipation that Afrikaans and English-African poetry seem to have suffered from too close a contact with Victorian literature. For Afrikaans is a language, one feels, that would achieve its finest effects when driven by some powerful intellectual or emotional motor.

II.

Anna von Schubert, a painting by whom we reproduce in this number, was a pupil of Matisse. She has outgrown whatever she derived from this master and with a great struggle has managed to escape from the almost irresistible influences of Cézanne—who is responsible for strangling the individuality of so many younger painters. She has lived in South Africa twice, but only for short periods. The "Native Girl's Head" which we reproduce is a striking contrast to the head of Gauguin. It exemplifies one of the healthiest tendencies in modern art which is at any cost to be vitally sincere. This tendency is spreading through the whole of modern art. "Querschnitt," one of the most brilliantly edited magazines in the world, comments with inimitable subtlety on this new tendency—by reproducing, without a word of explanation, a self-portrait by Corinth on the same page as one by Gauguin. No amount of verbal criticism could have expressed more than this juxtaposition.

The violent tactics by which Frau von Schubert has battered and built this head into shape out of raw paint, have succeeded in fixing an impression which more deliberate treatment could never have seized.

Correspondence.

Mr. Erich Mayer writes concerning the first issue of "Voorslag":

"I regret that I have to express my utter disappointment regarding the general tendency of the magazine as manifest in this issue. I am entirely missing the virile spirit of our young South African culture, the acquaintance with the best of which made me desirous to support any venture breathing that spirit, in every possible way—finding it now supplanted by the disillusioned spirit of the aged and over-civilised countries of Central and Western Europe.

I do not share the Oscar Wildean ideal of Art for virtuosity's sake, but regard Art as the extreme effort to reveal the soul of a nation, in this case of the healthy and ascending South African nation.

To me, the very *adolescence* of the younger white nations is an immense advantage over the super maturity of their older sisters, not glibly to be thrown away for the applause of the aesthetes beyond the ocean; and the healthful *childhood* of the numerous black races of Africa, not yet unduly tampered with by the 2,000 years older white civilisation, is something to be far better respected and protected than is the tendency of unscrupulous exploiters and shortsighted philanthropists alike.

Although, and even because, I believe that the black races are endowed with equally fine, though fundamentally different qualities as for example the European, East Asiatic, Semitic or Red Indian races, I regard as criminal foolishness all attempts to precipitate or divert the normally slow development of any race *or nation* by artificial methods, copied from nations 500 or 2,000 years their seniors who have not even yet shown that they are able to cut out the countless errors, hypocrisies and perversities that have led to their own degeneration.

Even if expressed with the most brilliant virtuosity of style and diction, the views on South African race questions held by the leading contributors of "Voorslag" can only tend to complicate these problems and to mislead and confuse the public opinion here and abroad, the writers being neither too well acquainted with the true mentality, character and aims of the leading classes of their Dutch-speaking compatriots, nor with the true psychology of the black and coloured races of Africa.

The result is bound to be equally harmful to the interests of all the races living in South Africa, whether these mistaken views are propagated in the form of political articles in our foremost daily papers, or casually but repeatedly ventilated in the book reviews of an outstanding magazine for literature and art, as "Voorslag" has all chances to be."

[We gladly print Mr. Mayer's letter as we are anxious that "Voorslag" should offer an open platform for the consideration of racial or other problems vital to South Africa. The opinions to which Mr. Mayer takes exception are those of the writers over whose signature they appear. "Voorslag" has no cut and dried policy on the racial questions of South Africa.—Ed.]

The Editor, "Voorslag."

Dear Sir,—

"Voorslag" is to be hailed with the joy and thanksgiving of our ancestors at the reappearance of the face of the sun after an eclipse.

Even in South Africa, then, not all that is characteristically human is dead. There are actually people here for whom the mind is something more than an instrument with which to sell a 2/6 blanket to a native for 12/6 and to lay out the profit on more 2/6 blankets; people who obstinately refuse to "worship furnaces" and whose vision is somewhat finer than "machines for making more machines."

Hooray and Hallelujah!

I have felt—reading "Voorslag"—what thousands of young people in this country must have felt—that there is now hope of life even here for us.

All success to you, Sir.

Yours,

A. RUBINS.

VOORSLAG

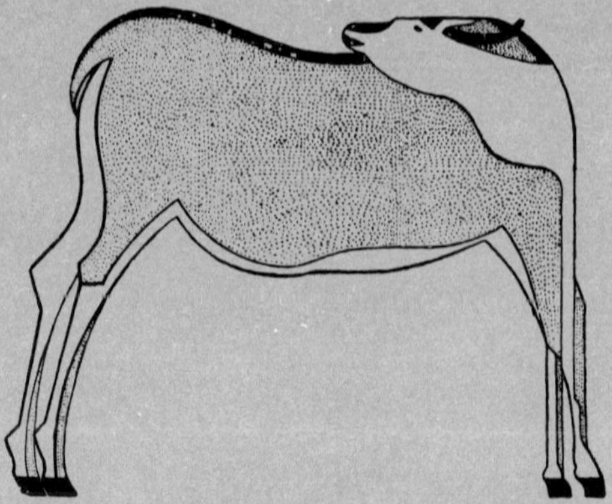

Vol. I AUGUST 1926 No. 3

Two Shillings and Sixpence

VOORSLAG

A MONTHLY MAGAZINE OF SOUTH AFRICAN LIFE AND ART

Price 2/6 per copy

Annual Subscription
25/-
Post Free

SUBSCRIPTIONS SHOULD BE SENT TO A. C. BRABY, PUBLISHER, P.O. BOX 731, DURBAN

VOORSLAG

A MAGAZINE OF SOUTH AFRICAN
LIFE AND ART.

Published by
A. C. Braby, Durban.

MSS. and all communications
should be addressed to Box 731, Durban.

Vol. I. August, 1926. No. 3.

Contents

ANNOUNCEMENT.

I have much pleasure in announcing my resignation from "Voorslag."

ROY CAMPBELL.

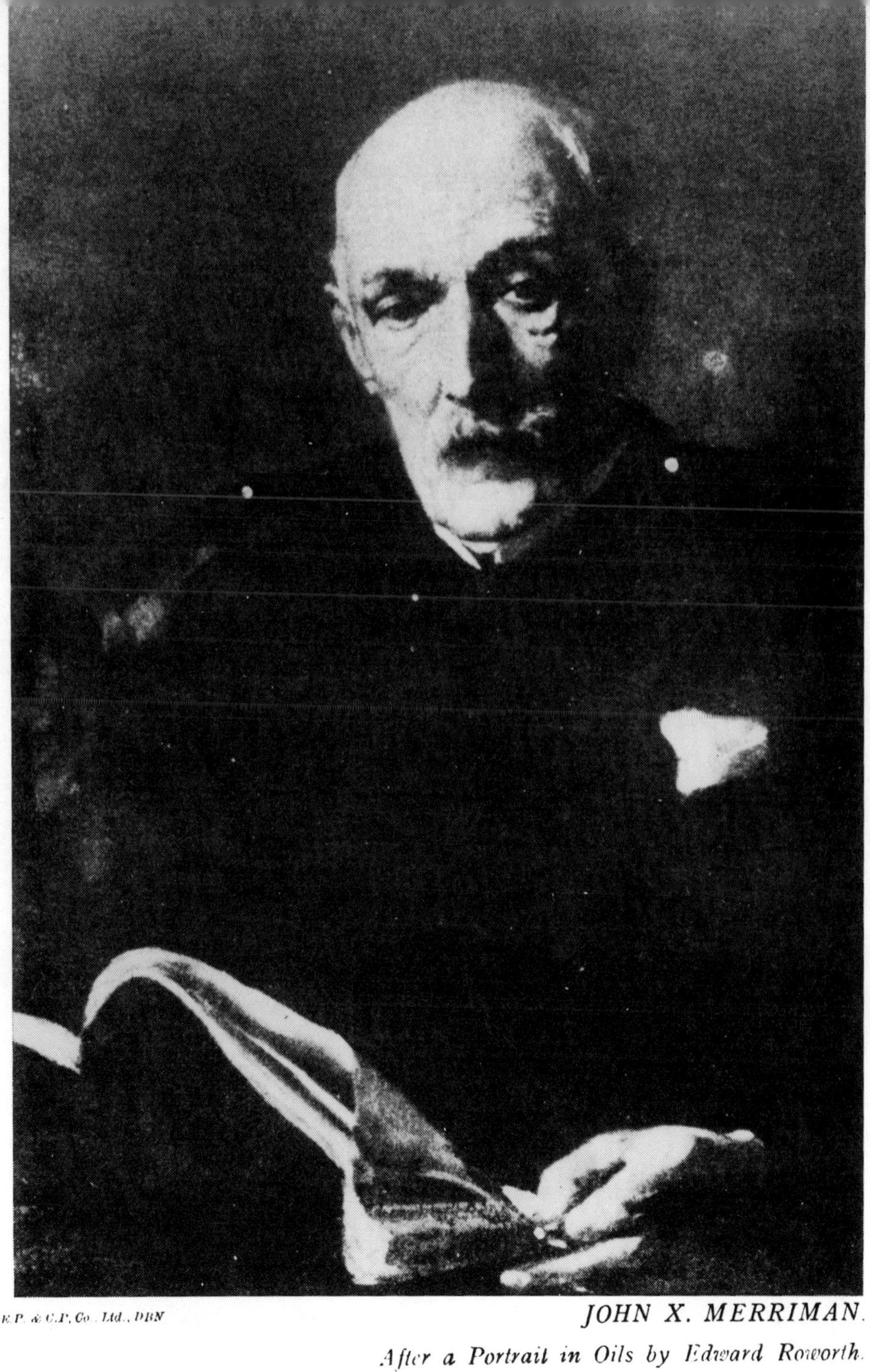

E.P. & C.P. Co. Ltd., DBN

JOHN X. MERRIMAN.

After a Portrait in Oils by Edward Roworth.

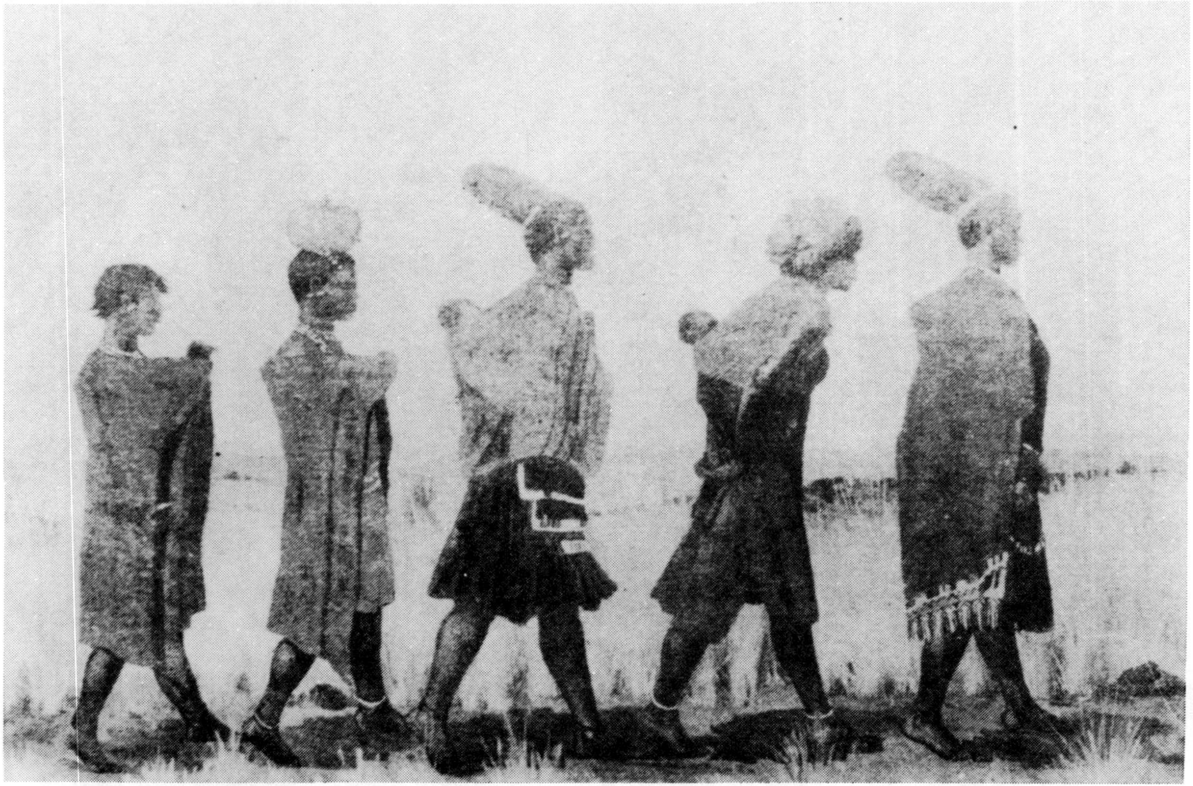

THE WOMEN

Margaret Jean Carey

(This picture was awarded the Karl Gundelfinger prize. 1926.)

VOORSLAG

Vol. 1 AUGUST 1926 No. 3

Bleached Spring

Prelude :

Pale sunlight filters through the window
and gleams on that red pot :
the fern droops.

Over the wall are three beeches
bursting into shrill green and beyond them the mountain
touched here and there with the keenness of spring.

The faded wallpaper
is almost covered with pictures
faded prints and photographs of dead people
stiff collars and blank unhappy expressions.

The room is grey
and chilly like linoleum :
dusk settles in the corners
and creeps over my heart.

Where are the songs of spring?
Did all joy vanish with the snow?
Has winter left no songs?

An icy wind blows down the street
scattering last year's dead leaves in the gutters.

The sun goes out and with all the bitterness of April
shiver the beech twigs.
The red pot in the window turns cold
the fern droops.

Spring's song seems dead at her heart.

Only the beech leaves in this April solitude
seem to hold spring's promise on their boughs
a wintry smile in pledge of April's laughter.

Sing me a song of spring, for spring
is entirely a creation of the poets.
Or tell me a tale of Love, for Love
is with us always.

This for a Spring Song:

If I were ||awakened one morning in Spring
I'd leap
        out of bed
                like the sun from the East||
throw off pyjamas and run down the stairs
out through the hall door and on to the lawn
dance in the dew and scatter the birds
gather tulips and daffodils
asphodel
holding them up in my two naked arms
to salute you, Spring and the sun
in the blue splendour of Spring dawn.

A picture of a certain austere beauty   but

nobody dares call me so early.

But were I . . . *da capo.*

And this for the Tale of Love:

A long dark wet street
puddles gleaming in the road under the gas lamps
drunk men stumbling and cursing, drunk women leering
ragged urchins shouting in the gutter or peering in at the tawdry shop-windows
York Street, Belfast.

And then suddenly from round the corner you:
a quick hand clasp a murmur of our names
And the long street glows with enchantment.
The night sings round us a magnificat.

Splendour falls from the dark it glows round us

Down the street a lighted tram reels like the car of Phoebus Apollo
the drunken men have sipped nectar
the women smile for they know the mystery
the children fish in the puddles for silver stars.

Love has lit up the street and we are his torch-bearers.

Return:

But Love goes over
And leaves only this grey room
with the chill of linoleum in every corner
and dusk settling down wearily over my heart.

Outside the window the three beeches
Shrill their green down the icy wind and

Autumn's dead leaves mutter peevishly to themselves in the gutter
they are discussing last summer
their dead life.

The sun dips behind the hill
And the cold wind penetrates every corner

the hard road glitters as if with frost.

There are no songs of Spring save in one's heart
and man's heart being brave sings loud to comfort him
through the long delays of Spring lest he lose heart.

Perhaps Spring is not what it was in the old days.

DAVID GAMBLE.

Pumpkins.

I.

EVERY year, Spring—the urge towards renewal, the yearning for creation—gets into Alita's Basuta blood. . . . I have discovered the real reason why Alita left her husband and came to cook for us in Johannesburg. It is not, as I thought, a question of higher wages at all. Alita left Bloemfontein because her husband beat her. And her husband beat her for the good reason that she would not obey his aged mother. As he pointed out: "A man may have many wives. But no man can have more than one mother."

The ruling thus laid down by Itumeleng, based though it is on an acute observation of natural phenomena, has had the not very surprising result of annoying Alita. And so, effectively, if not admittedly, she has deserted Itumeleng. And not only has she deserted him, but she has taken away with her their son, Sydney, and fitted him into the position of garden boy with us. It is a business that has left Itumeleng sullen and introspective.

And that, in short, is why it happens that Alita experiences the manifestations of spring, not in Bloemfontein, but in Johannesburg.

II.

All through the winter we have a drought, and by the time September comes the earth is dry and hard, the winds whistle harshly in all directions, and the loose red dust forms itself into gyrating columns which chase each other malignantly up and down the streets. Then, bodies and souls being parched and exhausted, we study the skies for rain. . . .

Finally, one day, Alita makes a pronouncement. The moon. The little thin new moon is in his heaven, and he is lying (Alita holds her two hands obliquely) at such an angle. And the significance of this is that we shall have rain. Did we know that?

We did not know that; and, besides, any importance we may have attached to Alita's richer meteorological training is dispelled by her next remark.

"We Kaffirs," she continues, complacently, "have not much book-learning, but we know our little things. I will tell you more about the moon. . . . When the new moon is lying on his back" (she puts her wrists together at the palms, and her curved fingers point upwards as the horns of the moon)—when the moon does that, it means there will be great sickness and death in the land."

Great sickness and death! But, again, why dismiss the portent contemptuously? The moon may not be quite wrong. Among the Kaffirs is there not always great sickness and death in the land?

But forget that to-day! Life is for the living. Spring is here. And Alita is going to plant.

She is going to plant mealies, water-melons, sweet-melons, and pumpkins. Alita knows there are other fruits and vegetables, but those she regards as being strictly white people's affairs. For herself she belongs to the old school. She plants the things her forefathers planted.

The sky is cloudless. There seems no prospect of rain. But the moon. . . . The moon is reclining as on an easy-chair.

Alita goes to work.

This is her procedure: She takes a little stick and makes, haphazard, a scratch in the ground. Into the scratch she puts a seed and covers it with a few grains of sand. Then she makes another scratch and puts in another seed. Then another scratch and another seed. Then . . . and so on. Alita's work is done.

In the circumstances you might expect her to eke out her labour with, at least, a little incantation. But Alita is not that kind of person at all. She relies solely on the forces of God and nature. "Now," she says piously, looking at the sky again, "the Old Man on High must send rain."

This, I understand from Alita, is the system of agriculture she has inherited from her ancestors.

Still, sooner or later it is bound to rain. And then, miraculously, little sprigs of green begin to poke through the earth. Most of them are weeds, but a few of them are the fruits of Alita's sowing, and she points them out delightedly.

"But the weeds, Alita," we ask. "Aren't you going to do something about the weeds?"

Alita shakes her head. "We Kaffirs don't trouble ourselves about those things," she says tranquilly.

Well, it may be that the soil of Basutoland is more hospitable than ours, but the fact remains that, with us, only the pumpkins come to maturity. However, Alita is satisfied. Pumpkins are her favourite food. "There are pumpkins enough," she says cheerfully, "to make a person sick. I could eat myself dead on pumpkins."

The difficulty is that she expects us to do the same. It is largely our own fault, of course. It was actually our suggestion that she should plant vegetables among the fruit trees, and we would buy the vegetables from her. The scheme was an excellent one, since poor Alita sends her whole wages home every month, and reserves for her own needs only "extras." Vegetables were, obviously, an extra, a legitimate source of personal income. . . .

Only, as I have said, Alita's vegetables are, in the end, represented only by pumpkins. The result is that, as Alita is anxious to make a little money, pumpkin has become with us a staple article of diet. But we are really not attached to pumpkin as a daily habit, and when we see the gross plants sprawling all about among the fruit trees, we are heartily prepared to agree with Alita that "there are pumpkins enough to make a person sick."

III.

Now see the workings of Fate.

At the height of the last pumpkin season Alita received a letter from Bloemfontein. All Alita's heart-beats are set in motion by letters from Bloemfontein, the home of her clan. As Alita is not "learned," it is my duty to read and answer her letters. This one ran as follows, and was in a handwriting strange to me:—

My dear Alita,—

I let you know for your child Emily is sik with a bad sikness. If you do not come at once you shall not see your child alive. I say come at once.

I am your dear husband,

JOHN ITUMELENG.

P.S.—We don't see the rain. Only this hotness.

I read through this letter quickly before passing on its contents to Alita.

"Alita," I said, "it is bad news."

I had not noticed that the moon was lying on his back. But Alita is ever ready for the worst, and Emily is her dearest possession.

"My child is dead," she said in a choked voice. "My only girl-child that I had."

"No, she isn't dead. But she is very sick. They want you to go to her at once."

I read out the letter.

"My child is dead," repeated Alita. "I know it." And she went to pack her belongings, her face grey under the brown skin, her hands shaking.

"But won't you come back, Alita?" I asked her.

Alita shook her head. "If Emily dies, I must stay to look after her child, Josephine."

Two hours later she left the house, followed by Sydney, carrying her bundles. As she walked away I heard a sound, which, at first, I took to be the wind in the eaves. And then it came to me that it was the savage bursting its way through Alita's civilisation. I stood on the balcony and saw her climb down the kopje which bears our street on its crest, and across the little spruit at the foot of the kopje. And unceasingly the high-pitched, long-drawn wailing came from her . . . until no sound came any more at all.

I watched the two figures grow small on the diagonal red line which was their path across the veld, separating suburb from city.

As I stood looking from the balcony, my eyes fell on the vigorous green that was the pumpkin patch. "It's no use leaving these," I thought. "We shan't need to eat them any more now. To-morrow they can be distributed among the neighbours!

A day passed. At ten o'clock the following morning a weary, dusty figure came into the kitchen.

"Why, Alita!" I exclaimed.

"Has missis got another cook yet?" she asked,

"No."

"Then I am back. . . . I have not eaten since yesterday morning," she continued, and made herself a cup of tea.

"And Emily?" I demanded. "How is Emily?"

"Emily is well."

"But the letter!"

"The letter was a lie. My sorrow was for nothing. Itumeleng wanted me back. He thought to cheat me with the letter. He believed that if I was once in Bloemfontein he could make me stay. But he does not know Alita yet. I came back with the next train."

She put down her cup.

"It is finished with Itumeleng," she said, and walked out of the kitchen, and towards the fruit trees.

As she did so, my heart failed before a sudden recollection.

"Alita," I said. "Your pumpkins. I thought you were not coming back. I have given them away."

"All?"

"Yes, all. To the neighbours. Yesterday."

I hurried on with explanations.

Alita ignored them, and came directly to the point.

"Then the people in this house don't like pumpkins?"

"That is not the question. I had no right to give away what belongs to you. I'll pay you for your pumpkins, Alita."

Alita stood silently looking towards her pumpkin patch. Then she spoke.

"It was right," she said, in heavy judgment on herself, "that Itumeleng should cheat me. For I am a cheat also. I cheated myself to think that missis liked my pumpkins. And I cheated missis to take from her money for things she did not want. Don't speak to me of more payment, my missis. I am shamed enough."

She turned away from the meaningless leaves and the barren stalks. And as she did so, I saw her raise the corner of her apron.

I waited until her straight narrow back and bulky skirts had disappeared from my view, and then I returned to the house.

SARAH GERTRUDE MILLIN.

Towards a National Art.

DURING the last decade there has been a marked increase in the appreciation of the fine arts throughout South Africa. There have been various causes for this minor Renascence: the foundation of the magnificent collection of modern art in Johannesburg chosen, for the most part, by the greatest connoisseur of his time, the late Sir Hugh Lane; the munificent gift by Sir Max Michaelis of works by the famous artists of the golden age of Dutch painting, every example being selected also by Sir Hugh Lane; the exhibitions so frequently held during recent years in all the principal towns of the Union by our leading artists; and, last but not least, the increased prosperity of our people which has enabled so many to become active patrons of the arts. All this has now made it possible to speak of a South African School of Art, its present outlook and its future goal.

There is one remarkable feature in the present situation and that is the insistent demand by our patrons that art in our country shall be "South African." I can remember the time when the pictures most desired by South African patrons were those which would harmoniously take their place on walls already occupied by the works of European artists. In those days the leading picture dealers of Cape Town imported quantities of European pictures, the majority of which, it must be confessed, were of mediocre quality, and they advertised from time to time exhibitions of oils and water-colours by "leading" English and "Continental" painters. The few South African artists had a pretty hard time, but the imported work sold freely. To-day exactly the opposite state of affairs prevails. There is no sale whatever for work which cannot be labelled "South African." In nothing else is the growth of a national sentiment more evident, and it is, moreover, entirely free from racialism, for the English patron, equally with his Dutch fellow countryman, demands a distinctly South African quality in any work of art which he desires to possess.

That our art should be led to attempt the portrayal of distinctively South African characteristics in nature and humanity is entirely to the good. All the great art of the past has indelibly impressed upon it not only the personality of the creative artist but also the spirit of the land in which it was wrought. The cosmopolitan art of to-day, swayed by every wind of fashion, is a modern phenomenon, and however amusing and exciting we may find its protean manifestations, I sometimes have doubts about the likelihood of our distant descendants building magnificent galleries to house any noticeable proportion of the work at present produced by so-called modern masters in Paris, London, Berlin, Munich or New York. The loss of national characteristics in art has been without a compensating gain.

The degeneration in English art needs no underlining, it is obvious to any reasonable person; to-day there is no English school of painting, and amidst the diverse 'ists and 'isms which flourish and decay with bewildering rapidity, there is no body of work being produced that can hold its own with the masterpieces left by such typically English manifestations of the art-impulse as the school of eighteenth century portrait painters, the old English water-colour school, the Norwich school, and the pre-Raphaelite Brotherhood.

Of course a prodigious clamour of deafening praise surrounds the efforts of present-day artists; but, when all this noise has resolved itself once more into silence, and only the work itself remains, what position will then be given to it? Hardly, I should imagine, the exalted place claimed for it to-day by its fervent and fevered advocates. I read recently that Mr. Clive Bell gave Mr. Duncan Grant a place beside Gainsborough—well! well!

So far, there has been no organised attempt made in South Africa to browbeat those who love art into accepting the strange cults that nowadays flourish so luxuriantly. Our art has been allowed to follow natural and healthy lines of development, and although still of an impressionable age it already shows signs of eventual vigour and independence.

One of the effects of this growth into consciousness of our national art has been the foundation within recent months of the South African Institute of Art. I am no lover of Academies or of what one may term "Institutionalism" in art. I think all fair-minded people will agree that there has been much in the histories of academies in the past to warrant a critical and distrustful attitude towards them. We need only glance at the record of the Royal Academy in England. None of the great painters of the Norwich school were admitted into the fold, it ignored the purely English and beautiful art of water-colour painting, and but for the opportune appearance of John Ruskin with his magnificent eloquence, the Academy would have crushed the pre-Raphaelites, under whose influence was produced the greatest work painted in England since the days of Hogarth, Reynolds and Gainsborough, as witness Madox Brown's "Work"; Millais' "The Carpenters' Shop," "Sir Isumbras at the Ford," and the "Supper at the House of Isabella"; Rossetti's "Girlhood of the Virgin"; and Hunt's "Hireling Shepherd."

The continued pursuit of the Academy's selfish policy led eventually to the foundation of the New English Art Club, where such men as Steer, Shannon, Tonks, Sickert, Orpen and John, found that appreciation denied them by the Academy. It is true that the Academy was glad eventually to open its doors to several of these, but they were refused recognition until it was no longer possible for the Royal Academy to honour them by admitting them, they rather conferred honour upon the Academy by consenting to put R.A. or A.R.A. after their names.

The evil that has been done by academies in the past in persecuting or ignoring vital and original movements in art has not been overcome by their frequent reversal of former wrong judgments. The sad welter of the present age in art, when any impudent decadent, devoid of all visible talent, can exhibit his tiresome rubbish, and then, if exception be taken to his vagaries, immediately claim exemption because Academies have in former years refused recognition to this, that, or the other great man, is the direct result of these Academical mistakes.

It is not unnatural, therefore, to adopt a waiting attittude towards our newly-formed Institute of Art. The inception and practical carrying through of the idea is due to Mr. Leo Francois, the Institute's first President, under whose guidance I feel confident that the foundation principles will be so broad and tolerant as to make it possible to banish some natural fears and misgivings. Mr. Francois is a man of energy and strong will, and he has for many years shown himself an unselfish and tireless worker in the cause of National Art, labouring at his self-imposed task with a single-minded and admirable devotion.

It is not from seeing merely the large annual exhibitions organised by the South African Society of Artists, the Natal Society of Artists, the Eastern Province Society of Arts and Crafts, or the so-called "Academy" in Johannesburg, that a fair estimate of the real quality of the art work at present being produced in South Africa can be made. One, at least, of our leading painters, and one of our greatest sculptors, do not contribute to any of these exhibitions. Other leading men exhibit only intermittently, and even so, frequently send inferior work, reserving the best for their own "one-man" exhibitions. It is also true that first-rate work does not gain, but rather loses by being shown in close proximity with a mass of work of lesser attainment, so that the actual achievement of our artists is on a higher level than is realised by those people whose knowledge of it is confined to the mixed works shown on the walls of our larger exhibitions.

It is possible to call to mind at once the names of a dozen or more artists who are producing fine and sincere work and building up the tradition of a genuinely national school of South African art. Let us glance for a moment at the work of some typically South African painters and sculptors. If we take the sculptors first, there is Kottler, an artist of the first rank, modern in every good sense of the term, whose portrait busts are masterpieces of strong characterisation and virile yet subtle technique; and Anton van Wouw, whose vigorous, vivid bronzes of native types give him an enduring position in the record of South African art.

Among the painters there is first R. Gwelo Goodman, our most celebrated landscape painter, who acquired his accomplished technique during many years' residence in Europe. In 1915 he finally returned home, and has produced during the last ten years a great volume of work, holding from time to time exhibitions in all the principal towns throughout the Union. Two years ago he organised an exhibition of his work in the Royal Institute Galleries in London, which showed convincingly his technical power in the various mediums of oil, water-colour and pastel.

Hugo Naude is a South African-born painter, who paints with charm and sincerity the mountains and valleys of his beloved home-land, and whose work is always characterised by freshness and an out-door spaciousness. Pierneef, born on the Transvaal high veld, is one of the most vigorous and interesting of our younger painters, and every year his work extends its range and increases its power. Another of our younger painters, Neville Lewis, has already achieved an enviable degree of fame, having held several exhibitions in London and being the only South African to be represented in the Tate Gallery.

There is a young boy at the Cape, the son of D. C. Boonzaier, the celebrated cartoonist, who gives promise of a brilliant career and draws with remarkable power; his landscapes and still-life's are well composed, strongly characterised, and good in colour; he already shows all the qualities with which the painter who would succeed must be endowed.

Among our water-colour painters, the work of Peers and Dumbleton is outstanding. Peers is an artist of refined sensibility, and Dumbleton successfully applies to the rendering of South African conditions the great tradition of Cotman. Mrs. Kay, both as an etcher and a painter of portraits, is an artist of much technical resource and freshness of vision. Miss Glossop has interpreted the more lonely aspects of mountain and veld, and Miss Vyvian portrays with considerable distinction the more sylvan aspects of the scenery of Natal.

The landscapes of Volschenk are the outcome of a deep, sincere love for the beauties of his native land, and though the circumstances of his early life did not enable him to enjoy the advantages of a technical training such as fell to the lot of his younger and more fortunate fellow-craftsmen, yet in spite of his enforced limitations,

Volschenk occasionally produces a landscape which more than holds its own by reason of its unforced realism, its unaffected simplicity, and its typically South African atmosphere.

In this short, incomplete review of the work of a few of our South African artists, it will be noticed that some of the most celebrated names mentioned are those of artists who, as I mentioned before, either do not exhibit at all at our mixed exhibitions, or else are chary of sending their best works. This tendency on their part is to be regretted, but the situation is not likely to be improved until the selection committees at the various exhibitions adopt a more critical standard. With the exhibitions as at present organised this is perhaps a counsel of perfection, but it is a point which should merit the attention of the newly-founded South African Institute of Art.

I do not intend to make foolish predictions about the future of our art, but I think present-day indications justify a feeling of optimism. Great art is the expression of the soul of the people, and our typical South African life, broad-based upon the soil, how fresh and real it is compared to the neurotic existence of the myriads in the overgrown cities of the old world! We may possibly be stolid, and to persons of a neurotic tendency it may even appear that we live in an intellectual vacuum, but I claim that our people as a whole have a spacious outlook, and bring to the art of life an inborn tendency towards dignity, beauty and sincerity, thus creating the right atmosphere for the growth of a vigorous national art.

EDWARD ROWORTH.

Psychology of Race.

AN AUSTRIAN THEORIST.

IN a recent number of *The Century* is an arresting article by the Austrian statesman-philosopher, Count Richard Coudenhove-Kalgeri. Writing with the precision and the monotonous but impressive thoroughness of a creed he impresses his philosophy of international harmony upon the reader.

Roughly analysing this creed of his we find that it is based on the assumption that mankind in any civilised country is divided into two classes—the man having aristocracy of the will (the squire or junker class) and the man having aristocracy of mind—the urban intellectual who may be socialist, journalist, artist, scientist or poet. These two types, says the writer, have been evolved from the psychological antipodes of Country and City. Country is separated from country by space, and city from city; but country is separated from city by time. "Centuries often separate a metropolis from the country that surrounds it." This is exactly true of Johannesburg, where the elemental kraals lie within a few miles. And yet we expect the black man to leap those centuries without self-destruction and with no harm to our social structure. Add to this unwisdom the taking away from the black man of his land, a return to which is always at the back of his mind, and the social chaos is complete.

"City life," we are reminded, "is abstract, mechanical, rational; country life is concrete, organic, irrational. The city dweller is sceptic, rationalistic, irreligious, progressive; the countryman is emotional, credulous, superstitious, conservative . . . Nature is the extensive, art (the urban spirit) the intensive form of visible beauty . . . Social or Christian morality is an urban phenomenon arising from the herding together of mankind. The typical city dweller combines

Christian morality with irreligious scepticism and materialism. From this results socialism, the religion of the modern metropolis. To the rustic Christianity is little more than a new edition of heathendom with new superstitions: his true religion is faith in nature, in force, in fate; even as the city dweller's faith is in man and his conquests over nature and fate. Townsman and countryman do not know each other and so live in a state of tacit or open enmity. There are many catchwords to conceal this elementary antagonism: the Red and the Green International: industrialism, agrarianism: Judaism and Anti-Semitism. All cities draw their power from the country: all country-sides draw their culture from the city . . . Cities grow and perish. The country is eternal."

On such familiar foundations—platitudes, truisms as some may call them—Coudenhove-Kalgeri proceeds to begin the building of a new international harmony. With his urban-derived intellect he proceeds to use this elemental soil of dead minds to some purpose. He is trying to bridge the gulf between the elemental and the intellectual man which in every country is the real bar to solidity of race, and in the world at present is the bar to solidity of action against the forces of evil, chief of which is war.

Who can doubt that in South Africa racial antagonism is partly the natural antagonism between the travelled and the untravelled colonial? Between the man who knows only the horizon beyond his mealie field, and the man who knows the chimneypots of London and Amsterdam, of Leyden and Cambridge?

The next stage of the writer's argument: "The flower of the rural type is the squire or junker: of the urban type the intellectual. The typical squire or junker combines a maximum of character with a minimum of intellect: the typical intellectual a maximum of intellect with a minimum of character. . . . [An exaggerated statement; but he is building on the grain of truth at the bottom of it.] The antithesis between squire and intellectual is based upon the fact that these two types represent the extremes rather than the summits of the nobility of blood and intellect. The highest visible form of the first is the ***grand seigneur;*** of the second the genius. Caesar the man of action, and Goethe the genius was each ***grand seigneur***. . . . The perfect aristrocrat is at once an aristocrat of the will and of the intellect, but neither squire nor litterateur."

As a perfect example of this type I should name Conrad: aristocrat, professional sea-captain, of high literary genius but never descending either to squire or litterateur.

"He combines," the writer goes on, "vision with strength of will. judgment with power to act, intelligence with character." Looking into our own country once more for an illustration, the character of Botha fits very beautifully into this conception of the perfect aristocrat. One might almost go further and suggest that in the friendship and cooperation of Botha and Smuts the two divergent aristocracies of will and intellect mingled with and were completing one another to the glory of their country and their race.

The writer then points out that it was this mutual misunderstanding between town and country which caused Germany to lose first the war and then the revolution. The junker party underestimated the strength of the city with its leaning to pacifism; and later, the socialist leaders working for revolution failed to grasp the conservative nature of the country people.

And then by a natural progression the writer comes to his theory of Germany's failure to find internal harmony at the critical moment. "Europe's nobility of birth and intellect (Country and City) created each its type: England's aristocracy of birth the gentleman, France's aristocracy of mind the Bohemian. Gentleman and Bohemian meet in the attempt to escape the ugliness of petty bourgeois life. The gentleman overcomes it by personal style, the Bohemian by temperament. The one brings order into the disorder of human relationships, the Bohemian freedom into their lack of freedom. The one ideal is the life-form of a caste, the other is the life-form of personality. Both ideals are phenomena of human crystallisation. Even as the crystal is able to develop only in a free environment so both of these ideals owe their existence to the English and French conception of liberty."

This necessary atmosphere, he says, was lacking in Imperial Germany and it was not possible for a similar ideal to develop. The German "lacked the courtliness of the gentleman, the flexibity of the Bohemian." And thereafter, finding no suitable life-form in his own actual life he looked for ideal embodiments of the German nature in his poetry. Thus it was that he found a physical ideal in Siegfried, the intellectual ideal in Faust. The first became distorted into the Prussian officer, the second into the German scholar. Mechanical ideals took the place of organic ideals—thus a rigid Siegfried and a rigid Faust. Only two Germans, it would seem, have given the German nation a glimpse of what this people might become living a truly organic and not a rigid life. The one is Bismarck, the hero of action, the German officer minus his stupid faults; and Goethe, the hero of the spirit, the German scholar minus his absurd faults.

In these two men, says the Austrian critic, "personality conquered the mechanical, the man the marionette." About these two a new German life-form equivalent to other Western ideals may be built up.

Count Coudenhove-Kalgeri is the founder of the "Pan-Europa League," a flourishing post-war society in Austria and other countries. His great value to Europe, a reviewer of his books points out, consists in his having once more begun with fundamentals; in disentangling truths which should have been patent, and racial and cultural harmonies upon which all civilisation must be built.

ETHELREDA LEWIS.

Music in South Africa.

WHEN considering Music in South Africa I am reminded of those fantastically statistical articles that were so popular in London magazines some years ago. If all the stamps bought at a London Post Office in a day were arranged end to end they would reach from the world to Mars; if an Atlantic liner were placed in Whitehall it would completely block the traffic—diagrams attached.

In such a manner one could perhaps make something impressive of a study of Music in South Africa. If all the money spent in giving music lessons to entirely unmusical people were employed in buying top hats for natives every native would be equipped with one decimal four top hats. If all the gold medal certificates issued at Eisteddfods were made into a bonfire and burnt the flames would be seen at Madagascar.

Only by regarding music in South Africa in some such way can the subject be made either cheerful or amusing. Regarded seriously it is very depressing indeed.

Of all the arts music is the worst served in South Africa. We have painters whose work is accepted throughout the world; we have more than one writer with a European and American reputation. South Africa has produced at least one architect of note. We have no great composers and such executive artists as South Africa has produced promptly leave its unappreciative shores for Europe or America, and return only very occasionally for a tour that can be financially justified only when regarded as a holiday.

South Africa is a vast country with an atmosphere of its own. It is a country of wide spaces, of fierce sunlight, of drought and famine, dried up river beds and raging torrents, gaunt mountain and burned dry veldt. Some indication of South Africa's character is to be expected in its art; in both painting and literature it is sometimes apparent, in music never. Such compositions as have appeared are thin timid things giving pale thoughts about the veldt at evening or shy whispers about Table Mountain. Nowhere do we find that strong, virile note that would suggest the inspiration of South Africa.

It must be admitted that the South African composer finds no store of traditional material ready to his hand. The native peoples have not made gay song and dance, rich in melody and rhythm as did the peasants of Europe, leaving behind them a great store of raw material for the composer of a later age to fashion into immortal works. All that the South African native can offer is a very strong sense of rhythm, the heart beat of music, and a subtle application of the significance of rhythms. Native music in point of rhythm is virile and vivid in the extreme, in melody it is poverty stricken. Out of the negroid sense of rhythm grew that evil smelling flower of decadent Europe and America, the modern jazz; and a South African native passing outside a ballroom of Capetown, Johannesburg or Durban may see white men and women in the flower of their elegant sophistication exploiting his traditional tribal dances, degraded into the "latest" dance from London or New York.

Yet that virile rhythmic sense is surely capable of other expression—of being exalted as well as debased, and on that sure foundation music that truly expresses South Africa and its character may one day be built.

South Africa appears to little better advantage when we consider the executive instead of the creative side of its music: the work of its singers and players instead of its composers.

It is probably true that South Africa spends more in money and talk on music in proportion to the amount of musical appreciation in the community than any other country in the world. Thousands of children receive expensive lessons in singing and playing and not only never learn to sing or play themselves but never even learn to appreciate the singing or playing of others.

When at last a genuine artist arrives, a pianist like Adolphe Hallis, or a singer like Jenny Sonnenberg, he must go to Europe for training and in order to find an audience. Does such an artist re-visit his native land he will be lucky if he can make the bare expenses of a concert tour, while tenth rate singers like Clara Butt or Coscia pass triumphantly through the country receiving the plaudits of packed audiences, and depart laden with riches.

Apart from a Hallis or a Sonnenberg, who find their audiences in Europe, there are the less talented musicians who seek an outlet for their abilities in their own country. Unless they are lucky enough to get into one or other of the two South African orchestras there is no place for them but the tea room or the cinema where their music is subordinated to the pursuit of pastries or the fervid excitement of the flickering film. Let them attempt to escape from the odour of buns or tobacco smoke and give a genuine concert and they will experience the cold indifference that South Africa preserves for its musically accomplished sons.

Our orchestras fare no better than our individual performers. There is much boastful talk about the orchestras of Capetown and of Durban. Neither can be regarded as first rate musical instruments, both are too small in numbers and have too many weaknesses to be accepted at their advertised valuation.

Mr. Theo. Wendt, a sincere musician, struggled for ten years to make the Capetown Orchestra a serious musical organisation and then had to find such solace as he could in a broadcasting studio. Dominated by the flambouyant personality of Mr. Lyell-Tayler the Durban Orchestra has been made a butt for jocular allusions, and trailed as a bait to lure up-country visitors into the meshes of rapacious drapers. It has been lent to the service of publicity and of mammon with ludicrous results.

Neither the Capetown nor the Durban Orchestra has received any adequate measure of support from the public, both have been made the subject of ignorant election speeches, both have cost ratepayers large sums of money, both have been liberally vilified by fools.

In one thing South Africa seems to be peculiar, it not only ignores music and the musical artist, encourages mediocre performances and wallows in the sentimental ballad, all these are common enough elsewhere, but it does more, it treats all music with a particular contempt and brands as "highbrow" all music of a higher level than jazz or musical comedy.

In matters of painting or literature or architecture the man of no taste does not adopt an attitude of scornful superiority. If a man has not read Shakespear or Charles Dickens he does not glory in his ignorance, more likely he will pretend a knowledge and an appreciation that are not his to claim; but for music the unmusical South African has unlimited derision and at it he flings the epithet "highbrow" as the gutter snipe flings mud.

Here and there a solitary worshipper worships the golden sound in secret and for the most part what good music is known in South Africa is known by means of the not to be despised gramophone.

He would be optimistic indeed who could see any signs in South Africa of a musical awakening. Yet to musical expression and understanding South Africa must come. Her wide spaces and her vivid colour, her power and her tragedy must find expression in sound as well as in word and pigment. But the signs of that awakening are not yet.

MAURICE WEBB.

Die Liefde Van Catullus

PASSER DELICIAE MEAE PUELLAE.

'n Navoiging van die Corspronklike Versmaat.

Mossie, lieflike skat van my geliefde,
Jy met wie sy gespeel het op haar boesem,
Wie sy eerste haar vinger aangebied het,
Wie se knypend gepik sy uitgelok het,
Wanneer sy, my geliefde, lieflik glansend,
Liefies so met jou speel en so plesier vind,
Troostend, dink ek, miskien, haar eie smarte
As haar vurige hartstog tot sy rus kom—
Speel met jou soos sy—O!, hoe verlang ek
So my hart te verlig van sware smarte.

Lygette o Veneres

Treur godinne van Liefde, treur, Erotes,
Treur O almal wat fyn gevoel besit.
Liefling mossie gelief deur my geliefde,
Liefling dood is hy nou,—hy was haar dierbaar.
Meer was hy vir haar werd dan selfs haar oë,
Heuningsoet was hy haar; ky ken sy nonnie
Beter ja, dan hyself haar eie moeder.
Nooit het hy van haar skoot hom ooit verwyder,
Nou hier dan spring hy daar, en altoos sing hy
Net alleen vir sy nonnie sing hy altoos:
Hy, wat nou langs die weg vol skadewee
Daar gaan waarvan, so sê hulle, niemand terug kom
Ai, mag julle vervloek wees, Duisternisse,
Dood se euwele Skadu-ryke somber
Alles sluk julle in, wat ook maar mooi is:
So mooi was my ou mossie: jul ontroof my.
Was dit mooi van jul: O my arme mossie,
Nou terwille van jou het my geliefde
Ogies rooi en geswel van al haar trane.

THEODORE HAARHOFF.

On the Humour of Milton.

WE do not regard Milton as a humorist: yet a reader will smile over his pages more often than over those of many avowedly frivolous authors. Not in his poems, not in his pamphlets, not even in his amazingly vituperative polemics, stands there, so far as I know, a single instance of a full-fledged joke. I am only aware of two occasions when he so much as tried to be funny: one was his answer to his daughter's request to be taught a foreign language, and the other his verses on the ill-starred Hobson, "the University carrier who sickened in the time of his vacancy, being forbid to go to London, by reason of the Plague." In neither case does his achievement prompt one to hope that deeper-digging may lay bare a rich reef of fun. And not only is all humorous purpose empirically found to be absent from his work; in attempting even to conceive of any association between the comic spirit and Milton's solitary, star-like austerity, the mind becomes involved in insuperable contradiction. The mere idea of Milton jesting is enough to call up a vision of the excellent man losing "in earnestness control of face," and by stress of endeavour coming to resemble his own conscientious but unwieldy elephant, who

> "To make them mirth used all his might, and wreathed
> His lithe proboscis. . . ."

"Comedy," as Meredith has instructed us, "is a game played to throw reflections upon social life, and it deals with human nature in the drawing-room of civilised men and women." Milton was not in this sense a social man, nor was he interested in human nature in such surroundings. But, however true this may be, the fact remains that laughter forms a considerable, though not certainly a predominant, element in the experience of the modern mind in reading Milton. This applies with special force to his poems, to which our attention here may be confined.

In our reading of Milton the springs of laughter are no doubt often touched merely by some archaic oddity of phrase. At other times, again, the quaintness is seen in some turn of thought itself, not in the outward habit but in the inner substance. Frequently, too, we may find the source of merriment in a chance resemblance to other and incongruous places of literature or life: Milton is amusing because he accidentally suggests something that has amused us before. A fourth typical case is where he forcibly carries over into English some peculiarity of classical syntax or idiom. Doubtless numerous other forms of the intrusion of the comic into his work could be distinguished. But whatever the difference we may mark in these forms, it will, I think, be found that certain general similarities are constant throughout them all.

In the first place, I would repeat, Milton, save in the two instances already noted, never means to be funny. This is sometimes hard to believe, but in the end I fancy we must come to accept it. Second, what strikes us as funny would probably not so have struck Milton's contemporaries. Again, bad writing is often comic, either through clumsiness of expression or insincerity of feeling. The comic in Milton is generally not of this kind, and does not seem to arise from his failure to say something that he is trying to say, or (what is a form of the same thing) from his saying more than he means. In Milton it appears almost always to be simply epiphenomenal to good writing. Lastly, this kind of involuntary and unsuspecting humour is in a real sense a Miltonic peculiarity. I do not mean that no parallel to it can be found elsewhere. It is, for instance, up and down the Bible.* But it seems to be much more frequent in Milton than anywhere in English before or after him; and it certainly is not common to his age.

The kind of fun that archaic quaintness provides is omnipresent in Milton. It is hardly possible to come upon two consecutive lines—I had almost said two consecutive words—which do not insinuate or re-inforce its suggestion in our minds. Where the whole is so deeply impregnated, it would be time's unserviceable expense to search too curiously for representative examples. This from the Hymn on the Nativity may serve for one—

> "Our Babe to show his Godhead true
> Can in his swadling bands control the damned crew."

And this from Lycidas for another—

> "Where other groves and other streams along
> With Nectar pure his oozy locks he laves."

Sometimes, too, the Miltonic orthography becomes so striking in its difference from the received usage of to-day as to reach a definitely comic value. A quotation from Samson Agonistes will exemplify this—

Chorus—This Idols day hath bin to thee no day of rest,
Labouring thy mind
More than the working day thy hands,
And yet perhaps more trouble is behind –
For I descry this way
Some other tending, in his hand
A Scepter or quaint staff he bears,

*e.g. in this passage from Leviticus The Lord is speaking. "When ye be come into the land of Canaan, which I give to you for a possession, and I put the plague of leprosy in a house of the land of your possession; and he that owneth the house shall come and tell the priest, saying, It seemeth to me there is, as it were, a plague in the house. . . ."

Comes on amain, speed in his look—
By his habit I discern him now
A Public Officer, and now at hand—
His message will be short and voluble—

Officer.—Ebrews, the Pris'ner Samson here I seek.

This moving passage may well rouse a modern to sigh, from beneath the weight of his own experience of governmental verbosity, for the golden days when public officers were of a stamp to achieve the apparently impossible and combine brevity with volubility. Nor need he modify his envy by the reflection that what the State servants of his own time have lost in these qualities of worth they have made up in their comparative mastery of the use of the aspirate. The form Ebrew is not an isolated realistic touch introduced to give verisimilitude to the character who here employs it, but is general throughout Milton's writings.

Samson Agonistes, presenting the admirably blunt and forthright character of Manoa, perhaps provides the best hunting-ground for the type of amusing piquancy which depends on the actual thought rather than on the form of its outward expression. The blind Samson is reviling himself and his too gullible love for Dalila as the true cause of his captivity and disgrace. He ends,

"These rags, this grinding, is not yet so base
As was my former servitude, ignoble,
Unmanly, ignominious, infamous,
True slavery, and that blindness worse than this,
That saw not how degenerately I serv'd."

Manoa.—"I cannot praise thy Marriage choices, Son. . . . .

The abrupt change of manner was no doubt not only apparent to Milton, but also intentional. Yet it will hardly be questioned that the effect he aimed at was not the comic one which represents our readiest response to Manoa's brisk rejoinder. It is interesting to note that Manoa returns to his son's matrimonial failure at the close of the play. He ends his most noble speech on the news of Samson's victorious death with these lines which I suppose always strike the modern reader (at least if he is unfamiliar with Greek tragedy) as anticlimax—

> "The Virgins also shall on feastful days
> Visit his tomb with flowers, only bewailing
> His lot unfortunate in nuptial choice,
> From whence captivity and loss of eyes."

I spoke above of a third origin of laughter in Milton—his accidental suggestion of incongruous things elsewhere in literature or life. This is more frequent than perhaps one would, in the abstract, suppose. We are wont, and on the whole rightly, to think of his method of expression as exceptionally distinctive, exceptionally personal to himself. It is not that his style is not on a narrow view and in many of its details derivative. Few writers have availed themselves of the fruits of their reading so fully or so fearlessly; and, as his reading was deeper than most, so are the sources from which he draws more copious in their supply. In this sense his debt to his predecessors is peculiarly heavy. But in the working of Milton's creative genius, all such external material is subjected to a complete metabolism; he makes it at once intrinsic to his own design and assimilates it into the very substance of his private idiom. Throughout the writings of his maturity the authentic Miltonic accent is always audible, unmistakable and unique. But this perfection of his style took time to achieve, and it is but natural that his earlier work should show many signs of uncertainty and experiment. This work, indeed, was literally verse-exercise, conscious and deliberate. He strove in it not only to fashion from the linguistic heritage of his tradition a medium through which he should be able to express his own intuitions in their unimpaired individuality, but also to select from his manifold poetic capabilities those and those alone which would genuinely subserve the high artistic purpose that he kept ever before his mind—I mean, of leaving "something to aftertimes as they should not willingly let it die."

I remember from my schooldays an entertaining pastime occasionally indulged in by boys interested in the poets. We may call it "Spotting the Author." It consisted, simply, in challenging a friend to a contest in which each read in turn some few lines of verse to the other, who then essayed to name their composer. Normally one guess only was given, but in cases of special difficulty the allowance was increased to three. He who scored the larger number of correct attributions was the winner. It was a game that received mild encouragement from the authorities, since they detected in it some educative value. Of general impressions won from playing it all I now recollect is that when one heard some fragment of striking beauty that nevertheless appeared devoid of all clue to its author's identity, it usually turned out to be by Shelley; and that of all poets comfortably the easiest to identify seemed to be Milton. But now, if I played that game again, I think my tactics would be to make my opponent the dupe of that accepted unmistakability, and to keep his score down by laying Miltonic traps for him. Take the lone line—

> Soft silken primrose fading timelessly. . . .

Might not even a skilled critic shudder at the grisly possibilities of error lurking for him here, if the verse's authorship were not known and he were asked to conjecture it? As for the harassed amateur guesser, he is often to be found sighting at targets wide of the proper mark by a couple of centuries and more. "Rossetti?" he queries tentatively. "No? Then possibly Tennyson somewhere?" Still you shake your head slowly and with feigned sympathy, as though you would help the poor flounderer if you could, while all the time inwardly you savour the relish of victory. "Well, what about Swinburne?" is his last shaft, desperate and defiant.

And even if you present that line, not alone, but with its immediate companions, the passage still seems far enough from the typical timbre of Milton—

> O fairest flower no sooner blown but blasted,
> Soft silken primrose fading timelesslie,
> Summer's chief honour if thou hadst outlasted
> Bleak winter's force that made thy blossom drie;

What is the likeliest guess now? An Elizabethan sonnet? I leave the point for the decision of those of subtlest sensibility. But I venture to think that all manner of answers would occur even to them before "On the Death of a fair Infant dying of a Cough" by John Milton.

Again, consider—

> If this fail,
> The pillar'd firmament is rottenness
> And earth's base built on stubble.

Will an even-minded judge deny that here the characteristic ring, the rhythm, and the splendid hyperbole of rhetoric are—dare I say it? —Shakespearean rather than Miltonic.

One more example is enough. I suggest that, could we come upon the following lines by themselves with no knowledge of their source or context, there would be nothing intrinsically improbable in ascribing them to Shelley—

> Lap me in soft Lydian airs,
> Married to immortal verse
> Such as the meeting soul may pierce
> In notes, with many a winding bout
> Of linked sweetness long drawn out,
> With wanton heed, and giddy cunning,
> The melting voice through mazes running;
> Untwisting all the chains that tie
> The hidden soul of harmony.*

I take such passages as these to be evidence that Milton had powers within him which, if he had chosen to develop them, would have resulted in poetry of quite different genres from any that he in fact gave us. Though Milton attained to a four-square and all-compelling individuality whose stamp made every slightest utterance inde-

* For the present purpose I have naturally not preserved here the tell-tale Miltonic spelling.

feasibly his own, it was not always so; and in and out of his earlier work there are scattered many suggestions of traits and mannerisms that ultimately became excluded from his poetic personality, as either unworthy of or unnecessary for his exalted intention. These suggestions point to unexpected affinities with certain of his predecessors and successors, who actually developed the traits that he eradicated or neglected in himself. We have heard him speaking in voices which sounded like those of Shakespeare, Shelley, and even Tennyson and Rosetti. One happened also occasionally on more curious resemblances, where the incongruous shades and descends and sometimes crashes into the comic. There is, for example, the rich close to the Epitaph on the Marchioness of Winchester. This unhappy lady died in childbed, when "Summers three times eight save one she had told" (3 x 8—1 = 23). The poet offers graceful condolences, and wishes the conventional peace and quiet on her grave. He wings his way steadily to the peroration in which he compares the dead peeress to the Biblical Rachel, who "fled to felicity" in giving birth to Ben-oni, called by his father, Benjamin. He concludes with the hope that—

> Far within the boosom bright
> Of blazing Majesty and Light,
> There with thee, new welcom Saint,
> Like fortunes may her soul acquaint,
> With thee there clad in radiant sheen,
> No Marchioness, but now a Queen.

The movement of the poem in these lines corresponds with what airmen designate by the term "stalling." After a period of level flight the craft slowly loses flying-speed, and falls nose-downwards in a vertical bathetic descent. The heroine's swift promotion, too, in consideration of faithful services on earth recalls those pious and improving ditties that formed the staple moral food administered to their young by so may Victorian mothers: while the last couplet of all more swiftly suggests the pointed fables in the Bad Child's Book of Beasts, which the ingenious Mr. Belloc has recorded as a warning and an exhortation to his kind.

Milton gets a somewhat similar effect in that queer passage of Euripidean Stichomythia in Comus. In the blackness of the night-enfolded forest the Lady has lost touch with her brotherly escort, and is wandering aimless, afraid, alone. To sustain her spirits and in the hope that her notes may reach her brother's ears, she sings. The sinister Comus, hearing, discloses himself to her, and they speak. She mentions her "extreme shift how to regain her sever'd company."

Co.: What chance good lady hath bereft you thus?
La.: Dim darkness, and this leavy Labyrinth.
Co.: Could that divide you from neer-ushering guides?
La.: They left me wearie on a grassie terf.
Co.: By falsehood, or discourtesie, or why?
La.: To seek i' the valley some cool friendly Spring.
Co.: And left your fair side all unguarded Lady?
La.: They were but twain, and purposed quick return.
Co.: Perhaps forestalling night prevented them.
La.: How easy my misfortune is to hit!

It would need, one thinks, all the assurance of the shameless scion of Circe to proceed with the conversation after such a buffet of sarcasm as that. Comus, hide all unbruised by the blow, continues without pause or diminished aplomb to chat amiably throughout another forty lines.

Passages like this and the closing verses to the Marchioness put the reader in something of a dilemma. It seems inconceivable that anyone could have written them without his tongue in his cheek. But Milton, jowl at bulge from the sly pressure, pointing down the ages at versifying Victorian pietists,—Milton casting a mocking glance at Euripides, then turning to his audience and slowly lowering the lid of one eye,—is not the conjunction of such indelicate and flippant gestures with the dignified severity of the man even more inconceivable still?

Of Milton's imposition of classical constructions on the English language and of his retention of the classical significations of words derived from Latin and Greek, regardless of accretions of meaning acquired in the course of their post classical lives—of these points so much has been written in Milton-literature that the barest mention may suffice for them here, where indeed it is only desired to point out that the idiosyncracy frequently produces sensibly comic results. Examples are so numerous as to occur on almost every page that Milton wrote. The following may indicate their characteristic effect—

> Nearer he* drew, and many a walk travers'd
> Of stateliest Covert, Cedar, Pine, or Palme,
> Then voluble and bold, now hid, now seen,
> Among thick-wov'n Arborets and Flours. . . .

or,

> That space the Evil one abstracted stood
> From his own evil, and for the time remained
> Stupidly good . . . . .

or,

> Greedily she ingorg'd without restraint
> And knew not Eating Death :

It would perhaps be of interest to speculate how for back in history Milton's readers began to feel the presence of the comic in any or all of the passages I have quoted, and for how long ahead posterity will continue to do so : or, if these questions are thought fruitless and unanswerable, to ask what are the features of the modern consciousness which make for the appreciation of the comic in such forms. I have to confess with some regret that I have no theory to propound, and find myself, willy-nilly, obstructed from any effective step beyond the more concrete ground on which I began, namely, of noting parts of Milton's work that appeal to that consciousness as comic. To cover the ground anew in search of omissions would be as tedious as, in an account which makes no pretensions of being exhaustive, it is unnecessary. I may therefore conclude by merely remarking that simple archaic quaintness, though no doubt the commonest, is probably the

* The Serpent.

least important factor in the comic appeal. Further, when Milton tickles his readers' sense of fun, it is by no means because their approach to his high-souled gravity is one of frivolous irreverence. It is certainly possible to be uplifted to the full by the nobility and grandeur of his poetry, yet still to feel, as it were as overtones, the comic effects at which I have tried to point. Of how much of the intended significance of Milton's work time has deprived us, who can say? But at least time offers the compensation of one aspect of significance unintended, the comic. It may be that this addition is a genuine enrichment of the beauty, diversifying the high seriousness not with intrusive barbarous guffaws, but with the serenity of humane and understanding smiles. True, Milton, himself, as we may gather unequivocably from his foreword to Samson Agonistes, would not have approved such adornment. But to our contemporary sense, steeped as it is in the Elizabethan tradition, laughter and the graver or more tristful emotions, rightly or wrongly, do not seem so incompatible. There is a pleasant irony in the reflection that though Milton abhorred and eschewed the "intermixing Comic stuff with Tragic sadness and gravity," time has insisted on compassing the mixture in his despite. The growth that he would have outrooted has sprung up posthumously, in the unprompted course of nature. And we may surely be forgiven if we submit so spontoneous a product to no sterner test than is applied to the fruits of the earth themselves; the thing is good if the taste pleases. To reject the free gift as a corrupt gratification or through fear of rousing the shade of Milton to wrath, would be to show too nice a scruple. Let us rather savour the pleasure it can give, while the human mind is attuned to its enjoyment.

LEONADE BARNES.

Nimrods van die See

DIT is laat op 'n Sondagaand. By die Point lê die Walvisvloot drie-drie langers mekaar, aan die kaai vasgemaak. Die sterk westewind van die more het weg gesterf en die barometer het eers ophou daal en toe vinnig gestyg. Op alle kante soos groot spookagtige figure gooi krane bewerige skadus oor die water. Op die verre einde van die kaai blaas kaffers skril op fluitjies waar hulle kool aan boord 'n skip dra en soos koue staal bore breek die geluid deur die stilte.

Die kapteine en manskappe van die verskeie bootjies het net van 'n diens in die klein Skandinawiese Kerk teruggekeer. Kaptein Kaspersen en een of twee van die manskappe is besig om 'n laaste pyp te rook voordat hulle na bed gaan en toe ek oor die kant van die Egeland klim was hulle besig om in Noors op die agterdek te praat.

Die kaptein herken my dadelik. "Ek is bly jy het weer gekom" sê hy. "Ons sal nie slegte weer soos laaste keer hê nie en daar is nou baie walvisse op hierde kus. Ons sal hierdie keer vir seker iets vang. Ek het Saterdag drie walvisse geskiet en was dit nie dat dit so gou donker geword het nie sou ek meer gehad het, want ons moet altyd taamlik vroeg op Saterdag terug na die hawe kom. Die een vloot sal more in die hawe bly want hulle kan alreeds nie die walvisse vinnig genoeg op die fabriek opsny nie."

Ek was al te vore met Kaptein Kaspersen op Walvisjag uit en ons staan nog 'n rukkie te gesels op dek. Hy het meer as ag jaar in die Suid-see en die Nu Georgia Eilande in Walvisbote deurgebring en hy het nou al meer dan ses seisoene walvisse op die Suid-Afrikaanse kus gevang. Hy ken al die streke en maniere van die monsters.

"More sal ons waarskynlik net Finn- en Blouwalvisse vang," sê hy. "Ons het nie die regte weer vir Sperm nie. Ons skiet hulle net op stormagtige dae of in die voortou van stormwinde. En more gaan die weer bepaald mooi wees."

Die Kaptein slaan sy pyp op 'n ystertralie uit. Hy kyk vir laas rond om te sien dat alles in orde is. Hy dink dat mens die kaffers wat heeldag op die kaai ronddwaal nie kan vertrou nie. "Verlede week," vertel hy my, "is daar twee goue ponde en 'n goue oorlosie uit 'n onderbaadjiesak van Kaptein Torsen van die "Odd" gesteel. 'n Mens moet maar versigtig wees. want die kompanie help jou tog nie."

Onder dek is daar nie baie spaar-ruimte nie. Die bouers van die Egeland het slegs op seevaardigheid en spoed gemik. Hulle het nooit aan onnodige weses soos passasiers gedink nie. Die manskap alleen kon nie almal in die bak van die skip bly nie en twee van hulle moes in die klein driehoekige eetsalon slaap. Die kaptein en die hoofmasjinis het elk 'n klein kajuit gehad, maar ook daar was ruimte skaars. Ondervinding het my geleer dat die bank waarop die matrose vir hulle maaltye sit, 'n goeie bed is en ek het toe weer daarop gaan lê.

Almal was gou in bed en al die ligte gou doodgemaak. In die salon, klop die stilte soos 'n koorsagtige pols. Net in die hoofmasjinis se kajuit kom die astrante getik van 'n wekker. Tik! Tik! soos 'n groot vinger stoot dit die nag aan. Tik! Tik! tot dagbreek en dan weer Tik! Tik! stoot dit die dag aan. Al die klokke in die wereld was op daardie oomblik Tik! Tik! besig dae, weke, maande, jare, eenue—Krrrkkkk—Die wekker het almal aan boord wakker. Dit is amper vier-uur, donker en bitter, bitter koud. Op dek is daar die sware getrap van voete. Stoom skreeu en spook benoud deur die yster pyp langs die koorsteen. Nou het ons van die kaai weg gestoot en swaai stadig om na die middel van die stroom. Daar is die gereelde geslaan van die skoef. Ons breek deur die skaduus van somber staal monsters wat hulle hoog in die nag bo die water verhef. Die Egeland se neus rys effens, byna onmerkbaar, soos die voorlopertjies van die groot seebrandens ons tegemoet snel. Dit is 'n wonderlike nag. Die sterre, hulle lig soos die fyn punte van koue blou staal, prik gedurig die duisternis. In die oë voel mens hulle geprik. Die sterre en die melkweg begin ronddans. In lang ligbesmeerde lyne slinger hulle deur die lug. Die mas van die Egeland waai die lug rond. Bo op dek het 'n deur begin slaan, oop en toe met die kom en gaan van elke brander. Ons is oor die baar en op die ope see. Die lang swaaiende lig op die Bluff en die skitterende duisternis van die hawe kwyn weg agter ons. Die Egeland en ons, die see en die sterre alleen bly oor.

Vir meer dan twee uur stoom ons reg Oos. Eindelik op die horison reg vooruit kom die eerste tekens van die dag. In die moreskemer klim 'n lang vorsgeboude matroos in die vaatjie hoog op die grootmas. Hy het 'n blcu seilbroek en dik grys wol jersie aan. Op die verre rand van die water skuif 'n dun strepie lig in die lug. Dit groei en grcei en bars uiteindelik uit 'n brander van lig in die Ooste en rol die son in die lug. Die land is nou 'n dun inklyn agter ons. Die more is kalm, en lug en see ontmoet in die verte in 'n duidelike skeidingslyn. Die dek van die Egeland is vir 'n wonder droog. Ons werk begin nou eers met erns. "Saterdag" sê die kaptein, "het dit hier van walvisse gewemel."

Die kaptein, die eerste offisier en 'n matroos, is op die brug en kyk skerp in die rondte. In die uitkykvaaitjie is daar nou twee matrose. Meteens roep een van hulle "Blaast" en wys opgewonde met sy hande in 'n seker rigting. Ons kyk almal waar hy wys. Daar kom dit weer. Eenmaal, tweemaal blaas die Walvis en 'n fontein van silwer wasem skiet in die lug. 'n Donkerblou liggaam het vir 'n oomblik in 'n boog uit die water geskiet en toe weer verdwyn. Die kaptein het van die brug oor die steil dek gestruikel en staan agter die kanon heel voor op die neus van die Egeland. Die skip stoom voort vir nog so 'n paar honderd tree en dan word die masjienerie tot stilstand gebring en ons dryf met die stroom, terwyl ons vir die walvis se her-vertoning wag. Die atmosfeer is elektries. Almal maak klaar vir die vis se vertoning. Mlangenie, die vuurman het ook vir 'n minuut of twee 'n glinsterende swart gesig op dek vertoon en gou 'n beker water gesluk. Hy weet wat met hom gaan gebeur. Die kaptein kyk nou baie op sy oorlosie. Tien, twintig, vyf-en-twintig minute, is al verby en die walvis het nog nie weer verskyn nie. Ons verwag dat hy nou elke oomblik sal opkom om te blaas. Selfs die kok het sy kombuis verlaat en staan op 'n kas oor die kant van die skip te loer. Dertig minute, en nog geen teken van die walvis nie. Die kaptein brom dat dit 'n groot dier moet wees. Hulle bly nie gewoonlik so lank onder water nie. Miskien het ons dit verloor. Skielik is daar 'n geroep van die mas-top. Die walvis kom boontoe. Hy kan onder die water aan swem gesien word. Bo op die oppervlakte is daar 'n gladde lap water. Die walvis gaan ver aan bakboord blaas. Die klein masjien op die brug rattel die stuur-ketting net so vinnig om as wat dit kan gaan. Mlangenie se graaf word al gouer en gouer in die kool gesteek. Dik swart rookwolke rol bo die skoorsteen. Die Egeland swaai om na bakboord. Elke plaat op die skip bewe en agter ons karring die skroef die water in skuim. Kaptein Kaspersen het die kanon al lank gelaai en hy swaai die loop in die rigting van die walvis. Kan ons naby genoeg kom te skiet voordat die walvis weer verdwyn? vra ons almal.

Ons ploeg diep vore en gooi groot walle van skuim op die water. Net 'n paar faam nader en dan kan ons skiet. Die kaptein buk laag oor die kanon. Vyf faam verder en dan kan hy 'n langskoot probeer. Maar die walvis het verdwyn en ons dryf weer stil op die water en kyk skerp rond, terwyl die kaptein by die kanon bly staan. 'n Halfuur later sien ons weer daardie gladde lap water teen die branders. Die walvis kom weer boontoe, maar die keer op die stuurboord en nader aan die Egeland. Die stuur word gou omgegooi. Die Egeland spring voorheentoe oor die branders. Amper onder die boeg van die skip, is daar 'n warreling van water en 'n donkerblou rug buig hoog uit die water. Met 'n dowwe kraak wat elke plaat op die skip skud word die harpoen in die rug geskiet. "Dis raak," skree die kok in my ore. Ons staan altwee op die kas. Uit die neus van die walvis kom daar 'n donker bloedstraal en dan duik dit weg in die water.

Van die mastop van elke Walvisboot hang daar 'n katrol aan die einde van 'n sterk veer. Die spanning wat daar op die kabel is word deur die lengte wat die veer rek bereken. Die hele proses werk amper net soos 'n reusagtige visstok en lyn. Deur middel daarvan word die walvis dan soos 'n gewone vis gespeel. Een van die masjiniste het nou by die masjien gaan staan en elke keer wanneer die walvis die kabel tot op sy breekpunt getrek het het hy die briek los gelaat en die kabel 'n faam of twee skiet gegee. Vir elke voet wat dit dieper gaan betaal die vis met 'n deel van sy lewenskrag.

Dit is 'n sterk walvis en baie groot. Elke keer as dit ruk kantel die Egeland gevaarlik oor na die water totdat die branders tot op die middel van die dek breek. Die briek gly een-of tweemaal en dan kan een man dit nie meer hou nie. Die walvis is te sterk en 'n matroos word gestuur om te help. Honderd en vyftig faam onder die oppervlakte spook die walvis vir sy lewe. Maar hy kan nou nie meer lang uithou nie. Met die harpoen is daar 'n klein bom van gegote yster in sy lyf geskiet, wat nadat die harpoen goed in die vleis gesink het, ontplof en klein stukkies gegote yster orals in sy liggaam blaas. 'n Uur na die ontploffing bewe die stert van die walvis in twee honderd faam waterdiepte flou, en stadig word die vis boontoe getrek. Soos koue swart gerimpelde marmer kom die walvis op die oppervlakte. Dit is heeltemaal dood en selfs die stert roer nie in die minste nie. 'n Lang staalpyp word in die lyf van die walvis gedruk en van die masjienkamer pomp hulle die dooie liggaam vol lug. Die walvis vul stadig uit tot dat dit soos 'n pap geblaasde lugbal in die water langers die skip dryf. Die stert word ingetrek en aan die kant van die skip vasgemaak.

Die hele dag stoom ons omtrent dertig myl van die land en paralel met die kus, na die Suide. Verskeie maal sien ons weer walvisse. Vyf maal probeer ons om van hulle te skiet. Maar die groot 75 voet Finn-walvis aan die kant is swaarder dan die Egeland self en ons is nie vinnig genoeg nie. Voordat ons kan draai en naby kom sink hulle almal in die dieptes. Toe dit donker word draai ons terug hawe-toe en kruip nader aan land. Die westewind het weer begin waai en soos ons nader aan die land kom word die see ontstuimig. Op die brug trek die stuurman sy groot oliejas aan, want die see spat tot teen die ruite van die kaart-kamer. Die dek self is gedurig onder water en die rook waai laag agter ons weg.

Alles kraak aan boord en wanneer 'n brander oor die boeg breek struikel die Egeland soos 'n gekwetste dier.

"Dit is 'n goeie ding dat ons na die hawe terugkeer" sê die kaptein vir my in die kaartkamer. "Dit gaan rof wees vannag. Ek is jammer ons het nie nog 'n walvis geskiet nie, die skip sou nie dan so kwaai gerol het nie." Ons praat goso 'n bietjie en dan gaan ons na bed. Vannaand slaap ek in die kaartkamer. Deur die vierkantige venster sien ek nou en dan die land en 'n rooi maan, wat laag oor die heuwels hang, soos 'n skeef gehangde portret. Die wind skeur soos 'n kranksinnige deur die sterre. Alles dans weer rond in die lug. In lang en ligbesmeerde lyne draai en struikel die sterre rond. Twee-uur in die more het ons weer onder die skadu van die Bluff gaan anker. 'n Matroos het my kom wakker maak. Ek het probeer om na buite deur die venster te kyk, maar dit is vaal van die soutwater gespat.

LAURENS VAN DER POST.

Translations from the French.

(Les Chercheuses de Poux is one of the finest of Rimbaud's poems—an example of how he could transform even the most prosaic details of life into great poetry without overlooking or trying to disguise their animality. Imagine with what glee the later Wordsworth would have seized on such an operation as that of two peasant-girls flea-ing the head of their brother, and what a mess he would have made of it! It is almost impossible even faintly to suggest in a translation the curious electrical concentration which charges this poem. Rimbaud is, with Mallarmé, supposed to be the most untranslatable of French poets. Aldous Huxley and Sturge Moore have both attempted translations of this poem and each has succeeded in seizing at least one of its many intrinsic qualities. But it is doubtful whether in fifty translations the whole strength of this poem could be captured. In translating the following poems the writer has sacrificed literary elegance and absolute literalness in order to give a sense of the emotional atmosphere of each poem.—*Lewis Marston.*)

LES CHERCHEUSES DE POUX (after *Rimbaud*).

When the child's brow, with torments flushing red,
  Implores white dreams to shed their hazy veils,
Two sisters, tall and fair, approach his bed
  Whose fingers glint with silver-pointed nails.

They seat him at a window where the blue
  Air bathes a sheaf of flowers: with rhythms calm,
Into his heavy hair where falls the dew,
  Prowl their long fingers terrible with charm.

He hears their breathing whistle, half-repressed,
  Flowing with ghostly pollen; and the hiss
Of indrawn spittle as if each suppressed,
  Upon her lips a hesitated kiss.

Brushing cool cheeks, their feathered lashes flick
  The perfumed silences: through drifting veils
He hears their soft electric fingers click
  The death of tiny lice with royal neals.

Drowsed in the deep wines of forgetfulness
  His soul a faint delirious music hears
And to the rhythm of their slow caress
  Wavers and pauses on the verge of tears.

L'ALBATROS.—(*Charles Baudelaire.*)

Often for sport the men of loafing crews
  Catch the vast albatrosses of the spray
That, indolent companions of their cruise,
  Pursue the swift ships on their restless way.

Scarce have they fished aboard these airy kings,
  When, helpless on those unaccustomed floors,
They piteously droop their vast white wings
  And trail them at their sides like drifting oars.

So proud before, now comical and meek
  Appears this soarer of celestial snows:
One, with his pipe, teases the golden beak,
  One, limping, mocks the cripple as he goes.

Like him the shining poet sunward steers,
  Buffets the storm and mocks the archer's hate—
But stranded on the earth to ribald jeers
  The great wings of the giant baulk his gait.

THE BURIAL OF A POET.

If on the night when you have died,
  Some Christian, pitying your ghost,
Beneath some dusty heap should hide
  This corpse of which you loved to boast,

Here, when the chastest stars have set
  And the nights with cloud are hung,
Will the spider stretch his net
  And the viper hatch her young.

And, through the year, unnumbered woes
Shall howl around your damned repose—
With the whistle of dead leaves,

With the snarl of staring bitches,
With the mumbled spells of witches
And the whispering of thieves.

DON JUAN IN HELL (*By Charles Baudelaire.*)

When to stark Charon having paid his freight,
  Don Juan embarked towards the sunless shore,
A surly ruffian, eyeing him with hate,
  Seized with a vengeful arm the rapid oar.

With hanging breasts, beyond the blackened water
  Dim twisted shapes of women met the eye,
And like a herd of cattle led to slaughter
  Lowed forth their lamentations to the sky :

There Sganarette reclaimed his wagers won :
  Don Luis, with one trembling claw thrust out,
Cursed, to the wandering ghosts, that rebel son
  Whose insolence had dared his age to flout.

Shivering in black, Eluisa strove meanwhile,
  So near her lover and her faithless spouse,
Once more to win from him that crowning smile
  With which they had illumed their early vows.

Braced at the oar the sombre, stone-like Titan
  Swirled the black wave. But leaning on his sword
The hero calmly watched the long wake whiten
  And all things else disdainfully ignored.

Reviews.

SLENDER SKETCHES, BY A STOUT GENTLEMAN; Durban; William Brown & Davis, Ltd.

Should one sing as the linnet sings, trill one's gamut I believe is the correct expression, and just make as many pretty noises as one can? Shall we all perch ourselves on tree branches and take a little gentle exercise in metre like birds? It is a wonderful thought. Let us all be birds and fly away up to the woody heights of the Berea, choose a tree that will stand for us, take a deep breath and just sing like linnets, hammerkops or whatever we think we are. Like the lady in "Tom Jones" we shall begin by appealing—in valse time:

Let me sing, let me sing, etc., etc.

And here is our latest singing bird: "Slender sketches by a stout gentleman." What can one say about them? Criticism of these amiable verses is at the outset disarmed by the explanation of it all given in the form of a short preface by the Stout Gentleman himself. And that preface gave me more pleasure than all the verses put together. In it he hints at war cries from the critics, but there is no need for war. One does not greatly do battle over a straw, and if these verses give pleasure to even one person—apart from that tolerant household of which he speaks—they will have attained an object. Pleasure may be absorbed by various people in various ways and though a pork butcher may be bored to death in a garden he may derive infinite pleasure from the contemplation of a pigstye. It is the same with verse. The stout gentleman himself would, I am sure, be the last to claim for his verses anything approaching immortality, and there are worse ways of spending one's leisure moments than even writing verses to one's dog.

There has been some talk in discussion of these verses of the lack of any false quantity to be found in them, and it has been said that false quantities in verse nowadays are as frequent as inspiration is rare. It is new surely to suggest that quantity—true or false—has anything to do with inspiration or that it is a better thing to count one's feet before the inspiration is hatched. Perfection of verse form can be a joy in itself, but without the shouting of inspiration behind it it becomes just a barren design. A meaningless arabesque.

As far as the Slender Sketches are concerned, a breath or two of inspiration might have knocked some of the quantities to hell and bucked things up enormously. Instead of this we find a neat facility, a Kiplingesque lilt now and again, a scholarly glamour over some of the lines, but most of it drenched in that sentimentality which many of us have at heart but which it always seems rather unpleasant to meet in print. Most of the verses deal with South Africa and South African things, and it is perhaps a tribute to the much vaunted Britanity of Durban to point out that all these things are looked at from an essentially English point of view: the verse, the manner, the outlook, all are English. I can imagine the wife of the Dean of Munchester writing about the Zulu cotton pickers in just this way:

There's a stirring in the kraals on the hill-top,
Though it wants a full hour to the dawn;
Girls are awake in the dark on the hill-top,
Though the quail are asleep in the corn.

Tumty tumty tumty tum tumty tum tum . . . and so on. You won't find the soul of a Zululand cotton picker there. And perhaps its just as well. The soul of a Zululand cotton picker might prove comfortless reading for the highbrows of Durban.

But the Slender Sketches will be alright. They won't upset anybody, and I don't think the Stout Gentleman need fear, as he so disarmingly puts it, that his family will be the main sufferers from this publishing. They have in them all the seeds of popularity so he won't have to make it up to them in any other ways.

D.G.

THE ETHICAL AND RELIGIOUS VALUE OF THE DRAMA, by Ramsden Balmforth. London: George Allen & Unwin, Ltd.

It will probably come as a surprise to South Africa to learn that drama may be considered to have any value at all save as a soporific or more or less innocent relaxation. And to suggest that it may have any ethical or religious value must, to a population fed on our popular drama which is either so sordidly social or hectically romantic as to have no value at all, seems simply affected nonsense. And it is nonsense to suggest that our popular drama has any significance at all save boredom.

> It was dullness, dullness all the way,
> With boredom mixed in my path like mad.

But drama did not begin at the Lyceum nor end in the multitude of the Theatre Royals throughout the world, and in this book Mr. Ramsden Balmforth makes an interesting though rather long-winded attempt to get at the meaning and significance of the long panorama of drama down the centuries. He begins with Job and ends with Thomas Hardy, Galsworthy and Bernard Shaw, so that though he certainly begins in time he leaves off a bit too soon. There are one or two of the moderns, such as Ernst Toller for instance, who would have fitted his theme exactly. And his theme is the problem of undeserved suffering. How can we reconcile the undeserved sufferings of humanity with supreme justice? Why should the good suffer? These are the questions and problems he imputes to the dramatists he has picked out and though the answers and half-answers he gets from them are tinged with a sentimental Christianity which becomes mawkish at times, he does put the questions and anyone who is interested may from his diagnosis discover a cure of his own.

This is a typical passage—he is discussing Goethe's "Faust." "In this we have the answer to our questionings—or, rather, such answer as our limited minds can give. In this we penetrate, in so far as we can, the secret mystery of personality, and bring a lamp of faith which helps us to look with steadfast eyes on the secret of Nature herself. We see that Love and Duty at their highest, are one, and that, rightly conceived, our life is one with the Spirit which binds the stars in their courses, which prescribes the bounds of the oceans and moves and throbs in the myriad forms and combinations which feed and minster to our senses. There is a Faust in each one of us, and also a Marguerite, a heavenly messenger, calling us with heavenly voice, if we will but listen, to follow the promptings of the higher self—the spirit of God within." And here follow some uplifting lines which sound like Browning-and-water and end up with what I have heard vicars describe as "a nice thought to take home with us."

"The Woman-Soul leadeth us
Upward and on."

It is easy to pick faults in this book. Its style is for the most part undistinguished even commonplace, and there is this rather windy rhetoric which I have noticed and which seems to blow from the churches. But one can skip the wind and dive in under the style, and though the exercise becomes fatiguing at times it is worth it. His subjects are great and few people can treat of greatness without getting some of its quality into themselves. Besides this he has discovered that Shaw is something more than a brilliantly funny turn: and that is more than can be said for many people. He quotes him: "I want to be thoroughly used up when I die, for the harder I work, the more I live. I rejoice in life for its own sake. Life is no brief candle for me. It is a sort of splendid torch which I have got hold of for the moment. . . ." and from this he deduces a doctrine which he suggests runs through the whole of the Shaw plays: a cry for "more abundant life." And from this, too, he gets what he conceives to be the one great message of the drama down the ages: freedom through service.

For all its air of research and profundity this book is for the most part very elementary, and in discussing the "Prometheus Bound" of Aeschylus Mr. Balmforth even "says a word or two about the Greek drama in general," explaining that the chorus in a Greek play was "something altogether different from our modern idea of a chorus." One would have thought that sort of thing hardly necessary in a serious work. But these explanations give the clue to the book: it is, for all its impressiveness, a simple work, and will upset nobody. It may even help a good many, and if it only sends its readers back on to the men of which it treats it will have done something.

Portraits in the Nude—concluded.

"'No'! Who are you saying 'no' to?" Dirk exclaimed, striking him suddenly on the head with his hand.

"No, baas," said Shilling, without even raising his voice, "you mustn't strike me, I am not a child."

"O, you're not a child?" said Dirk. "Go and fetch me a reim."

While he was fetching a reim the two brothers exchanged a few words, and then took off their coats and laid them on the wall. The morning was calm and cool. The sun was tranquil in a windless sky. Shilling returned with the reim.

"Do you know what this is for?" said Dirk, dangling it before him.

"No, baas," said Shilling, with his gentle smile.

"Undress yourself," said Dirk, "Make haste."

"No, baas," said Shilling, with his gentle smile.

The two brothers bound his wrists with the reim. He made no resistance. Frans produced a knife and ripped off Shilling's clothes. When he had done this, he jabbed the point of the knife, here and there, into the Kaffir's flesh. The two brothers bound Shilling to the wheel of the waggon. While they were whipping his face and stomach with their sjamboks, Takhaar, who had seen, from one of the windows of the house, what was going on, came out with his holy bell. He saw, in the scene before him, a symbolic sacrifice. He did not interfere with his sons. He stood, at some distance from them, his eyes half closed, and rang, slowly and solemnly, his bell.

Sara, who was returning, baby at back, from the valley, with a vessel of water on her head, heard the bell, and turned towards the house by a different path in order to see if anything was happening, that the master should be ringing his bell on a weekday, on a week-day in the morning. She arrived, past the eucalyptus trees, suddenly upon the scene, and screamed. She seized the bucket of water she was carrying and flung it with all her might at Frans. It fell short and wide of him, on its side. The water sprang out in the sun like a flash of glassy fire, and the bucket clattered on the stones with a tinny hollow sound. The frantic Sara ran to Takhaar, clutched at his arm, and cried to him to stop his sons from killing her husband. But Takhaar, whose lips were moving rapidly in prayer, changed the bell over into his other hand, and continued his sacrificial tolling. Sara caught sight of her husband's eyes. She pulled, dragged the baby off her back, and ran forward, holding it out at arm's length before those eyes, before those eyes, those eyes. But Shilling didn't see the child. Shilling was bound. Shilling offered no resistance. Shilling didn't utter a sound. Sara put the baby down on the ground, and flew at Dirk. But he waited for her, as he had waited once before, with open arms. The impact of her assault bore him over backwards, and he sat on the ground, holding Sara in his arms, tightly in his arms, while she struggled and trembled and panted and struggled. With the black woman quivering in his arms he could think of nothing but Poppy Fitzmichael. Sara's baby, which was fat, stood happily on all fours, collapsed, sat up laughing, grasped its feet with its hands, began to gurgle unknown words of innocence, tumbled like a baby mountebank. Frans kicked Shilling on the buttocks with his heavy boots, once, twice, three times. Sara screamed.

It was at this moment that Lily appeared, who had hurried down the mountain at the first ominous sound of Takhaar's bell. She was in time to hear the sickening sound of Frans's boots on Shilling's flesh. She felt, she told Cormorant afterwards, quite hollow, as though there was nothing inside her.

"Give me your knife," she said to Frans.

He gave it to her. She approached Shilling. His eyes were shut. His mouth was open, but his teeth were clenched, white and bloody. Blood was oozing out between them. His face and body were lacerated. Lily cut through the reim which bound him to the wheel. He fell forward on the ground, rolled over. There was dust on his wounds. She stooped and kissed his forehead.

"Come here," she said to Dirk and Frans. "Carry him into the house, and put him on my bed." The two brothers obeyed her without any hesitation. She followed them into the house. But as for Sara, she began to beat her body, her swaying body, with her hands, and began nodding her head, nodding her head, and screaming and screaming and screaming. Lily came back to console her. She could not be consoled, but suffered Lily to lead her by the hand into the house.

17. A LETTER.

BUDA-PESTH,
WEDNESDAY.

My Dear Lily,

I will come back to-morrow morning. Mr. Winterhalter says will you ask Mr. Van Ryn to have the rams brought down from the berg? He is coming over with me, and wants to get ten or twelve rams more, as he finds he will need them. Have you got any meat in the house? Don't worry, anyway, because Mr. Winterhalter had a fat hamel slaughtered this morning, and we are bringing half over with us to-morrow. It will be nice to get back.

With love,
M. VAN RYN.

18. A FAMILY GROUP.

When Cormorant got back to Obeliskal Zonnebloem Lily came out of the house to meet him. The day was hot for early spring. She wore a loose white dress embroidered with yellow. She had just come out of the kitchen and her arms were all powdery with flour. From the heat of the day and of the kitchen her face was flushed, and as she stood in the shade, laughing, her teeth seemed very white, her eyes sparkling with a brilliant langour. She seemed to quiver with laughter as gracefully as a tree quivers in the wind, or a fish in the water. How quiet it was at Zonnebloem! All you could hear was the distant, the almost inaudible, mountain-weeping of a bird. They both heard it. It must have been a signal for them to embrace. They embraced. He smelt of tobacco and she smelt of cloves.

He followed her along the passage. She stood at the dining room door and winked. Then she opened it and went in. It was an exciting moment.

The whole household could be seen grouped above and beyond her, it seemed, like a company of angels. They were all standing—that was what gave the heightened effect—and the room was cool and dark. All in that moment they seemed to Cormorant entirely united as a family, standing here, this warm morning, with warm colour in their morning flushed faces, bright-dark-eyed, full of an astonishing tenderness. It was charming, this exciting moment.

Under the lamp stood Takhaar, lean and clean and dignified. He is silent, as you might expect of a man who dwells in the perfect security of a saint. His face has acquired that delicate wax-like look, which in the beauty of life suggests the beauty of death, a mask-like look that is only found in certain faces between middle age and old age. Takhaar is silent, his hands, those hands, breaking the patriarchal bread.

Almost her husband's serenity rests in Minta, that admirable slapper-slippered houseloving woman, whose lips do not at present wear that fantastic smile with which she went to nagmaal, whose lips are now slightly compressed, at this time when she walks through a tranquil plain of life, a bunch of keys swinging from her slowly-swinging skirt. As a glass is filled with white wine she is filled with love. Her voice is tenuous and clear like tinted glass. Her eyes are clear like tinted love. She stood at the end of the table. In her hand was the brass coffee pot. So she would stand till the day of her death. That was her figure, the squareness of her breasts under a frilly white blouse, her bottlewaistedness, her fat stomach, the fullness of her skirts, her hair dragged up from her Mongolian cheeks; those were her wide white hands, her nearly old eyes.

Frans chews food and laps up coffee, Frans with his jutting beard, his dumb hands, his vague eyes. He walks in his sleep. Unlike Takhaar he does not indulge in religious speculations. He does not test propositions. He is one who follows his feet; the shadow of the old European; an inconstant friend; a dangerous lover. What child is hidden in this womb of silence?

Dirk has on a bright blue cotton shirt. In his face is the light of uninjured innocence. One regrets nothing if one is a Van Ryn.

Golgo is here, reclaimed, in a lace collar. The man-child becomes the child-man, and reverses the order of the world.

"It's nice to see you back again," Cormorant said to Mrs. Van Ryn.

"You're quite like one of the family, I'm sure," she said after an awkward pause.

Cormorant regarded this sentiment doubtfully. He turned it over as you would turn over a tickey to see if it had a hole in it. Lily could hardly contain her laughter. She winked so earnestly that Golgo said, with his mother's precise solemnity:

"Miss du Toit's winking."

Lily blushed.

"What are you winking at, Lily?" asked Dirk.

"Who's winking?" said Lily.

19. A PORTRAIT IN THE NUDE.

Lily was standing, late that night, before the looking-glass in her bedroom. Her clothes lay in a heep on a chair. They were still warm from contact with her body.

She balanced the candlestick on the top of her head, and watched, in the looking-glass, all the downglancing, shadows on her body. A spider on the ceiling felt on high the heat from the candle, and hurried away. She lifted her hands (and muscles and many lights and shadows moved with them) and took hold of her hair on either side of her head, and ran her fingers through it, in the candlelight. She took the candlestick and put it down on table. She stood, hands at hips, in an easy attitude, looking at herself in the glass. She clasped her hands at the back of her head. I shan't have to wait long for him, she thought. How I wish he would come to-night! If he could see me now——!

But there was his face—she could see it reflected in the glass, through the crook of her arm.

No, these things do not happen, she thought. How could he possibly be here? Her heart beat frantically. She turned round. Yes, there he was. She had a beautiful body; she gave it to Cormorant. You, O you, O Cormorant!

WILLIAM PLOMER.

THE END.

Correspondence.

To the Editor of "Voorslag,"

Sir,—

I hasten to rescue the remains of Mr. Mayer from the Charybdis of his colliding arguments. The argument by which he shows the superiority of Colonial to European culture is identically the same as that by which he shows the inferiority of native to Colonial culture. After claiming that we are so much "younger" than Europe, he does not hesitate to claim that we are 2,000 years "older" than the native. However, he allows himself a margin of 1,500 years, and says we are "2,000 or 500" years "older" than the native. If 1,500 years is of so little importance that it can be so sweepingly discarded, why make such a fuss about the remaining 500? If as Mr. Mayer suggests the opinions of two of your leading contributors were formulated to catch the applause of European aesthetes, is it likely that we should be expounding them out here for the benefit of South African anaesthetes? Yet even a world-wide aesthetic reputation is less ignominious than the local anaesthetic oblivion which envelopes most of the artistic efforts of Mr. Mayer's young and "virile" culture. God forbid that art should ever express the "soul" of such a small, rancidly-racial nation as ours. The soul of our nation is always being expressed in Eistedfodds, exhibitions of paintings by South African artists, and anthologies of bad poetry. If this is art, then the soul it expresses must be suffering from senile decrepitude. Let us rather believe that art is the conscience of a nation, troublesome perhaps, but like most consciences allowed no say in daily affairs. Mr. Mayer deplores our knowledge of European literature, art, and history. Having such a history of blunders behind us—what right have we to benefit by the experiences of other nations? Are we "degenerating" into a nation of thinkers? No, we are too "virile"!

With this comforting thought, "breathing" some fiery South African "spirit," let us resume our local anaesthesia and protract our childhood as a nation into a second childhood.

Yours faithfully,

ROY CAMPBELL.

Dear Sir,—

Miss Pamela Willmore by perpetrating—I know of no better word—"The Strandloopers," and with your aid, foisting it on unsuspecting readers, has a duty to perform. It is her bounden task to explain what she means by it. Perhaps my intelligence is lacking, but being inclined to be conceited, I decline to acknowledge the fact. Perhaps it has a subtle humour, too advanced for mere males to appreciate; perhaps it has a serious underlying warning to humanity, and South Africa in particular.

Still one more perhaps. If you as Editor, passed the "Strandloopers," perhaps you'll publish this letter despite my closing lines.

To Miss Pamela Willmore.

Madam, perform an easy task,
And answer questions I would ask.
Is it funny, is it sad?
Is it you or I who's mad?

Yours faithfully,

"ANTON."

VOORSLAG

A MAGAZINE OF SOUTH AFRICAN
LIFE AND ART.

Published by
A. C. Braby, Durban.

MSS. and all communications
should be addressed to Box 731, Durban.

Vol. I. September, 1926. No. 4.

Contents

VOORSLAG

A MAGAZINE OF SOUTH AFRICAN LIFE AND ART.

Published by A. C. Braby, Durban.

MSS. and all communications should be addressed to Box 731, Durban.

Vol. I. October, 1926. No. 5.

Contents

VOORSLAG

A MAGAZINE OF SOUTH AFRICAN
LIFE AND ART.

Published by
A. C. Braby, Durban.

MSS. and all communications
should be addressed to Box 731, Durban.

Vol. I. November, 1926. No. 6.

Contents

VOORSLAG

A MAGAZINE OF SOUTH AFRICAN LIFE AND ART.

Published by A. C. Braby, Durban.

MSS. and all communications should be addressed to Box 731, Durban.

Vol. I. December, 1926. No. 7.

Contents

VOORSLAG

A MAGAZINE OF SOUTH AFRICAN LIFE AND ART.

Published by A. C. Braby, Durban.

MSS. and all communications should be addressed to Box 731, Durban.

Vol. 1. January, 1927. No. 8.

Contents

VOORSLAG

A MAGAZINE OF SOUTH AFRICAN
LIFE AND ART.

Published by
A. C. Braby, Durban.

MSS. and all communications
should be addressed to Box 731, Durban.

Vol. 1. February, 1927. No. 9.

Contents

VOORSLAG

A MAGAZINE OF SOUTH AFRICAN
LIFE AND ART.

Published by
A. C. Braby, Durban.

MSS. and all communications should be addressed to Box 731, Durban.

Vol. 1. March and April, 1927. No. 10

Contents

VOORSLAG

A MAGAZINE OF SOUTH AFRICAN
LIFE AND ART.

Published by
A. C. Braby, Durban.

MSS. and all communications
should be addressed to Box 731, Durban.

Vol. I. May-June-July, 1927. No. II.

Contents

Published for the Proprietors by A. C. Braby, Box 731, Durban and Printed by The Knox Printing & Publishing Co., 36, Little Grev Street, Durban.

ERRORS IN THE 'VOORSLAG' TEXT

Vol. 1 no. 1 June 1926

p. 12	line 17:	for *bye-product* read *by-product*
	line 25:	for *vestigal* read *vestigial*
p. 13	line 1:	for *conspicious* read *conspicuous*
	line 2:	for *savory* read *savoury*
	lines 3, 5, 6:	for *palateable* read *palatable*
p. 17	line 4:	for *artizan* read *artisan*
p. 19	line 10:	for *whch* read *which*
	line 19:	for *Danmier* read *Daumier*
p. 20	line 18:	for *intelligencies* read *intelligences*
	line 21:	for *freize* read *frieze*
p. 21	line 4:	delete apostrophe in *still life's*
p. 22	line 12:	*in a* – not italics
p. 24	line 12:	for *Louve* read *Louvre*
p. 28	line 14:	for *wss* read *was*
	line 25:	for *selectd* read *selected*
p. 29	line 24:	for *kerel* read *kêrel*
p. 41	line 24:	for *affiicted* read *afflicted*
p. 42	line 20:	for *oruselves* read *ourselves*
p. 43	line 12:	for *tpye* read *type*
	line 26:	for *absorbtion* read *absorption*
p. 48	line 20:	for *sensilities* read *sensibilities*
p. 60	line 10:	for *imagiative* read *imaginative*
p. 63	line 2:	for *stubbonly* read *stubbornly*

Vol. 1 no. 2 July 1926

p. 4	line 5:	for *ones* read *one's*
	line 25:	for *catastrophies* read *catastrophes*
p. 5	line 20:	for *mass-conscious* read *mass-consciousness*
p. 13	line 5:	for *Your* read *You*
p. 15	line 6:	for *gleans* read *gleams*
p. 18	line 19:	for *after life* read *after-life*
p. 21	line 11:	for *Deceber* read *December*
p. 22	line 31:	for *bourgeoise* read *bourgeoisie*
p. 25	line 13:	for *he share* read *to share*
	line 25:	for *effected* read *affected*
		for *by reason by* read *by reason of*
p. 26	line 9:	for *L' Occident* read *L'Occident*
	line 13:	for *eloborately* read *elaborately*
p. 28	line 21:	after *knobkerries* insert comma
	line 22:	for *matelpiece* read *mantelpiece*
p. 32	line 11:	for *Ghandi* read *Gandhi*
p. 35	line 11:	for *An* read *And*
p. 39	lines 11, 15, 16:	for *ammuniesie* read *ammunisie*
	line 21:	for *vercordel* read *veroordeel*
p. 40	line 17:	for *ambiesie* read *ambisie*
	line 20:	for *by* read *hy*
	line 20:	for *rmy* read *rym*
	line 26:	for *geskiendenis* read *geskiedenis*
	line 33:	for *Partiot* read *Patriot*
	line 35:	for *Wêrde* read *Wêreld*
p. 41	line 1:	for *kinkerlik* read *kinderlik*
	line 10:	for *oorals* read *orals*
	line 18:	for *vroeér* read *vroëer*
	line 30:	for *gerôer* read *geroer*
p. 42	line 6:	for *veroorsâak* read *veroorsaak*
	line 7:	for *Langehoven* read *Langenhoven*
	line 9:	for *gebeurtinisse* read *gebeurtenisse*
	line 24:	for *verassend* read *verrassend*
	line 27:	after *lewe* delete *e*

	line 27:	for *Twede* read *Tweede*
p. 43	line 8:	for *twede* read *tweede*
p. 51	line 10:	after *Minta* close quotation marks
p. 52	line 2:	after *back?* close quotation marks
p. 64	line 15:	for *General* read *Generaal*

Vol. 1 no. 3 August 1926

p. 8	line 2:	for *Basuta* read *Basuto*
p. 16	line 1:	for *attittude* read *attitude*
p. 25	line 24:	for *flambouyant* read *flamboyant*
p. 27	line 3:	for *Corspronklike* read *Oorspronklike*
p. 28	line 7:	for *ky* read *hy*
p. 36	line 9:	for *Rosetti* read *Rossetti*
p. 38	line 3:	for *idiosyncracy* read *idiosyncrasy*
	line 17:	for *for* read *far*
p. 39	line 22:	for *spontoneous* read *spontaneous*
	line 28:	for *Leonade* read *Leonard*
p. 41	line 28:	for *eenue* read *eeue*
	line 31:	for *koorsteen* read *skoorsteen*
	line 33:	for *skoef* read *skroef*
	line 33:	for *skaduus* read *skadus*
p. 43	line 31:	for *katrol* read *kastrol*
p. 45	line 2:	for *goso* read *nog so*
p. 47	line 8:	for *neals* read *nails*
p. 51	line 20:	for *Munchester* read *Manchester*
p. 58	line 13:	for *heep* read *heap*

NOTES ON 'VOORSLAG'

To avoid repetitive notes, biographical information – on people who are mentioned frequently in the text of *Voorslag* or in the editorial material – has been given in the Index.

Voorslag, Vol. 1, No. 1 (June 1926)

Page

1 'Voorslag' means whip-lash.

3 'Why *Voorslag*' by M.W. – Maurice Webb. See Appendix D for Campbell's comment: '. . . such an apologetic little preface.'

5 'The Albatross' subsequently appeared in the volume *Adamastor* (1930).

10 'Beauty in Nature' is an extract from *Hollsm and Evolution* (1926) by Jan Christian Smuts. In *The Wayzgoose* Campbell satirized Smuts's 'Button-Holism' and Plomer, in *Double Lives* (1943), said: '"Beauty in Nature" advanced the proposition that beauty would be there even if we were not there to behold it. . . . [S]peculation of this kind has been to General Smuts what his paintbox has been to Mr Churchill' (p. 193).

17 'Cézanne' by Edward Roworth.

25 'Portraits in the Nude' subsequently appeared in *I Speak of Africa* (1927). See Plomer's comments on textual alterations, *Voorslag* Vol. 1, No. 3, p. 58 and note. Of Plomer's story Geoffrey Haresnape has written:

> Both works ['Portraits in the Nude' and *The Story of an African Farm*] exploit the motif of the farm in its empty landscape as a symbol for the isolation of each individual human being. Puritan dogmatism, which can lead to authoritarianism and to repressed behaviour, is explored in both. Olive Schreiner's Boer woman is in some respects the prototype for Plomer's Minta van Ryn, whilst Plomer's mountain-scaling, watchful and solitary Cormorant follows in the tradition of Waldo. Lyndall's questing

> spirit and her criticisms of conventional moral values find their fulfilment in the natural freedom of Lily du Toit. ('The *Voorslag* Movement and Olive Schreiner', Van Wyk Smith, Malvern & Don Maclennan (eds), *Olive Schreiner and After: Essays on Southern African Literature in Honour of Guy Butler* (1983), pp. 110–111.)

In his forthcoming article Stephen Gray adds:

> His 'Portraits' deals with crude power, sexuality and madness in an offensively patriarchal puritan environment. . . . Only Doris Lessing in 1950 (in *The Grass Is Singing*) would catch up with what we would now call this Fanonist-type insight into the interrelatedness of the horrors and crude beauties of the colonial enterprise and its apartheid psychology. . . . [Plomer] was the first modern psychological fiction-writer in South Africa. . . . ('William Plomer's Stories: The South African Origins of New Literature Modes', *Journal of Commonwealth Literature*, Leeds, Vol. 21, No. 3, 1986.)

Takhaar – literally 'branch-hair' (Afrikaans); contemptuous term for a backveld Afrikaner.

40 Slawkenbergius, an imaginary author in Sterne's novel *Tristram Shandy* (1760–67). He had a long nose himself and wrote a Latin treatise on noses.

52 Mary Ann Hughes, pen-name of Roy Campbell.

53 'The Strandloopers' (beachcombers), by Pamela Willmore, pen-name of William Plomer. The author did not include this poem in his *Collected Poems* (1960; 1973).

56 General J. B. M. Hertzog (1866–1942), Prime Minister of S.A. 1924–39.

57 'A Contemporary View of Van Gogh'. This was written by William Plomer. Mr E. J. Horniman was Plomer's uncle by marriage: see Plomer's *Autobiography* (1975 and 1984), pp. 40–41, 115–116.

Voorslag, Vol. 1, No. 2 (June 1926)

Page

13 Tielman Roos (1879–1935), Minister of Justice and architect of National Party victory at the polls 1924.

15 'A study of South African Poetry'. Campbell chooses his example from one of the many late nineteenth-century volumes of verse which hymned the 'mystery' of the wide outdoors. He was severely critical of 'veld and vlei' poetasters – who nevertheless helped to lay the foundations for his own successful incorporation of African elements in his poetry.

15–16 'the flag question'. In 1926–27 there was in Parliament a great deal of heated debate about the exact composition of the South African flag. The issue was related to the recent history of the country and to South Africa's status in the British Commonwealth, but Campbell's point is a very valid one.

16 Colonel F.H.P. Creswell (1866–1948), leader of the S.A. Labour Party.

20 'Gauguin' by Edward Roworth. This article draws heavily on the writings of artists and French art historians, e.g., *The Complete Letters of Vincent van Gogh* and *The Letters of Paul Gauguin to Georges Daniel de Mondfreid*, as well as (acknowledged on p. 31) Robert Rey's *Maîtres de l'Art Moderne*. Roworth's article prompted the following letters at the time in *The Star*, Johannesburg:

> The second number of *Voorslag* has a signed article on 'Gauguin'. The contributor adds this foot-note: 'For the extract from the letter of the Rev. V. and for much of the data of the foregoing article I am indebted to the monograph by M. Robert Rey in the *Maîtres de l'Art Moderne*.' Out of curiosity I turned up the book on Gauguin, and compared it with *Voorslag*'s article. I expected to find the same facts expressed and ordered differently. There were, however, so many sentences lifted almost intact that my curiosity was whetted. Therefore I read on and searched the *Voorslag* article for something which would not seem to be covered by the author's acknowledgements as to the origin of his data. Here is the passage I picked on: 'M. Ch. Chasse has told in detail the life led by the group in 1889 at Pouldu, while Armand

Seguin published in *L'Occident*, in 1903, an amusing description of the inn at Pouldu as adorned by Gauguin and his friends, the walls covered with arabesques and designs, window panes painted and turned into stained glass and lintels adorned with encouraging and arrogant phrases.'

Alas! it is straight from M. Rey, with the alteration of a couple of commas and two words. Is that covered by the expression of 'indebtedness' to M. Rey for 'data'?

* * *

It will be noted that the author of *Voorslag*'s essay expresses his indebtedness to 'the monograph by M. Robert Rey in the *Maîtres de l'Art Moderne*.' I am not a linguist, and my knowledge of the Frenchman's book was gained from a translation by F.C. de Sumichrast. If the editors of *Voorslag* wished to interest people in Gauguin why couldn't they have been frank about it? Why couldn't they have acknowledged that their article is a mere boiling down of Rey's book? And if they wanted to be very sincere they might have added that a complete English translation, with 40 illustrations (one appears in *Voorslag*) and bound in stiff covers, is published by John Lane for the price of two copies of *Voorslag*.

facing 21 'Head of Native Girl' by Anna de Schubert, amateur painter, wife of wealthy expatriate Estonian who was befriended by the Campbells.

32 '"Eunuch Arden" and "Kynoch Arden"', by Lewis Marston, pen-name of Roy Campbell. The article on the demise of the Romantic spirit in English poetry and the rise of Georgianism was inspired by Osbert Sitwell's pamphlet (see *Voorslag* Number 3, p. 34) *Who Killed Cock-Robin? Remarks on poetry, on its criticism, and, as a sad warning, the story of Eunuch Arden* (1921). Sitwell's pamphlet holds up, as examples of the second-rate in poetry, Tennyson's 'Enoch Arden' and several poems by Georgian poets, as in the following reference to Sir John Squire's 'The Rugger-Match':

> Poetry is not, as our 'man-in-the-street' reviewers imagine, a football kicked down any mean, squat street by any fool who passes.

Whistle! A kick! A rush, a scramble, a scrum
And now I'll go home, and open a bottle of port.

Poetry is more like a crystal globe, with Truth imprisoned in it, like a fly in amber (p. 6).

The Georgian poets were those who came to prominence during the reign of George V. Campbell, however, uses the word as a term of abuse for those writers whom he associated with Edward Marsh's 'Georgian Poetry' anthologies, especially Vita Sackville-West, Sir John Squire and Marsh himself.

37 Campbell was inspired by and translated works by both Baudelaire and Rimbaud; the latter's 'Le Bateau Ivre' provided a model for *The Flaming Terrapin*.

40 Die Patriotbeweging. Often called die Eerste Afrikaanse Beweging, this was a vigorous cultural movement which flourished from about 1870 till about 1900. Its aim was to promote Afrikaner language, literature and values. Its main vehicle was the weekly journal, *Die Afrikaanse Patriot.*

General Piet Joubert (1831–1900), leading official, politician and commandant-general in the South African Republic (Transvaal).

Gustave S. Preller (1875–1943), journalist, historian, critic and poet.

41 Eugene Marais (1871–1936), poet, fiction-writer and ethologist.

Pieter C. Schoonees (1891–1970), literary critic and theorist.

42 Jan Celliers (1865–1940), popular poet.

Jan de Waal (1871–1937), writer of novels of intrigue.

Cornelis J. Langenhoven (1873–1932), versatile writer and politician.

Die Tweede Taalbeweging, or die Tweede Afrikaanse Beweging. This was the second important Afrikaner cultural movement. Set in motion after the Anglo-Boer War, it was far more broadly based than the earlier movement (see Note on p. 40, above). It fought on two fronts (against Milner's anglicizing policy, and against the proponents of Nederlands), it brought about the recognition of Afrikaans in schools, in the N.G. Church and in the State, and it produced some literature of high quality.

Totius, pen-name of J.D. du Toit (1877–1953), poet, scholar and theologian.

C. Louis Leipoldt (1880–1947), versatile writer and journalist.

62 'To a Young Man with Pink Eyes', which is evidently addressed satirically to Lewis Reynolds the sponsor of *Voorslag*, subsequently appeared in the volume *Adamastor* (1930).

64 'Marginalia' contributed by Roy Campbell.

66 Anna von Schubert. See 'Head of Native Girl' referred to above, where she is called Anna de Schubert.

***Voorslag*, Vol. 1, No. 3 (August 1926)**

Page

8 'Pumpkins' by Sarah Gertrude Millin (1888–1968). See Appendix D for Campbell's comments on possible contributions by Millin to *Voorslag*. By the time 'Pumpkins' appeared in Number 3 Campbell no longer exercised editorial control.

15 South African Institute of Art, founded by Leo François in 1926.

16 Leo François (1870–1938), president of the Natal Society of Artists during the late 1920s and of the South African Institute of Art.

17 Hendrik Pierneef (1886–1957), S.A. painter, one of whose San sketches appears on the covers of *Voorslag*.

'. . . the son of D.C. Boonzaier', the S.A. painter Gregoire Boonzaier (1909–).

19 'Psychology of Race' by Ethelreda Lewis (1875–1946), S.A. author best known for her editorship of the 'Trader Horn' books in the late 1920s and for her novel *Wild Deer* (1933). See Appendix I for Campbell's comments on Lewis.

23 'Music in South Africa' by Maurice Webb, who, in the mid-1920s, lectured on the appreciation of music at the Technical College in Durban.

27 'Die Liefde van Catullus' by Theodore Haarhoff (1892–1971), a well-known professor of classics. ('I am not going to have any

"mossies", even Roman ones, twittering in the pages of *Voorslag*' – Campbell quoted by Van der Post in a letter to the University of Natal Press, 1979.)

29 Milton's 'On the University Carrier'.

40 'Nimrods van die See' was to form the basis of Van der Post's book *The Hunter and the Whale* (1967).

58 In the Preface to *I Speak of Africa* (1927) Plomer commented on the concluding section of his story 'Portraits in the Nude':

> In June we started a monthly review, *Voorslag*, and in spite of continual interference we were able to produce two tolerable numbers in which the interests of business men, party politicians, paint fanciers, half-dyed blue-stockings, and half-witted catch-penny ink-sprayers were reduced to a minimum; and in which life, art, and letters were judged by international and aesthetic rather than by parochial or patriotic standards. Before the appearance of the third number, however, we were asked to put ourselves in submission to a 'business editor'.
>
> We consequently resigned, abandoning *Voorslag* to this commercial dignitary, a genial and respectable trades-person, to whom I conceded the right of publishing the conclusion of 'Portraits in the Nude' (most of which had come out in the first two numbers), in order to preserve for readers of the paper the integrity of the story. For this concession I was rewarded by seeing my work printed in a form differing from that in which I wrote it. Colonial squeamishness had demanded in the last scene not only a fig-leaf but an illegal operation. The deliberate and inexcusable mutilation of a MS. is typical of the colonial attitude to culture, an attitude which might be compared, not unjustly, with that of a dog to a lamp-post. However, that artists cannot live in South Africa is a fact that has been fully demonstrated by the lives of Thomas Pringle, Olive Schreiner, and others.
>
> 'Portraits in the Nude' is here printed for the first time as it was written.

A PORTRAIT IN THE NUDE

Lily was standing, late that night, before the looking-glass in her bedroom. Her clothes lay in a heap on a chair. They were still warm from contact with her body.

She made grimaces. She experimented with her smile and with her eyebrows. She put the candlestick on the floor, and tilted the looking-glass to see what lights and what shadows found themselves on her legs, loins, belly, breasts. She raised her arms slowly, and slowly waved them, to watch the increasing and decreasing shadows in her armpits, like two dark yawns, and the bulging and extending repose of her pectoral muscles. She turned round. She looked over her shoulder. She admired the curves of her back and bottom. There was a faint network of veins on her hips. She wagged her hips. She stooped down (and long shadows flew out behind her, along the floor, and up the wall) to pick up the candlestick, and although she wasn't fat several tender creases appeared across her flanks.

She stood up again and balanced the candlestick on the top of her head, and watched, in the looking-glass, all the downglancing, formerly upthrown, shadows on her body. A spider on the ceiling felt the heat from the candle on high, and hurried away. She lifted her hands (and muscles and many lights and shadows moved with them) and took hold of her hair on either side of her head, and ran her fingers through it, in the candle-light. She took the candlestick and put it down on a table. She stood, hands at hips, in an easy attitude, looking at herself in the glass. She clasped her hands at the back of her head. I shall not have to wait long for him, she thought. How I wish he would come to-night! If he could see me now–!

But there was his face – she could see it reflected in the glass, through the crook of her arm.

No, these things do not happen, she thought. How could he possibly be here? Her heart beat frantically. She turned round. Yes, there he was. She had a beautiful body; she gave it to Cormorant. You, O you, Cormorant!

60 The reply, by Pamela Willmore (William Plomer), to this letter by 'Anton' is reprinted here from *Voorslag* Number 4:

Sir,–

Your correspondent, Mr 'Anton', insists that it is my bounden duty to reply to his questions. To the pathetic little interrogatory billet-doux with which he serenades me, the following reply may be a little callous, but he is welcome to whatever satisfaction he can derive from it.

You ask if it's you who are mad–
  Ah no, let me lull the suspicion!
You ask 'is it funny or sad?'
  And here is my humble admission–
It is sad that a mooncalf should hurry
  So rashly to question a bard,
And I must be mad that I worry
  Poor creature! to squash you so hard.

PAMELA WILLMORE

APPENDICES

A Roy Campbell to Edward Roworth, 1925.
(Campbell Collection, South African Library, Cape Town.)

My dear Ned,

I enclose my belated poem for Sibbett. I could work nothing into a really satisfactory form and was therefore forced to wait until I did this. I shall write to Sibbett and explain my slackness.

Lewis [Reynolds] has returned. He and Webb had a discussion about the magazine, in which Webb converted him to a 'business' point of view. The 'business' part of it seemed to be procrastination, vagueness and miasma. I said to Lewis that it would be impossible for me to co-operate with anything but the most decided enthusiasm: That you and Plomer and I had decided that nothing ambiguous or shilly-shally was to be allowed: and that if affairs were not ready in a month we would have to seek help elsewhere. The effect was satisfactory. Lewis has buckled to like a sensible fellow.

The most important thing is to have one meeting just to satisfy Webb and Lewis. Webb must be treated with an appearance of respect. We must pat him on the back every now and again and tell him he is all right. I had to explain to him that his manifesto was a little in the air but he took it very well. It is most unfortunate that you can't come to this bloody meeting.

You are the only person that can save the thing from being run in a gregarious fashion with six or seven editors from the appearance of things at present. I can't thump my fist and say 'I am the only competent person!' But I know from experience that for a little gang to run it is impossible. It'll degenerate into a Library Group[1] or a Natal

Society of writers. Garnett[2] in writing to me the other day from England says: 'It is great news about *Voorslag*. It should be of great importance of gathering into a focus the most intelligent people in the country. But everything depends on the man at the tiller. Principles and intentions are all very well but they must take form in the Man, and if he is wanting, nothing happens.' This is the real crisis of the whole thing and I am depending on you to pull it through. I could, with an effort, get all the power into my own hands, as I am not faced with much moral resistance. But I fear that Webb and Lewis look on *Voorslag* in an all too human way and it might prejudice my position as editor if I were to do so.

It would be better if you could take a holiday and come up here.[3] But if not, write to Lewis. Do not write as if I had warned you about what I fear is possible about the running of *Voorslag*. None of my fears have taken a definite form but I am quick in sensing an atmosphere. Lewis is very well disposed to both of us and it will be very easy, if you throw in your vote on my side, to save it from being run as a lady's home journal. I know that it will only need a word from you.

Write to Lewis at once, if you can't come, and write as if you had not heard from me. I'll write again soon.

Your article to the Tech. magazine was fine!! That's the stuff.

I see Neville Lewis has had a successful show in the Leicester Galleries. It's fine that S.A. is getting decently appreciated at last.

Mary and Tess send their love.

Yours affectionately,
Roy

B 'A South African Magazine: Is *Voorslag* What It Should Be?' by Sarah Gertrude Millin (*Rand Daily Mail*, Johannesburg, 16 June 1926)

Something is happening in South Africa. Something is stirring. There is consciousness in the land. There is the ferment of growth. These are a few of the manifestations of the rising spirit: A social restlessness, a political awareness, a concern – not necessarily beneficial – about the natives and the problems they present, an artistic awakening.

At this appropriate moment comes to birth – of all places, in the reactionary Durban – a halfcrown monthly magazine which calls itself *Voorslag*, and proposes to devote itself to 'the life and art of South Africa and the development of the South African people,' to the 'attempt to keep in contact with contemporary thought in Europe and America,' and to 'the consideration of social and political questions free from party and racial prejudice.' . . . 'Whatever concerns South Africa,' says the Foreword, 'concerns *Voorslag*.'

Now this is splendid. This is what we need very badly. Yet, in the circumstances, is *Voorslag* quite what it ought to be? Ought it really to be so reminiscent of *The* (American) *Dial*?

The Dial, for those who can admire sincerity, whatever its form, who can see the straining towards freedom and advancement through a fog of pretentiousness, lit here and there by a flash of real genius, *The Dial* is for such people a production of a certain significance.

But America is a great and rich country, full of literary vehicles. It has not only the gargantuan dailies and Sunday papers, the lavish weeklies and monthly magazines; it has also periodicals of first-class quality like *The Nation, The Atlantic Monthly,* and *The American Mercury.* It has, in addition, the largest reading population in the world. America can afford to gratify whatever taste it chooses. There is room – not much room, according to statistics, but still, a foothold – for papers like *The Dial*. But dare South Africa, in its barrenness and need, so limit itself?

Narrow in Appeal

For, in effect, *Voorslag*, with all its gallant ambitions, is deliberately narrow in its appeal and deliberately wide in its contemptuous exclusions. Its prophets are the prophets of *The Dial*: the Sitwells, Mr Clive Bell, Mr Roger Fry and Mr T. S. Eliot. Its gods are Van Gogh and Cézanne, Dostoevsky, Marcel Proust and James Joyce – though, in spite of Mr Eliot, one sincerely hopes not Miss Gertrude Stein.

Some of these names occur in this first number of *Voorslag*, someone ventures to assume. The fact of the matter is that *Voorslag*, for all its South African flavour, is a branch of a well-defined overseas group, and one may therefore guess fairly accurately what its attitude towards Life and Art is going to be.

However, that doesn't matter. *Voorslag* is not exactly what it thinks it is. It is not quite original – for it has merely adopted one ready-made set of ideas instead of another ready-made set of ideas. But it is young and honest and romantic and vigorous, and because it is young and honest and romantic and vigorous it is also interesting and rather moving, and worthy of assistance and support.

In addition, there is some first-rate capacity behind it, and it is excellently produced.

It has secured for its opening number a contribution by General Smuts. General Smuts, as everyone knows, is more than a politician – he is a philosopher and a scientist, with a great gift of language. His opening address at Oudtshoorn to the Association for the Advancement of Science most deeply impressed scientists overseas. His essay on 'Beauty in Nature' gives *Voorslag* weight and serenity.

Mr Roy Campbell has a poem, 'The Albatross', which is after the style of *The Flaming Terrapin*, and if only one had not seen that really magnificent performance first, one might have been more startled by the conception and imagery of 'The Albatross'.

Mr Edward Roworth writes with clarity and vigour on Cézanne – his life, work and his personality.

Mr William Plomer, the young author of *Turbott Wolfe*, a novel of genuine talent, quality and underlying feeling, but too violent and self-conscious, does a series of notes and sketches, which he calls 'Portraits in the Nude'. They exhibit the same capacity for handling words as *Turbott Wolfe*, and the same sense of style, but, except in two or three of the longer essays, they rather fail to come off. Mr Plomer, if one is prepared to consider placidly a negrophile bias which is so strong that it causes a lack of general balance, contributes also the best review in *Voorslag* – one on Dr Norman Leys's book, *Kenya.*

Other Reviews

The other reviews are by Mr Roy Campbell, Miss Mary Ann Hughes and Miss Pamela Willmore.

Miss Mary Ann Hughes writes offensively and inaccurately about Leo Tolstoi. 'Tolstoi's kink is fairly obvious. As a young man he rioted himself sick. He gave way to his lusts and thoroughly gluttonised himself, with the result that his constitution suffered. At the age of thirty he was bald and toothless. What was there left for him to do but to become a moralist? He fled to the arms of middle-class respectability for protection. Surfeited to sickness, his whole attitude to the joys of physical existence was soured and warped. He was irritated by the physical paradise which he could no longer enjoy and turned his face away in a doleful scrutiny of the soul. He became the trumpet of the Philistines.'

This is truly terrible. It must not be allowed to happen again.

Miss Pamela Willmore contributes some verse, and is of the opinion that Mr George Moore is as to one-half of him a querulous, irritable spinster, whose 'rather treacly taste in poetry, pure and watery prose and petulant jealousy of his contemporaries' may be forgiven him, since, in any case, he is no longer taken very seriously by people of subtler understanding.

Finally, Mr Roy Campbell reviews very justly and appreciatively *Turbott Wolfe*, and the collected works of Mr T. S. Eliot. 'To read Mr Eliot's poems,' he says, 'is to realise the necessity for new values in modern life. There must be a great distinction in human consciousness; we must gibe, sneer and ridicule our venerable reviewers into epileptic fits. We have plenty of muck to clear out of the way before we can start the great work of reconstruction.'

He here, apparently, crystallises the spirit of *Voorslag.*

C 'Poet Resents Criticism. Roy Campbell on *Voorslag* – Not Exclusive' (*Rand Daily Mail*, Johannesburg, 24 June 1926)

Sir,

As the perusal of the first number of *Voorslag* seems to have deranged Mrs Millin's equilibrium, I feel that it is up to me, as literary editor, to help her to regain it.

She has, curiously enough, identified the aims of *Voorslag* with those of *The Dial*, an American monthly, and she hastens with superb impertinence to attribute to our contributors a long list of 'gods and prophets' in whom they believe. It is neither a law that contributors to the same paper should believe in the same 'gods or prophets,' nor is it a necessity that a well-run magazine should have any 'gods or prophets' at all. Half of those, which she attributes to us, I regard more in the light of Aunt Sallies than of prophets.

Surely it is possible for one paper respectfully to mention such household names as Cézanne, Dostoevsky and Van Gogh without either being suspected of deifying them or being identified with any other paper which happens to do so? The *Huisgenoot* has published some extremely intelligent articles on Cézanne and Van Gogh. But that is no reason why it should be identified with *The Dial*. Why *The Dial*? There must be at least five thousand papers in the world which are capable of mentioning great writers and artists with respect.

All intelligent readers are prepared to 'consider placidly the strong negrophile bias' which characterises the work of Herman Melville, Gauguin, Olive Schreiner and Couperus, who are about the only great artists one can associate with the Southern Hemisphere. Why should not intelligent South Africans do the same with their only living novelist? Alone among South African journalists, Mrs Millin fails to realise that 'Portraits in the Nude' by William Plomer is a story and not a series of 'sketches and essays.' She should read things before she ventures to criticise them.

Leaving out of account the fact that the circulation of *Voorslag* is not limited to South Africa, the success of the first number shows that there is ample foothold for it in South Africa. Good taste is not limited to America. Mrs Millin again underrates the intelligence of

South African readers by saying that *Voorslag* is 'contemptuously exclusive.' 'In our barrenness and need,' she says, 'dare South Africa so limit itself?' At the time she wrote these words, I believe, a letter was rapidly traversing the veld in the direction of Mrs Millin from the business editor of *Voorslag* to invite Mrs Millin to submit contributions for our approval.

So far from worshipping the 'gods' of *The Dial*, so far from being at all exclusive, *Voorslag* in its 'barrenness and need' had been driven to pay homage to the 'gods' of *Good Housekeeping*! Yet even *Good Housekeeping*, bulky as it is, has probably to exclude a few of the MSS. sent to it, if not from any sense of discrimination, at least from the point of view of space.

Yours biliously,
Roy Campbell

Natal

D Roy Campbell to Maurice Webb, June/July 1926. (Campbell Collection, Killie Campbell Africana Library, Durban.)

My dear Webb,

I had already replied to Mrs Millin's article when your message came. It was a far more impertinent article than the *Mercury* snippet had led me to believe, and I could not pass it over. It only concerns the literary part of *Voorslag* and the literary prestige of the paper, for which I am solely responsible. Both Roworth and Plomer agree that it was essential to retaliate. People must not be led to believe that they can misrepresent the aims of *Voorslag* with impunity. She attacks. I retaliate. Now we are quits, I shall be quite willing to consider any of her work for *Voorslag*. I took no advantage of her – I simply applied her own form of reasoning to herself to show what an ill-bred little hussy she is. I have since verified every single word of Mary Ann's article, it is accurate in every detail.[4] Don't accept anything from

Mrs Millin unless I see it first. It will be fatal to *Voorslag* to publish anything as muddle-headed as was her article to the *Rand Daily Mail*. Every article in *Voorslag* must be like armour without a single chink, and it must have here and there a few spikes sticking out to warn off the journalists. We will never relieve the 'barrenness and need' of South Africa by being 'barren and needy' ourselves which is evidently what Mrs Millin wants us to be.

One can't introduce new ideas into a stale country by being meek and modest. We shall merely have the flies sitting on us. If you had not put in such an apologetic little preface and if you had left at the back that list of extracts which I put there, journalists would not have dared to be so patronising. You removed this without asking my permission – damn you! Why don't you look after the business part of it and leave the literary part to me. You would be far better looking after the business. Castle, Sibbett and even unknown people have written to Roworth and myself asking why it isn't in such bookshops as Anderson's in Jo'burg and why it can't be got in Capetown. That's your job. It takes me hours of thinking to balance the magazine properly; a magazine is like a very delicate machine and one can't allow people to go and put their clumsy feet through it behind one's back. For God's sake don't touch a word of this number. I know exactly what I am doing with it. If you play any more tricks behind my back I'll chuck the whole thing up.

Don't read anything to your library group. I understand that you read my 'Albatross' *before it was published* without asking my permission – good God, man, what are things coming to? It's the damnedest bit of impertinence I ever heard of in my life. You will have to change your tactics if we are going to get on together.

Yours sincerely
Roy Campbell

If you can't observe the ordinary laws of editorial etiquette you must not expect me to take any notice of messages warning me not to write to Mrs Millin. Even if it had come in time, it had nothing to do with me. For God's sake don't put anything into *Voorslag* without letting me see it.

E '*Voorslag* Again' (*Cape Times*, 31 July 1926)

A cryptic message, sent from Natal, which appeared yesterday, announced changes in the staff of *Voorslag*, the second number of which has just appeared. Mr Roy Campbell and Mr William Plomer, it seems, are no longer to be responsible for the editorial side of the venture. It would be polite to express surprise and disappointment at this; but need we be polite? To tell the truth, the second number of *Voorslag* is as disappointing yet as provocative as the first; there is little quality but considerable stimulus in it. Unfortunately, the provocativeness is largely due to inaccuracy, and this dooms the stimulus to be ephemeral and unsound. Inaccuracy is the strength of satire but the weakness of criticism, and in their high-astounding way the Voorslagians are aspirant critics; yet being inaccurate they are very bad critics. Mr Roworth, who contributes blameless and slightly Victorian commentaries, and who is entirely in the wrong galley here – even Mr Roworth is not a good critic. The beefy gentleman who cuts cigars with a twenty-foot stock whip upon the music hall stage may not be intellectual; but he could teach Messrs Campbell, Plomer and their coterie the essentials of their enterprise, since his lash falls in the proper place to do its work. An inaccurate lash is a debased instrument, and it is childishness to snap it at all and sundry. Nor can there be any great achievement in using it as a scourge instead of a guide to the herd. *Voorslag* is inaccurate both in its purposes and in their development. Its sponsors may feel with the Jesuits that the errend pardoneth much, and that the mission of fertilising the vegetable intellect of South Africa is sufficient to atone for all shortcomings. Must Shelley pause to con his line? But Shelley's purposes were crystal-clear, and there was more in his *credo* than destructiveness and flippancy. A *credo* is *Voorslag's* earliest need. When the *Yellow Book* appeared as the mouthpiece of one of the best-fortified minor movements in literature, Symons expounded in the first number the decadent gospel with unequalled directness and delicacy. This exposition focussed decadent impulses, provided a dynamic nucleus, boxed the decadent compass. Without some similar directional indication, *Voorslag* will never be dynamic, and unless it becomes vastly more accurate, it will assuredly never be dynamitic, as its parents seem fondly to expect it to be. It is a sad thought, but let's face it; even beautiful young men must aim at something if they wish to hit anything.

The departure of Mr Roy Campbell and Mr William Plomer from *Voorslag* may show that its promoters understand all this. Even if a certain sneering ferocity did constitute an artistic method, and if the sad assurance of futility did guarantee an exploitable point of view, *Voorslag*, under its original control, would still be a long way from acquiring merit as an organ of purpose, since it is not even accurate in ferocity and futility.The truth of the matter is that Mr Roy Campbell has been a most unfortunate leader for this enterprise. Like many better men before him, he has succumbed to the vice of epithets. Epithets are the most unmanageable device of words. They killed Positivism before its time, and they ruined all but a fraction of Walt Whitman. Mr Campbell probably handles epithets better than Whitman; they are rarely less than art with him, but that does not make them arguments. This distinction is well illustrated in his two contributions to the second number of *Voorslag*. He addresses a poem in his customary style to a man with pink eyes, and a clever little poem it is. It is compounded of epithets which, under close scrutiny, reveal themselves as largely inaccurate. Yet the sprightliness of their employment, and the dash of their mode, do go some way to excuse their inaccuracy. Pride of place in the same number is given to his long article upon the subjection of the world in general and of South Africa in particular to bourgeoise ideology. Here the epithetal method is again employed, and the result is a *mélange* of foolishness which might be talked – but assuredly would never have been written down – in second-class circles in Chelsea. The most inarticulate member of the bourgeoise herd could be very impolite to what Mr Campbell conceives to be his facts but what are in reality only his epithets. Premises and deductions alike are grossly inaccurate, and some of the attempts at paradox would make even Chelsea writhe. Mr Campbell is much too clever – and much too much the artist – to have been led into such a display if his literary method had not betrayed him. He cannot make arguments out of epithets, and he would do well to remain in his original milieu.

The herd, says Mr Campbell, are the prey of fetishes. That is very true, but so are these impermanent Voorslagians. Their twin 'Mumbo-Jumbos' are youth and damnation, and neither is a very certain obsession. The current number of *Voorslag* praises Whitman and sneers at General Smuts; yet at Cambridge, when very young, General Smuts praised Whitman too fulsomely to find a publisher. He was too youthful even for the emancipated 'nineties. As for damnation, the vegetable mind has compensations that the Archangels do not share. Yet if there is damnation for the one, there does not seem to be any particular escape for the other. The slanging of the other man's fetish is amusing only if it is well done. This second number of *Voorslag* contains very little else; and as a whole it is pitiably poorly done. This seems to have been a pretty general verdict; so exit Mr Roy Campbell and Mr William Plomer. It will be interesting to see what their successors make of *Voorslag*, which, hitherto, has been sacrificed to a fetish of adolescence. Youth is a grand thing; but it is not uncommon or very remarkable after all.

F Roy Campbell to C. J. Sibbett, July 1926.
(Campbell Collection, South African Library, Cape Town.)

Umdoni Park
Sezela

My dear Sibbett,

I have just had a violent row with Roworth and *Voorslag*. Myself and family are completely stranded and I have neither employment, health nor money.

For political reasons, because Plomer and I are negrophilists, the founders of *Voorslag*, including Roworth, have intrigued to get me to resign. The others were perfectly clean but Roworth was extremely dishonest and when I showed him what he had been doing could only make a feeble attempt to defend himself. He has throughout pretended to be on my side and encouraged me in what I was doing – only to join with the others at the last moment and use some very dishonest arguments which, when I exposed, he made no attempt to defend but just blushed and looked silly.

Mary is trying to find work as a lady-help and I have a very bad lesion in my spine which I can only get cured in England.[5] Therefore I am asking you to send me fifty pounds.[6] I shall never be able to repay it. I am asking it as a gift. You are about the only person in the country I have not made enemies with. My mother is in England and I am without any resources whatever. I am too ill to work. We are going to put our children in a crèche and wait till I can get money to go to England, where we have friends. None of my relations will look at me because of the opinions I have expressed in *Voorslag*. I can only offer as a feeble return for your help to dedicate one of the three sections of my next book of poems (now complete) to you.[7] As the other two dedicatees are Mary and Plomer, I cannot offer you any higher honour in my own way.

We are staying on here for another two weeks and I should be grateful if you could help us.

Yours sincerely
Roy Campbell

P.S. Please answer me at once whether you can help me or not, I am absolutely on tenterhooks.

G Edward Roworth to C. J. Sibbett, 5 August 1926.
(Campbell Collection, South African Library, Cape Town.)

The Marine Hotel
Durban

My dear old Cecil,

I was delighted to meet Cecil [Mrs Sibbett] yesterday. It was a lucky chance as I had not been in town for over three weeks and will not be back again until the 18th. You will be glad to hear that I never saw her looking better and ever so bright and charming! I gave her a full and intimate account of all that has happened since my return in regard to *Voorslag*. I have reluctantly come to the conclusion that after all you were right in your fears that his (Campbell's) first poem might also be his last. The man who reaches the height of pure poetry once only and then is 'cleaned out' is a far from uncommon type in literary history. In a year and a half he has produced 'The Albatross', a painful effort to recapture the fervour of the *Terrapin*, the poem which you did not think up to the standard of *The Waste Paper Basket*,[8] 'The Young Man with the Pink Eyes' [sic], unmitigated tripe, (intended for Lewis Reynolds by the bye) and as a prose effort 'Fetish Worship in South Africa'. Well, I need not ask what you think of *that* cheap nonsense! *Voorslag* has been a bitter disappointment to me. Not one of its aims as put forward in the preliminary statement has been even attempted, not to say attained. I think Plomer's influence has been bad. I am pleased to think that I told them all, including Mary Campbell, who says 'no one in South Africa is fit to criticise *Turbott Wolfe*', that I did not like the book at all and thought it was a pity he published it! This was received in complete silence – probably a silence of horror not unmixed with pity.

I see poor old John X.[9] has gone. If the Old Mutual or any body of admirers are thinking of a memorial to him I want to let you know that my portrait of John X. since its return from Wembley has been stored at Isaacsohn and Wollen and could be seen there or sent anywhere required. It is *the* portrait of Merriman.

Always your friend,
Edward

H 'The Voorslaggers and their Victims' (*The Natal Advertiser*, Durban, 21 August 1926)

Thackeray said once that to be mentioned by Gibbon was like having one's name inscribed on the dome of St Paul's Cathedral. It is a great declension from Gibbon to the editorial columns of *The Natal Advertiser*; but it is no less decline from Henry Fielding (about whom Thackeray was speaking at the time) to *Voorslag*. What, probably, associated this hotchpotch of notions in the present writer's head was the remembrance that Thackeray's *mot* was contained in his lectures on the 'English Humorists,' and one cannot, for the life of him, think of the *Voorslag* gentlemen as anything other than South African humorists. There is humour – and humour: nor is the word being used in the present instance in the high and rare sense that is its proper attribute. A great humorist, like Dickens, Thackeray himself, or Swift or Goldsmith, makes you smile wistfully through eyes glinting with tears. *Voorslag* merely makes one grin.

The third issue lies before one at the moment, and, speaking quite soberly, one doesn't quite know what to do about it. It is so obviously well-meaning; its writers are so obviously impressed by one another; it has so obviously youth's utter finality about it; and it is, oh! so barren of the ghost of a smile at its own fathomless fatuity. Where but in *Voorslag* would one find on the very first page (a whole page to itself, by the way) this sort of thing?

ANNOUNCEMENT

I have much pleasure in announcing my resignation from *Voorslag*.

ROY CAMPBELL

How fearfully banal! How inimitably absurd! How charged with the ethics of the nursery or, at best, the lower fourth! *Voorslag* is supposed to set the tone in plain living and high thinking in South Africa. Frankly, both Mr Roy Campbell and the present editors of the paper ought to be slapped for such a public pageant of mutual childishness.

Poor Old Journalists

That announcement – admirable only in its clarity and briefness – may be regarded as the First Depression in the issue. But it is not the only one. A month ago, the then contributors made mighty laughter over the third-rate platitudes of modern journalism. Well, all we want to say is this: that a great deal in this month's *Voorslag* comes very near itself to being journalism of a fair standard. Its chief failure lies in the fact that it is hard to say precisely what the writers are getting at, or even to believe that they themselves know what they are talking about. With these deficiencies remedied (and Voorslaggers have youth on their side) they may yet live to adorn the pedestrian calling of the daily chroniclers or political pamphleteers; a calling not despised by poets like Milton, moralists like Swift, philosophers and critics like Coleridge and humorists like Dickens. But they have a long way to go!

Meantime *Voorslag* introduces its readers to more South African poetry. The King is dead; long live the King. (No! That's not the title of any one of its contributions; heaven forbid!) But, just to show that Mr Roy Campbell's resignation has not dammed the spring of poetry at its source, another Celt steps into the poet's place of honour. It is true the spring he talks about is called 'Bleached Spring' (we don't know whether that is the kind of spring that is not far behind the Double Dyed Winter that Shelley wrote about and that Mr Hutchinson, the eminent novelist, made so popular) but it is good going all the same. It shows one how poetry can be written nowadays. All you have to do is write a slab of readable prose and then cut it into uneven lengths. Any lengths will do, so long as no two commit the unpardonable offence of being equal, which (as Euclid would declare) would be absurd. And, after all, why not? God made countless millions of men and women and no two of them ever looked alike. Why, then, should the modern poet – a man made in God's image, but, of course, much less old-fashioned – be content with a less diversity of gifts. Says our *Voorslag* poet, as he clinches his outburst: *'Perhaps spring is not what it was in the old days,'* and one of two rejoinders leaps to the lips at once. Either, *'Perhaps poetry is not what it was in the old days,'* or (apologetically), 'Eno's, my dear chap, Eno's always at the change of the season.'

The Empire of Dullness

Poetry first – then the unleashed and contradictory chatter of the highbrows. Mr Edward Roworth – that painter of delightful pictures – forgets Ruskin's maxim that directly a man can do anything well he ceases talking about his craft, and he writes engagingly about art in South Africa, ending up with the claim that 'our people as a whole have a spacious outlook, and bring to the art of life an inborn tendency towards dignity, beauty and sincerity'. He may be right. If he is it makes it a trifle awkward to Mr Maurice Webb, straining at the next leash to say what he thinks about music in South Africa. For Mr Webb finds the land barren, from Dan to Beersheba. There are no signs (he declares) of a musical awakening. Clara Butt is 'tenth rate'; and we brand as 'highbrow' all music above the jazz. And much more. You can have this, or you can have Mr Roworth's 'inborn tendency towards dignity, beauty and sincerity'. But you cannot have both, despite the accommodating gentlemen who have unearthed a long-felt *flair* for putting the culture of South Africa to rights.

Evil communications corrupt good manners. We have strayed from our opening charge, have even (hateful but purging confession) had to re-read our opening folios to recall what it was. For these enormities *Voorslag* must be held to blame. If it were such a thing as might be burnt by the public hangman, we could find it in our hearts to commend it. If it were such a thing that the Bishops denounced or the Pope banned, we would reprint whole chunks of it and risk the consequences. If it said, in terms unequivocal and direct, what was wrong with South Africa, and pointed out the way helpfully, encouragingly and not superciliously, to a better order of things, we would praise God and hold it might be, after all, a latter day Star in the East leading us all to the Way, the Truth and the Life. But, shaking off the heavy opiate of this latest issue, we must be true to the canons of our daily craft, and act as interpreter between man and his fellow-man. *Voorslag* has committed the one unpardonable sin that art knows – *It is dull.*

When Prince Hal searches the pockets of the sleeping Falstaff and finds his reckoning at the Boar's Head Tavern:–

Item:

Sack, two gallons 5s. 8d.
Bread . . . . ob.

he cries out, 'O monstrous; but one halfpenny worth of bread to this intolerable deal of sack!'

In *Voorslag* it is the other way about. It is nearly all bread, and stale bread at that. Are those responsible for the production afraid of the sack?

I 'The Future of Roy Campbell: A Manifesto for South Africa' (*The Cape Argus*, 11 September 1926)

Literary quarrels are invariably absurd affairs. Some writer, drunk with ink, blurts out in print a frank criticism of a friend which he would never have said in conversation. Immediately there is retaliation, knives, or rather pens, are out, and dagger thrusts are delivered. There is no quarter, no reconciliation. A literary duel is usually one to the death.

South Africa has lately been witnessing such a literary duel. A melancholy business which seems destined to play havoc with a brave literary publication such as *Voorslag*, and drive two most promising writers out of the country.[10] The duel seems to have developed into a general free fight, for many journalists, scenting battle from afar, have joined in, apparently for the fun of it. Much ink has been slung in Natal and, no doubt, all who joined in this literary quarrel are thoroughly satisfied with themslves.

An English Quarrel

What Mr Roy Campbell and Mr William Plomer think of the other contributors to *Voorslag*, or what the other contributors think of the 'pushful' poet or the 'naughty' novelist, does not concern me here.

It is all very much like another little literary quarrel which I witnessed in London two months ago. Mr Scott Moncrieff, the translator of Marcel Proust into English, had said something unkind about the Sitwell family. He tried to make amends by going up to Osbert Sitwell one evening and saying: 'My dear Osbert, I am an older man than you are and I am sorry for what has happened. Let us shake hands.' Osbert looked at the proffered hand and then at Scott Moncrieff. He shook his head, sadly. 'I'm sorry, Scott Moncrieff. I admire your translations awfully, but you'll have to go on growing old.' And so Scott Moncrieff seized his pen and wrote a satire in the Pirandello manner: 'Four Authors in search of a Character'.

All very absurd, and somewhat pathetic. So I regard Roy Campbell's quarrel with literary South Africa. It leads nowhere except to a general damnation.

It is rumoured that before Roy Campbell and William Plomer depart from South Africa they will riot in the form of a manifesto.[11] It is said to contain some of their best work and will, no doubt, raise a storm of controversy in this country. That, I have no doubt, is their object. 'We want, for the first time, to apply international standards to South African art, literature and criticism', writes Roy Campbell in a letter to a friend,[12] 'a thing which we were not allowed to do in *Voorslag*. We are going to have separate articles on all the outstanding writers in the past and to try to set them in a proper perspective. It is a thing which has to be done. Hitherto we have been too timid and friendly and amateurish. Our artists and writers (excepting Pringle, Olive Schreiner and Lady Duff Gordon) have been for the most part tradesmen, and in the interests of trade they have decided to live and let live, with the result that we have no artistic pride as a nation, and no taste at all. It was partly our intention of doing this in *Voorslag* that led to a panic on the part of others.'

One can imagine that very sensitive South Africa would be alarmed at such a project. Yet, we need criticism so badly, for as a country we are so often praised. There is, perhaps, some little self-complacency about us which needs rudely correcting at moments. But quite rightly we shall not love the young man who is brave enough to criticise us. In fact, there will be many who will openly rejoice at his departure from our shores.

But it is a pity that a poet should make himself a modern 'enemy of the people.' It was a mistake, in the first place, to expect a poet to be an editor. The friends of Francis Thompson kept him in comfort while he produced poetry; the friends of Roy Campbell should have allowed him to write poetry and persuaded him to avoid controversy. The position of Roy Campbell reminds me vividly of the clown in Andryev's *He Who Gets Slapped*. He has been the butt of many buffetings by clever journalists, the experience has left him bitter and deadly aggressive.

I have never met Roy Campbell. He may be egotistical, cruelly indifferent to the feelings of others, youthfully impatient of the meanderings of middle-class minds and the commercial art of the day. He may delight to stir up strife and insist upon his own self-opinionated individuality triumphing. On the other hand, he may be as 'mild a mannered man as ever slit a throat.' But I am not concerned with the temperament of the man; it is his work that matters. And when the hounds who are now in full cry have done their yelping – something remains. That something is the verse which Roy Campbell has written.

'Twopenny Coloured'

I think there are more people who detest poetry than like it. The deadening process begins at school, where one is asked to swallow as literature verse which even Irving Berlin would reject as stuff for syncopation. So it is rare to find someone really enthusiastic about verse. And even among those who appreciate verse, there is an immense variation in taste. Tennyson to many is a great poet; to others he is a doddering rhymester. Kipling to many is an inspiration; others find him vulgarly blatant. There are poets rich in verbiage to contrast with others who obtain their effects with a pruning sparseness. There are the twopenny coloureds and the penny plains.

I mean no disrespect to Roy Campbell when I term him a twopenny coloured poet. At a first reading he staggers you with the richness of his verbiage and the rioting of his imagination. There is a flood of colour from his pen which imprisons you like a mere insect in a kaleidoscope. His world is a titanic coloured cosmos, and you swirl through it at a dizzying pace. There is always the danger of coming away from his verse satiated with fervid imaginings and colour blind.

Those who want the penny plain in verse will be bitter critics of Roy Campbell. They who want the naked sunshine will not be content to see it through a stained glass window. That is the provoking element in Roy Campbell's verse – it is sunshine through a stained glass window. Reading *The Flaming Terrapin* again and again – and it is not easy reading – one discovers a rich turgidity. There is too much richness in this verse; the turgidity needs to be swept away by the clear stream of limpid verse. But time will rid Roy Campbell of this fault – if fault it be. He is, at the moment, full of the heady wine of youth, has drunk too deep, and there are occasions when he vomits. A hard head comes with years, and a little less verbal intoxication will be all the better for his verse.

Yet, though he has none of the intellectual sparseness of Francis Thompson, but more rather of the exuberance of Byron, his verse lures one again and again. If anyone doubts that Roy Campbell is a poet born, let him read of the tree-felling in *The Flaming Terrapin*.

Some criticism has been levelled against 'The Albatross', the poem with which Roy Campbell launched *Voorslag*. It may not be as pretentious as *The Flaming Terrapin* but it has its fine stanzas. I read 'The Albatross' while in a ship at sea, and I came away from the reading with my blood singing with the tempestuous zest of it.

It is poetry that can no more be ignored than the pundits of the musical world can ignore the Hungarian Rhapsodies of Liszt. It may suggest titanic cataclysms and worlds in travail, and it is difficult for many poetasters who have been wrapt in the contemplation of odes to daisies to feel other than frightened in this awful loneliness of chaos. As that fine Irish poet A. E. (George Russell) wrote when *The Flaming Terrapin* appeared: 'No poet I have read for many years excites me to more speculation about his future, for I do not know of any poet who has such a savage splendour of epithet or who can marry the wild word so fittingly to the wild thought.'

Yet there are many in South Africa who have not hesitated to declare that this poetry is merely a splendid bonfire of the imagination and that the ashes are already cooling. But even if his verse be damned, the poet will still live in art. Two months ago, in a gallery in Chelsea,

I saw the portrait of Roy Campbell by Augustus John.[13] The face of the poet shows all the keen hunger of a man who has found life a rich rioting for his imagination. There is the stamp of intellectuality and sensitiveness on the features, combined with a contemptuous expression which may explain much.

The iconoclast is subtly revealed. John never flatters. There is no more disturbingly frank portrait painter today than this wild, shaggy man of art who is chained to the bricks and mortar of civilisation. But I agree with the critic who found the portrait of Roy Campbell as beautiful as an El Greco angel painted in golds and browns. George Bernard Shaw once laughingly said that he would go down to posterity merely as the 'subject of a bust by Rodin'. Whether Roy Campbell achieves or does not achieve, all that his first book of verse would promise, he will still go down to posterity as 'a figure painted by John'.

But Roy Campbell is leaving South Africa. These literary squabbles have embittered him. Many have wondered when the poet who wrote *The Flaming Terrapin* is again going to assert himself, and I hear that the time is very soon. He has written two new long poems, 'Danaid' and 'The Pitso'.[14] These will be published by Jonathan Cape. 'They have already outclassed *The Terrapin* in every direction', declares the author in a letter to a friend, and he then proceeds to give some idea of the working day of a poet.

12 to 36 Hours a Day

Despite the physical and mental troubles of the past few months, he has produced a good deal. 'I have never done better work than I have lately', he writes. 'I have never worked less than 12 hours a day, besides journalising for *Voorslag* for four months: and in one or two cases I have worked 36 hours on end without sleeping.' Few of the poet's critics could claim the same devotion to work.

It is a great pity that the iconoclast should become a scapegoat in South Africa. I sometimes think that for all our stark sunlight, glowing mountains and amber sunsets of the veld, South Africa produces many drab minds. There are moments when many of us are as neutral as the khaki of the veld. Softened by that soporific of glorious sunshine, we lull ourselves into a comfortable torpor of mind and body, believing that all is well with the world and life. And we have been roused from this comfortable state by a young man who will insist on talking loudly. The drab minds have been flooded with rich colouring. Ruskin said of Whistler that he flung a pot of paint in the face of the public. Roy Campbell is doing the same with his verse, although it must be admitted that this young man is inclined to fling the empty pot as well.

London is the smiling, complacent mother to all these intransigents in art. It is there that Roy Campbell will find his home. But he will always be the exile. Hatred is often the precipice edge of love, and a fierce quarrel often leads to a still fiercer reconciliation. Roy Campbell and South Africa may yet claim each other.

W.J.M.[15]

J Edward Roworth to C.J. Sibbett, 16 October 1926.
(Campbell Collection, South African Library, Cape Town.)

Sezela
Natal

My dear Cecil,

Very many thanks for your letter and the flag[16] design enclosed. I have been intending to write to you to ask when you expect to be in Durban as Cecil [Mrs Sibbett] told me that you would be here some time in October. I also wanted to ask you to send the design for the flag in for consideration by the commission. As I told you, I consider it to be excellent and would like to see it chosen as our national flag. I suppose I am at liberty to forward your design to Pretoria under a *nom de plume* as you say you do not wish your name to be signed to it – your letter does not make this quite clear but I hope I shall be doing right in sending it forward? Very many thanks for your efforts in connection with the Merriman[17] portrait, I think I told you it could be seen at Isaacsohns in Long Street? You ask if I am satisfied with *Voorslag* – it has been a great disappointment to me since the first number. Cecil will have told you how badly Campbell behaved. We have all acted with the best motives and Campbell was treated with the utmost generosity – by both Lewis Reynolds and myself, but as you always say it is 'character' that really counts and in Campbell we were unfortunately dealing with a type devoid of character, without generosity or any sense of responsibility and a very despicable liar. In a letter which he wrote after he resigned from the paper he said that the owners of the paper 'even refused me the salary owing to me' and that also he had been 'turned out of my house by my landlord who regarded my tenancy as prejudicial to his political future'. The facts are that Lewis paid him £60 for his two months' editorship of the paper and that for over eighteen months he occupied the bungalow fully furnished in every way (after they had smashed all the valuable china we had collected I twice renewed with common china at a cost of nearly eight pounds) absolutely free of all cost and in addition *every day* without fail Lewis sent down from Lynton Hall eight bottles of milk, vegetables, salad, and fruit, eggs and butter weekly, frequent presents of legs of mutton, fish, etc., besides giving him a present of a typewriter. So much for the hard-hearted landlord who turned him out of his house! What happened is that when Lewis saw a vilely scurrilous letter that Campbell wrote to me he sat down at this very desk at which I am writing and sent a most polite note to Campbell saying that he thought it would be pleasanter if he sought a fresh environment and giving him two months in which to make fresh arrangements. What annoyed Lewis so much was I think that at the same time that Campbell wrote the 'Billingsgate' letter to me he had written the most servile letter to Lewis. In my letter he said that he was 'glad to have had the opportunity of preying on me' – I suppose he thought he would still have the opportunity of 'preying' further on Lewis! As you feared, Campbell has proved incapable of following up the *Terrapin*. He himself says that his best work is in the *Voorslag* – he might have added his only work. Cape of course has never seen and never will see these long poems and important works that Campbell talks about. (I see poor Makin[18] was taken in by these statements and wrote a pathetic article on the 'future' of Roy Campbell.) You may tell Makin that there is nothing in manuscript by Campbell but some short poems, of which the one you rejected for *The Waste Paper Basket* is the best[19] – there is hardly enough to make one slender volume. Campbell is today incapable of writing poetry and it is fortunate for him, unless he finds some other well-meaning persons to 'prey' on, that his father left a fortune of thirty-six thousand pounds. Love to yourself and Cecil.

Always your friend
Edward

K Roy Campbell to C. J. Sibbett, received December 1926. (Campbell Collection, South African Library, Cape Town.)

My dear Sibbett,

Yes I know and admire Pauline Smith's work. She is the only woman-novelist that is any good out here. *The Little Karoo* has some very fine work in it. *The Beadle*, though not so good, shows that she is capable of developing. Most of the women-writers I know would have gone on repeating themselves once they had discovered so excellent a mannerism as that employed in 'The Pain'. To repeat oneself is the secret of popular success – it is called 'fulfilling one's promise' – and it should be shunned like Hellfire by an artist. Most women-artists are unable to resist 'fulfilling their promise'. But here is one who isn't. Good luck to her. Olive Schreiner's *From Man to Man* will add to her reputation. Have you read it yet? One gets the feeling of tremendous electricity – not quite organised: and brilliant illumination – not quite focussed. However it is a really fine work: nobody but she could have written it. She makes all other South African writers seem a little tame, because she *feels*, gets angry, and throws her weight about. Olive Schreiner is not exactly a 'restrained' writer but her work *lives* (in spite of Cronwright), her words burn, and she thinks deeply. Olive Schreiner is a genius: Plomer, Pauline Smith and myself are talented people. And Mrs Millin and Mrs [Ethelreda] Lewis are a mess. Mrs Millin's famous 'restraint' is like a dog-collar without a dog in it. Mrs Lewis is purely a comic: but she is a good-hearted old thing: the trouble with her is Elephantiasis of the Soul.

Do you read Pringle ever? Most of his work is villainously bad: but in his five or six best poems he is head and shoulders above every one else out here. Plomer says he is by far our greatest writer: I say 'next to Olive Schreiner,' for his good work occupies so very little space. Olive Schreiner, though she never can compress it like Pringle into one terrific punch, could always sustain her best work.

Some day I shall start a printing press out here. I will bring out a series of perfectly printed little books at about 1/- each and try to make South Africa realise that it has a literature. I will write appreciations myself. My first book will be Pringle. It will contain only about 10 poems: ['Song of the] Wild Bushman', the 'Captive of Camalú', 'Afar in the Desert', 'The Tornado', 'Makanna's Gathering', 'The Kaffer' ['The Caffer'] etc. etc. My next will be Lady Duff Gordon:[20] in the preface I will demolish once and for all that braying she-ass of a Lady Anne Barnard.[21] Then I shall bring out *The Story of an African Farm*. I shall also produce Boniface's work.[22] He is completely unknown out here. He was a fine poet who committed suicide in Natal in 1860. He wrote in French. He carved his last sonnet on a big Umkuhla tree in Durban which is still standing but the letters are almost illegible. It contains some fine lines the best of which is (translated):

> Here where I fall, the accusing victim
> of the *christians* of Natal.[23]

I shall also print selections from Cripps,[24] myself, Plomer, Pauline Smith etc. etc. . . . But that is a long way ahead.

I enclose a satire called the *Waysgoose* [sic] which I have just written but not had time to correct. The typing is my own and the whole thing crawls with misprints. It is really quite amusing I think: and in case I can't get it published out here, I would like you to keep it in your 'archives'. I don't know if you'll be able to read it. Funnily enough it is the first bit of 'inspired' writing I have ever done. The words and phrases formed themselves automatically and only 48 hours elapsed between its start and finish. My best poetry generally takes me a year and the poems grow only by means of assiduous cultivation. But this stuff just gurgled out like water through a plug-hole. However on re-reading it, I find it has a certain amount of kick in it and I shall make alterations and polish it up. Every one to whom I have read it goes into fits of laughter. Although I am still under medical treatment and still get fits,[25] I am as happy as the day is long. I am keeping regular hours over my work – four in the morning, four in the afternoon and three at night. And my work is going ahead like a steam-engine.

I shall bring out the *Boomslang*[26] at Xmas. I wonder if you could give me some advice about how is the best way to advertise it. I am fed up with Makin but not disagreeably so. His article landed me with more than 100 letters of sympathy[27] – mostly from unmarried virgins. Curse him! I wrote and asked him henceforth to be my enemy. His article was a bit too 'knowing' and fatherly. I don't mind being slanged by journalists but I can't stand being sympathised with by them. I don't lay any blame on you for this: nor on him for that matter: but he took extraordinary liberties I thought: and Plomer was fed up at being stuck up for as a 'naughty' novelist: he said he would rather be slanged. There is nothing 'naughty' about Plomer – he is almost too much the other way: he converted me to teetotalism which I must admit has improved my work by 25 per cent and he almost managed to cure me of smoking: he is an absolute Puritan though he is human enough not to be a prig and absolutely understands and pardons the vices of others – except dullness and bad writing. Every word Plomer writes is written in burning sincerity: he is witty but has absolutely *no* sense of humour: and he does not know when he is being funny in his own work. To approach Plomer's work from the point of view that it is 'naughty' and over-sophisticated is simply to misunderstand it. If you read Plomer's review of Leys's *Kenya* in the first no. of *Voorslag* you will see what he is really like – absolutely sincere, in deadly earnest and quite fearless.

It is one of the greatest luxuries in life to meet a man who is absolutely uncompromising. Plomer and I get on like a house on fire even though we never agree on a single subject. Plomer is pro-native for the ideals of democracy. I am pro-native for the ideals of aristocracy. I know that you think that my work on the native question is associated with the poetic imagination but this is not so. My whole education has been purely scientific and I am not nearly so rhetorical or sentimental or unpractical as are the most matter-of-fact politicians. You will see when my book on the native mind comes out.[28] It is easy for journalists out here to say 'Mr Campbell is young.' But I have sent my work to Sir James Frazer and Levy Bruhl and they are both enthusiastic over it. It will come as a shock to S.A. to find that I can interest the greatest scientists in the world, when instead of trying to grapple with my arguments the S.A. intelligentsia are pooh-poohing them because I am young. At the same time they are hailing Smuts as a scientific thinker for no other evident reason than that he is old. 'Holism' is a hopeless wallow of emotionalism and mysticism and anyone who is capable of incisive thought cannot read it without puncturing something on every page. Poetry by no means precludes scientific thought. The writing of a good poem is as much of a feat in engineering as the building of a big steamship. And a mind that has been trained to express its abstract imaginations in a material form will necessarily be far more materialistic and solid when it comes to tackle scientific material. The scientific treatises of Goethe, Lucretius and Erasmus Darwin (all poets) are the clearest and most logical ever written. You will see nothing abnormal in my views on the native question if you live for another 30 years. The general attitude of the S.A. Whites to the native question is due to the fact that only one in 1 000 can speak a single native language – which is only the *first step* to understanding the native mentality: and only one in a thousand can realise the fact that the ultimate issue depends as much if not more on the emotional side of the native psyche than it does on that of the white man. The white man passes his laws and makes his plans for segregation etc. sublimely oblivious of the fact that he is not doing it of his own accord. He does not realise that he is merely reacting to the moral forces of native mentality: he thinks that as long as the native is not passing laws and sitting in parliament, he has therefore no power. But every law that is passed and every plan for segregation that is made is the direct result of the unconscious conflict, and the native mind is its indirect agent.

The Romans understood colonization: but we are utter babies at the job. Caesar never had any trouble with subject races: and he treated them in such a way that when Rome was swamped politically, the Roman civilization remained unimpaired and went on growing wherever it had been planted. What are we civilized Europeans but the Roman Empire? – save that we have lost two great arts (1) that of making war *successfully* and for the good of the state (2) the art of planting our own culture among barbarous peoples so that it will continue to grow and be beneficial to the rest of humanity. The mentality of Caesar compared with that of Rhodes[29] is like the mentality of Nietzche [sic] compared with that of Mr Vine Hall:[30] you have only to compare the Gallic War with the activities of Rhodes out here. Rhodes simply appears like a shambling muddle-headed old barber. Rhodes had far bigger advantages than Caesar – fire-arms etc. and money. Yet he only exploited the country commercially. Caesar would come along with a couple of legions: he would have law and order established in two months: in four months the inhabitants would have become Roman citizens. In two or three years their children (black or white) would be imbibing Roman Culture. What the Romans left to Europe has lasted 2 000 years. What we have left to Africa would disappear in 10 years if we were to be knocked out like the Romans. All we do when we arrive in a country is to uproot and destroy the traditions of the inhabitants and at the same time to refuse them the right of imbibing any other traditions.

In the end South Africa (whites) will suffer terribly economically for their short-sightedness. The potentiality of the nigger as a skilled labourer is enormous. We refuse to let him enter into competition with us in order to keep our 'racial purity', which would stand far more chance if the native were allowed any racial pride. Slavery only increases half-castes.

Anybody with a sound knowledge of history can see what a preposterous figure the white African makes who in order to hypnotise himself into believing in his mental superiority to the blacks is *forced* to retard the blacks *artificially* from entering into competition with him. The competition would only sharpen and invigorate the white man, and it would bring into play all the tremendous physical and mental resources which are at present paralysed and inert. But how is it to be done? etc. etc. People are always terrified of the obvious. The obvious thing is to reform native education. No more Noah's ark and Adam & Eve. Mechanics, chemistry, geometry is what he needs: and he needs to have at least ¾ of what he contributes in taxes spent on his education. Then you will see South Africa go ahead: but not until then. No country can go ahead which keeps the greater part of its mental and physical resources *artificially paralysed*. A man might just as well cut off his ears and nose and tongue on the grounds that it helped him to see better when his other senses did not interfere with his sight. However this is a departure into politics. My book deals only with psychology. I am not printing it in my own name, because if it were known that it was written by 'a poet' it would immediately be used as an 'argument' against it. *I want nothing to be said about it* until it has been published and reviewed and then I will divulge my identity. As soon as I get it typed I shall send you the Mss. and also the complete Mss. of my poems for your collection. My Mss. goes up in value: Garnett[31] has had some high offers for the *Terrapin* Mss. the whole of which is printed like this only very neatly and carefully [i.e. not in longhand]. I am also sending you the first *rough draught* I made of the *Terrapin* with alterations etc. It might be a curiosity some day. I shall send it in another envelope, as it is at present packed.

I am sorry you aren't coming to Durban. I may have to go home for a month at Xmas time to get my spine righted: but I shall have to return as I am absolutely piling up data for my book every day. I have got a great friend V. Tutton who was at school with me and whom I have taught my methods thoroughly. He attends law-courts for me and knows exactly what I want: he makes notes in shorthand. In return I am helping him with experiments for a book he is writing on the effects of light on animals. It is fascinating work. We play with chameleons, snakes and fish and we are getting on finely. He has found out a great deal about chameleons: and I made the discovery that if a chameleon is green and you kill it on a ground of a different colour it will lose its colour after death: but if you kill it on a green ground it will keep its colour: and we are following this up with many wild theories!! But it is all great fun. He is so terribly earnest about it all:

but I can't help laughing sometimes when he rushes round to my house in a terrible state to tell me that one of his mosquito-fish has eaten its youngsters or some other terrible tragedy that has happened to the chameleons-guts that he had just taken hours to prepare for the microscope. However he is a sincere, good fellow and one of the few who, in Durban, have any interest outside their pockets. He lives about 2 miles away but he rushes in every two hours or so to borrow my microscope. I am well enough now to accompany him on fishing expeditions but I have to go very quietly. I have always been passionately interested in Natural history so he suits me down to the ground. My only other associate is Bill Payn, the Springbok footballer.[32] He used to be my form-master at school and he always took an interest in me as a kid: he lives only a few doors off and he comes in for a smoke every evening for about half an hour. He is very much with me on the native question and has often used his avoirdupois and his fist to correct the aggressiveness of colonials towards the natives. He is a great, strapping fine-looking animal and it always puts me in a good temper to talk to him.

Mary is well and so are the children. Mary is giving me invaluable help with the *Boomslang*. I should never be half the writer I am, I'm afraid, if it weren't for her. She positively keeps me alive. She is the perfect model of what an artist's wife should be. But I get all the damned credit for it.

Well you see this letter leaves me very busy and very happy (thanks largely to you).[33] My brother[34] turned out very well, though I hardly know him, and he insisted on *giving* me £15 a month (he wanted to make it 20) until my books come out. He turns out to be a good generous fellow – though he is terrified of my poetry and my ideas. We get on very well however and keep off all other subjects except fishing which is his favourite occupation.

That is all the news. Good-bye and thanks for your letter.

Yours very sincerely
R.C.

P.S. For fun, I wrote to François asking him what he meant by his atmospheric denunciation of me and Plomer. I wrote in extremely sarcastic terms and reminded him that he had no right to use 'mutual admiration' as a reproach seeing that under his own *nom de plume* he never does anything but write about himself – seldom without awe and reverence. I wrote 'I had always thought that your multiple personality was purely a fiction, and I never believed that you were anything but an imaginary local deity, akin to the TOKOLOSH of the Zulus – but to be denounced from the heavens themselves! This removes all my doubts about your existence'. He was not only low enough to stomach all these insults but he wrote back asking me to come and see him, blaming Roworth for his misunderstanding, and confessing his boundless admiration for the *Terrapin*!! By Jove they are a fine lot. As soon as I am better I *will* go and see him! It is all great fun. I don't feel the least bit annoyed with any of them now that I have come to understand their mentality. They are simply amazing. I am putting it across him beautifully in the *Boomslang* – but not unkindly. Webb is the only one I feel unkind towards, because he is a bit more crafty than the others. Webb is Jubb in the *Waysgoose*.

Since writing this letter all my plans have been changed, I shall be leaving at once for England – in about 3 weeks. I have had a bad time with my neck again and the only thing is to go and see Sir Herbert Barker.[35] If we pass Capetown I shall call and see you.

R.C.

Anyway we may meet in London.

L 'We hear from Roy Campbell: A "Long Range" Attack' (*The Cape Argus*, January 1927)

Sir,

A long review of William Plomer's *I Speak of Africa*, which recently appeared in *The Cape Argus*, accuses that writer of having taken advantage of his 'safe distance' from Africa to speak his mind about that unfortunate country. Charmingly naive as the supposition is, it might mislead the more credulous of your readers: and I should be grateful if you would allow me to dispel the notion. As a matter of fact, the whole of *I Speak of Africa* was in my possession during my editorship of *Voorslag*, and Plomer, who was still in the country, authorised me to print as much of it as I wanted. Had that magazine been able to stand the strain of my editorship, the whole of *I Speak of Africa* would have appeared in it. It was because both Plomer and I insisted on getting to close quarters with South Africa that we were asked to resign from *Voorslag* – after refusing to modify our tactics. It was South Africa who kept at a 'safe distance' from us, by refusing to publish our correspondence, or to come openly into the ring with us. We were never afforded a single opportunity without wiping the floor with our adversaries; South Africa's only way out was to prevent us from coming to close quarters with her. She must not accuse us of timidity if we choose our own range now. She will find that our range is much longer than hers, and that we can shell her even better from countries which are as honoured to publish our work and our correspondence as she was afraid to. It was only after we found that South Africa refused to face us that we took advantage of the honours which had long been offered us by more civilised countries. Lest the same allegations of timidity should be made in the case of my forthcoming satire on the South Africans, *The Wayzgoose*, may I state that I made every financial and moral effort in my power to get it published in South Africa before leaving, but was everywhere confronted by the horror of the printers and their legal advisers.[36] In any case, both Plomer and I are returning shortly to South Africa for a rest, and also to see if our work has had any salutary effect. If any proof is needed of our desire to keep South Africa at a 'safe distance,' let any South African paper accept an article or two from our pens! While we were in South Africa she called us 'bullies,' 'cruel,' 'self assertive' and 'callous,' and she pleaded her right, as a 'young country,' to be senile and fatheaded, and to be left to decay in peace. Yet as soon as we turn our backs, it is South Africa who affects to be 'dangerous,' who puts on the swagger of a 'bully,' accuses us of timidity, yes, and even dares to show her poor old false teeth. Truly, the rage of the sheep is terrible! If we had been at all timid of that moronism which has come to be associated with the name of South Africa, we should not have attacked it in the regions where it takes the most virulent forms. For, be it remembered we edited *Voorslag* not only in South Africa, but in Durban, that Mecca of moronism, the unbroken ignominy and dullness of whose history is only relieved by the inexplicable phenomenon of my birth there.

Yours faithfully,
Roy Campbell

NOTES

1 Webb had founded the Library Group (Durban) in 1923.
2 Edward Garnett (1868–1937), English writer and critic, co-author (with his wife Constance) of translations of a number of great Russian novels. In the 1920s a reader at Jonathan Cape, Campbell's original publishers.
3 Sezela.
4 Refers to 'Tolstoy and Dostoevsky' by Mary Ann Hughes (Roy Campbell) in *Voorslag* Number 1.
5 See Note 25, below.
6 Sibbett sent Campbell money, as he was to do on several other occasions.
7 The section entitled 'Early Poems', in the volume *Adamastor* (1930), is dedicated to C.J. Sibbett.
8 Journal of the Owl Club, a club founded in 1894 for literary and musical gatherings. The journal appeared annually from 1921 to 1926 (excluding 1924) and again in 1934. Contributors included Sibbett and Roworth, and Campbell's poem 'Tristan da Cunha' appeared in the issue of 1926.
9 John X. Merriman (1841–1926), statesman; has been called 'South Africa's greatest parliamentarian'.

10 Plomer and Van der Post left S.A. for Japan in 1926, and Campbell had plans to return to England.

11 This proposed 'manifesto' is frequently referred to by Campbell, but did not subsequently appear.

12 Quoted from Campbell's letter to Sibbett, received in August 1926. (Campbell Collection, South African Library, Cape Town.)

13 See the dust-jacket of Peter Alexander's *Roy Campbell: A Critical Biography* (1982).

14 There is no evidence of these poems having been written.

15 William J. Makin was the author of eleven novels including *Two Moons* (1925) and *Redhead of the Red Sea* (1937).

16 Refers to the 'flag question'. See *Voorslag* Number 2, pp. 15–16, and note.

17 See Note 9, above; portrait by Roworth.

18 W.J. Makin, author of the article printed as Appendix I.

19 See Note 8, above. According to Roworth (Appendix G), the poem referred to is 'To a Young Man with Pink Eyes'.

20 During her brief stay in the Cape Colony, 1861–62, she wrote *Letters from the Cape*, which appeared in 1864 (republished, 1927).

21 Her letters to Henry Dundas have been collected as *South Africa A Century Ago (1797–1801): Letters Written from the Cape of Good Hope and Extracts from a Journal.*

22 Charles Etienne Boniface (1787–1853), early Natal author and wit, wrote among other pieces *Kockincoz, or, The Pettifogging Lawyer's Plot* (1843).

23 See Nienaber, G.S. (ed.), *Bluettes*, by Charles Etienne Boniface (University of Natal, 1963), for Raymond Sands's translation of the poem to which Campbell refers.

24 Arthur Shearly Cripps (1869–1952), Rhodesian novelist, short-story writer and poet.

25 Campbell at the time claimed to suffer from a neurasthenic complaint. In *Broken Record* (1934) he says that later, in 1933, X-rays finally confirmed that he had had a broken neck for twelve years, dating back to an earlier accident (pp. 140 & 178).

26 Plans to produce a journal entitled *Boomslang* did not materialize.

27 See Appendix I, 'The Future of Roy Campbell . . .', by W.J.M.

28 No evidence has been found to suggest that Campbell was engaged in research for such a book.

29 Cecil John Rhodes. Plomer published a deflating biography of Rhodes in 1933 (republished, 1984).

30 Revd Arthur Vine Hall (1862–1957), prolific South African versifier.

31 See Note 2, above.

32 For nearly forty years from 1915 Bill Payn was a legendary master on the staff of Durban High School, where Campbell had been a pupil. Famous for his sporting exploits: Springbok rugby player, provincial colours for cricket, baseball, athletics and boxing; Comrades' Marathon participant whose famous run in 1922 was characterized by frequent stops for hearty meals and drink. Fought in two world wars, winning Military Medal for bravery. Voracious reader whose amazing knowledge of words was reflected in speeches affectionately remembered. Died 1959. Hero-worshipped by Campbell who penned the following tribute:

> You say you are no poet, but
> You're more than one, great Bill!
> The whetstone though it cannot cut
> Can sharpen swords that will.

For details of Campbell's schooldays see Jennings, *The D.H.S. Story* (Durban, 1966).

33 Refers to financial assistance from Sibbett.

34 George, an older brother, who was a medical doctor. In later life, he became Chancellor of the University of Natal.

35 Specialist in manipulative surgery and friend of the English painter Augustus John, who in turn had befriended Campbell during his days at Oxford.

36 In *Broken Record* (1934) Campbell writes: 'I publicly offered in the *Cape Argus* to publish my *Wayzgoose* in Africa at my own expense rather than take it to England. My brother, Dr George Gordon Campbell, was kind enough to offer to pay the expenses of the publication. Only Desmond Young of the *Natal Witness* had the spunk to take it up, but was forbidden to do so by his firm's lawyers' (p.174).

REFERENCES

Alexander, Peter, 'Campbell, Plomer, Van der Post and *Voorslag*', *English in Africa*, Grahamstown, Vol. 7, No. 2 (September 1980).

Alexander, Peter, *Roy Campbell: a Critical Biography*, (Oxford, O.U.P. and Cape Town, Philip, 1982).

Black, Stephen, 'An Epidemic of Imitators: *The Sjambok's* Success and Why', *The Sjambok*, Johannesburg, Vol. 1, No. 8 (7 June 1929).

Campbell, Roy, *Broken Record*, (London, Boriswood, 1934).

Campbell, Roy, *Light on a Dark Horse*, (London, Hollis and Carter, 1951).

Campbell, Roy, 'Poetry and Experience', *Theoria*, Pietermaritzburg, No. 6 (1954).

Campbell, Roy, Unpublished Memorandum to William Plomer, August 1926, Durham University Library.

Cape Times, Cape Town, Centenary Supplement, (27 March 1976), 'A Remarkable Team and a Remarkable Period'.

Gray, Stephen, *Southern African Literature: an Introduction*, (Cape Town, Philip, 1979).

Gray, Stephen, 'William Plomer's Stories: the South African Origins of new Literature Modes', *Journal of Commonwealth Literature*, Leeds, Vol. 21, No. 3 (1986). Forthcoming.

Hallett, Robin, 'The Importance of *Voorslag*: Roy Campbell, William Plomer and the Development of South African Literature', *Theoria*, Pietermaritzburg, No. 50 (May 1978).

Haresnape, Geoffrey, Introduction to *William Plomer: The South African Autobiography*, (Cape Town, Philip, 1984).

Haresnape, Geoffrey, 'The *Voorslag* Movement and Olive Schreiner' in Van Wyk Smith, Malvern and Don Maclennan (eds.), *Olive Schreiner and After: Essays in Southern African Literature in Honour of Guy Butler*, (Cape Town, Philip, 1983).

Haresnape, Geoffrey, 'The Writings of Roy Campbell, William Plomer and Laurens van der Post with Special Reference to their Collaboration in *Voorslag* ('Whiplash') Magazine in 1926', Unpublished Ph.D. Thesis, University of Sheffield, 1982.

Jennings, H. D., *The D.H.S. Story, 1866–1966*, (Durban, D.H.S., 1966).

Jennings, H. D., 'The Enigma of Roy Campbell', *Contrast*, Cape Town, No. 57 (1984).

London Magazine, Vol. 13, No. 5 (December 1973–January 1974), 'About William Plomer'.

Miller, G. M. and Howard Sergeant, *A Critical Survey of South African Poetry in English*, (Cape Town, Balkema, 1957).

The Natal Advertiser, Durban, (19 March 1926), 'A Nasty Book on a Nasty Subject'.

The Natal Witness, Pietermaritzburg, (19 March, 26 March, 2 April, 16 April, 23 April 1925).

Plomer, William, *The Autobiography of William Plomer*, (London, Cape 1975).

Plomer, William, *Double Lives*, (London, Cape, 1943).

Plomer, William, *I Speak of Africa*, (London, Hogarth, 1927).

Plomer, William, 'South African Writers and English Readers', Proceedings of a Conference of Writers, Publishers, Editors and University Teachers of English, University of the Witwatersrand, 10–12 July 1956, (Johannesburg, Wits University Press, 1957).

Plomer, William, '*Voorslag* Days', *London Magazine*, Vol. 6 No. 1 (July 1959).

Sitwell, Osbert, *Who Killed Cock Robin? Remarks on Poetry, its Criticism, and, as a Sad Warning, the Story of Eunuch Arden*, (London, Daniel, 1921).

Van der Post, Laurens, Introduction to Plomer, William: *Turbott Wolfe*, (London, Hogarth, 1965).

Van der Post, Laurens, Unpublished letter to the University of Natal Press, November 1979.

Van der Post, Laurens, *Yet Being Someone Other*, (London, Hogarth, 1982).

INDEX

To avoid repetitive notes, biographical information – on people who are mentioned frequently in the text of *Voorslag* and in the editorial material – has been given here.

The Introduction, Notes on *Voorslag* and the Appendices have been numbered in one sequence; the *Voorslag* facsimile is between pages 26 and 27. Index references to the facsimile text are distinguished by bold type and the part number and page are given thus: **1.22.**